# FREEMAN OF THE HILLS

*Also by A. H. Griffin*

Inside the Real Lakeland
In Mountain Lakeland
Pageant of Lakeland
The Roof of England
Still the Real Lakeland
Long Days in the Hills
A Lakeland Notebook
A Year in the Fells

# Freeman of the Hills

## THE LAKELAND TWO-THOUSANDS AND OTHER FELLS

A. H. Griffin

*Photographs by Geoffrey Berry*

And in the darkest hours of urban depression
I will sometimes take out that dog's-eared map
and dream awhile of more spacious days; and
perhaps a dried blade of grass will fall out of
it to remind me that I was once a free man
on the hills. . . .
A. H. Sidgwick, 1912.

ROBERT HALE · LONDON

First published in Great Britain 1978
ISBN 0 7091 7222 2

Robert Hale Limited
Clerkenwell House
Clerkenwell Green
London EC1

Photoset by Ebenezer Baylis & Son Ltd.,
The Trinity Press, Worcester.
Printed in Great Britain by
Lowe & Brydone Ltd.,
Thetford, Norfolk
and bound by Weatherby Woolrough, Northants.

# Contents

# Illustrations

# Acknowledgements

I am especially grateful to Francis G. Falkingham of Shipley for allowing me to use his list of the Lake District 'two-thousands'—extracted from his list of the English 'two-thousands' published in the 1966 *Journal of the Gritstone Club*—and for his agreement to its publication as an appendix to this book. My thanks are also, once again, due to Geoffrey Berry, consultant secretary to the Friends of the Lake District, for his splendid photographs and to Alfred Wainwright for his beautifully-drawn map, also used in my *Inside the Real Lakeland*.

Companions accompanied me over about one-third of the Lakeland 'two-thousands', and enlivened several days with their good humour and conversation. They were Ted Stacey of Levens, Ivan Waller of Crosthwaite, Sid and Jamie Cross of Clappersgate and my son, Robin, of Bonnyrigg, Scotland. My wife also accompanied me on one short walk but I am principally indebted to her for her hours of patient typing and her valued help with the index—one of the most frustrating chores of authorship.

Mr R. A. G. Powell of the Ordnance Survey, Southampton provided some useful information, and Ordnance Survey maps have been an invaluable source of study and inspiration to me for half a century.

*Cunswick End, near Kendal* A.H.G.

# 1. Mountains Galore

The mountain challenges and delights of the English Lake District—even after an active life among the fells—remain virtually inexhaustible. When you have been up and down every mountain, summer and winter, by every generally accepted route and—if you are a climber—done most of the climbs, on every crag, of which you are capable, you have by no means completed the exploration of the fell country. Indeed, perhaps nobody has ever done so. Nobody, living or dead, has been into every corner of every mountain, scrambled up every mountain beck, and squirmed round every crag and outcrop. So the young, with a lifetime of walking, scrambling and climbing ahead of them, and the elderly, with a thousand active days recorded in their mountain diaries, still have unlimited scope for adventure in the Lakeland hills.

Challenges, either mental or physical, are the very essence of living. Without them we merely exist or become cabbages. We all need to be stretched, as the late Lord Reith used to say—elderly people as well as the young. Too many retired people claim they are bored because they've nothing to do, whereas retirement from a possibly boring job can often provide a wonderful opportunity to live a new life of one's choosing. The challenge need not be energetic—a new hobby perhaps, learning a new language, growing one's own vegetables, redecorating the house or even a brisk few-miles' walk every morning, no matter what the weather—but, ideally, both mind and body should be stimulated. Seeking some simple stretching, I set myself the very modest challenge, in my sixty-seventh year, of revisiting all the mountain summits of the Lake District that are more than 2,000 feet in height. A time limit of three months was set and the project was easily completed within this period. With very little extra effort the round could have been completed within two months, and I afterwards wished I had been a little more enterprising. Indeed, with better planning and single-minded dedication to the job, to the exclusion of everything else, I believe the whole project could be completed in a month, for I only spent twenty-seven separate days on the round and several of these provided me with only one or two summits. It should be emphasized that this peak-bagging orgy was, in no sense, a meritorious achievement. Anybody, with average energy and able to spare the time, could do the same or better.

There were slightly more than 200 summits in the round and most were collected in 'horseshoe' circuits, starting and finishing at the same point. The book describes these walks*, and also attempts to assess the wonderful potential of the Lake District for this type of ridge wandering, travelling all round the compass and seeing changing views with every mile. In no other part of mountain Britain are the possibilities for horse-shoe rounds more marked—a circumstance largely due to the 'spokes-in-a-wheel' formation of the Lakeland valleys and their containing ridges. I have also tried to suggest other ways up the more interesting mountains—better ways, in many cases, for in travelling along the ridges you sometimes miss the best features of the hills—and a chapter has been added on the more worthwhile fells that fail to reach 2,000 feet above sea-level but, sometimes, prove more rewarding than some of the higher tops. Black Combe, Haystacks and Illgill Head are examples of these. The book, therefore, seeks to embrace all the highest mountains and most of the best fells in the district but, at the same time, I am very conscious of the great deal that has had to be left out. If all these walks and suggested routes are followed the reader, like myself, will still have much to learn about the Lake District hills but, hopefully, his appetite might have been whetted for further exploration. It must be realized this is not a guide-book—there are guide-books in profusion for those who wish to be taken by the hand. The book is merely a personal appraisal of the mountains of Lakeland by a life-long admirer who has the good fortune to live in their midst. It is written in humility and in deep wonder at the majesty of homeland mountains that can still bring exaltation though I see them every day. Every year I go into the hills, walking, climbing or skiing, more than 100 times—up to 150 days in some years—but every day I find something new, and I will never know the whole. So the hills will remain a joy forever.

* See my *The Roof of England* (Robert Hale 1968) for more detailed descriptions of sixty of the best Lake District mountains.

Many people have traversed all the summits in the Lake District that are over 2,000 feet in height—the Lakeland 'two-thousands', as they are called. Several particularly diligent walkers, prepared to trudge across miles of tussocks and bogs to reach indeterminate summits in lonely places, have collected all the tops in England above 2,000 feet, of which there are about 350. I was not interested in this larger project—mere peak-bagging, before my fall from grace in the summer of 1977, had not been one of my failings—but to revisit all the Lake District mountains within twelve weeks seemed an interesting exercise. A friend of mine had recently done them, in rather more leisurely fashion, in his seventieth year, and this gave me the idea for my series of walks and, indirectly, for this book. Readers, I thought, might be interested in a fairly concise study of all the mountains of the Lake District and, especially, an assessment of the area's horseshoe possibilities.

When I came to study the lists and maps I found there were only two summits I had not previously visited in fifty years of wandering the fells—an outlier of Caw Fell, on the western fringe of Lakeland, and Coomb Height, the unimpressive shoulder of Knott in the hills to the north of Skiddaw. All the rest had been walked, quite incidentally, in tramping or rock climbing expeditions—many of them dozens, or even scores, of times. Indeed, before this project, the only Lake District mountain that I could recall ascending solely because I had never been up before had been Sheffield Pike. Until this late spate of peak-bagging I had never bothered to tick-off summits but had simply walked them in casual rounds, as circumstances or company disposed, or to round off a climbing day. Rock climbs were a different matter; these were always ticked off in the lists, most assiduously.

Being lazy by nature I did not take the trouble to prepare a list of the Lakeland two-thousands, which can involve hours of study—with a magnifying glass, in my case—of map contours and, sometimes, detailed examination of the ground. In preparing a list of mountain heights you also have to lay down rules—exactly how the summits are to be determined, how much of a dip between tops should be accepted, and whether or not certain doubtful summits should be included. All this seemed to smack of too much hard work and research, so I took the easy way out and used somebody else's list. Between 1961 and 1964 Francis Falkingham, a well-known Yorkshire mountaineer, walked over all the summits of England that are more than 2,000 feet high and published his list in the 1966 *Journal of the Gritstone Club*. This is one of the small handful of lists of the English two-thousands that have been published in various climbing club journals and, for years, these remained the only information about the subject—information only normally available to club members, and not to the general public. Then, in 1974, Nick Wright published a list in book form* detailing 345 summits of 2,000 feet or more in height that he had walked. But, in making my modest rounds, I used Falkingham's list which I found admirably precise, although I did not agree with his nomenclature in one or two places. There are slight differences between his list and that of Nick Wright that I will discuss later, although only the most dyed-in-the-wool peak-bagger will be concerned with these. I wrote to Francis, an old friend, who kindly sent me a copy of his list and generously agreed to the publication of its Lake District section. (Readers will find the list in the appendix—published in its original form, despite my minor quibbles about his naming and location of some of the summits.)

At this stage I must deal with the metrication of mountain heights and confess that one of the aims of this book is an attempt to keep the Lakeland two-thousands alive and unforgotten. Many people have wondered to what extent metrication will eliminate our mountains, since, in this country, the name 'mountain' has often been taken to imply a height rising more than 2,000 feet above sea-level. Which, they ask, will become the 'mountains' of the Lake District after all the heights are given in metres instead of feet and when, if ever, will the two-thousanders disappear? And for how long will the collection of the two-thousands remain a modest achievement available to everybody? One dictionary defines a hill in Great Britain as a height below 2,000 feet and a mountain as a higher natural elevation. This is a slightly curious definition since Scottish mountaineers are apt to describe all their mountains as hills—although 277 of them are above 3,000 feet in height, or 545 if you count every point and excrescence—while mountains in the Lake District are locally called fells. Outsiders, however, have generally regarded heights in the fell country above 2,000 feet as mountains, although this arbitrary rule excludes such notable hills as Black Combe (1,970 feet) and Illgill Head (1,978 feet), the summit of the Wastwater Screes. In Scotland the pursuit of the 'Munros'—separate

* *English Mountain Summits* (Hale, 1974).

mountains more than 3,000 feet in height—is an increasingly popular challenge. If the 'Munros' were regrettably to disappear, because of metrication, and the continental 'thousanders' substituted, there will be only 132 of these. But my guess is that the 'Munros', hallowed by long tradition and with all the detailed tables readily available, will be with us for many years to come, and, in some form, may always remain. The Lake District two-thousands, however, are not nearly so avidly collected—there is little challenge in the achievement, unless the round is made in a very short time—so that clamour for their retention may not be so vociferous.

Lists of the Lake District two-thousands are normally worked out from the Ordnance Survey's one-inch map, supplemented by the new 1:25,000 maps. At present, mountain heights are given in feet on these maps, as also are the contours. I understand from the Ordnance Survey that their intention is that their one-inch tourist map of the area should remain available as long as sales warrant and one senior officer's guess is that this map should still be on sale after 1979. The one-inch seventh series is being replaced, throughout the country, by more than 200 sheets of a new map at the scale of 1:50,000. Basically, the first series of this is an enlargement of the one-inch map, but the second series is being completely redrawn to a new specification. Some sheets in this second series have a ten metres contour interval; contours on other sheets, both first and second series, are at 50-feet intervals derived from the one-inch map and relabelled in metres. The Ordnance Survey say it will take "many years" to resurvey the contours at metric intervals for the whole country. The 1:25,000 Outdoor Leisure maps. styled 'The English Lakes', and showing the contours in feet, are new productions and I am told the contours will not be shown in metres until the second series becomes available. And this, I am assured, is not likely to happen before the mid-1980s. Altogether, therefore, the Lake District two-thousands should be on the maps for a few years to come although, eventually, they will disappear. But the summits will always be there, and the various lists—together with this book—will be available for reference. And, even after the maps have all gone metric, some walkers will still treasure the former two-thousands and, perhaps, occasionally collect them. After all, the athletic world continues to retain the hundred-yards and mile. Perhaps the mountain world will be just as traditional.

For what other convenient collection will remain? When all the two-thousands have finally disappeared from the maps which of our summits will be regarded as mountains? Surely not, arbitrarily, those summits above the curious height of 609.6 metres—the metric equivalent of 2,000 feet? And certainly not only those fells that exceed 1,000 metres for there are none of these in the Lake District. Scafell Pike, the highest mountain in England, rises only 977 metres above sea-level—71 feet below the new magic height. Some day, perhaps, somebody will suggest some arbitrary metric height as the new plimsoll line between 'hill' and 'mountain'. If a standard of, say, 600 metres was to be selected this would bring in several more Lake District summits than the present total of two-thousands, while a 700-metre standard would reduce the collection by about one-third. Perhaps the new aristocrats of our Lake District mountains will, one day, be the 'nine-hundreds'. There will only be a handful of them—the Scafells, including Broad Crag and Ill Crag, as well as Helvellyn, Skiddaw, Great End and Bowfell. Even proud and shapely Great Gable would fail to make this grade—by exactly one metre. But, far better in assessment of mountain worthiness, would be the end of mere height as any sort of criterion. After all, mountain heights are purely relative, for at 8,000 feet in the Alps you may be only on a cow pasture while at the height of Mont Blanc in the Himalayas you are only in the foothills. And it must be accepted that some of the two-thousands of the Lake District are disappointing humps whereas, for example, Haystacks, at only 1,900 feet, is an outstandingly fine little mountain. All the same, some of us will be sorry if we had to lose the Lakeland two-thousands through the mathematics of officialdom. Let us, therefore, when the time comes, and they are lost on paper, keep them in our hearts.

Falkingham's patient poring over maps and study of the ground yielded 203 two-thousanders in the Lake District, and these were the ones I walked—besides a few others. Readers may be surprised to learn that these totals may vary—Nick Wright, for instance, found exactly 200 and others have come up with slightly different figures. "Surely," readers may say, "all these lists should be the same. A mountain is either more than 2,000 feet in height, or less than this." But it all depends on how you define these summits—which maps you use, how much drop there should be between neighbouring tops, how accurate or clear the contouring is, and so on. Falkingham, like the others, worked out his own rules and finally came up with his definition of a two-thousander as any piece of land with a separate contour ring at 2,000 or over on the Ordnance Survey seventh series one-inch map, together with any points where the map was obscured by hachuring but which, after visiting and reference to large-scale maps, were obviously adequately separated from other tops. Even so, his list produced several anomalies. For instance, his strict rules excluded the distinct little top of Helvellyn Lower Man—one of the 3,000 footers of Lakeland—as well as High Pike, one of the summits on the well-known Fairfield Horseshoe, although these are naturally traversed when you are collecting neighbouring tops. On the other hand he included a curious handful of summits on Rydal Fell, four on Birkhouse Moor and three on Gray Crag—mostly unremarkable tops, merely thrown up by the slightly switch-back nature of their ridges, which serve to swell the total with almost no extra effort. Falkingham rightly included High Man on Pillar Rock as a separate summit—this, the only bit of rock-climbing, made a neat finish to my rounds—and I think a case could be made out for the inclusion of Scafell Pinnacle as an extra summit. Nick Wright does not include Pillar Rock among his summits and eschews two or three of Falkingham's tops, but adds four not included in the latter's list. These are Helvellyn Lower Man, already mentioned, Black Brow, near Little Hart Crag, Little Carrs and Pavey Ark and I refer to them later in my descriptions of the walks. Altogether, however, I am satisfied that Falkingham's list is generally accurate and painstaking, and his eyesight, for studying crowded contours, unimpaired.

My own collection of the two-thousands was singularly—and rather stupidly—unplanned. I merely decided at the beginning of May 1977 to revisit all within twelve weeks, and just went off to walk over a selection of them, in any part of Lakeland, whenever I happened to be in the mood. The walks had to be fitted in among climbing and other mountain activities, gardening, house-decorating, writing and other interruptions. Half-way through the first month I went off to Scotland to do some snow-climbing, which slowed down the process but provided a welcome change from peak-bagging in familiar hills. Some sort of planning and a less casual approach would have cut down the number of walks and provided a far neater completion. As it was, towards the end of the project, I had to go off to collect odd summits, missed in my previously unco-ordinated attack, that could have been included in other walks. Walkers who take the trouble to plan their circuits beforehand should easily be able to achieve better rounds, avoid some of the back-tracking that I had to do, and complete the collection in fewer journeys. As it was I made twenty-seven expeditions—some of them to collect only one or two summits—and fourteen of them were done alone. Actually, I went on my own over two-thirds of the summits but had the pleasure of company over about seventy of them. A lone walker generally goes more quickly than if he is accompanied, and my two biggest daily totals—in each case thirteen summits—happened to be made when I was on my own. The Lake District two-thousands include six summits over 3,000 feet—or seven, if you count Helvellyn Lower Man.

To have collected the two-thousands during the winter, with much shorter days and snow and ice about, would have been a much more demanding, and probably more interesting, exercise. My winters, however, are normally spent snow-climbing and skiing and I was not prepared to devote these exciting months to straightforward pedestrianism. When you approach your seventies you begin to wonder, with some alarm, how many more energetic winters you may have left, and tend to try to make the most of those that remain. So the walks were done in the longer and generally brighter days of early summer when only rock-climbing, where my standards have sadly deteriorated, had to be set aside. And the longer days enabled me to do three of the walks, including the well-known Fairfield Horseshoe, in the evenings. There were some wet days and several days of low cloud but, mostly, the walks were done in good and, occasionally, excellent weather which made for easy and enjoyable rounds. Since most of the summits were traversed in mid-week very few people were seen on the tops, and it seemed clear that the Lake District fells are only visited by considerable numbers at weekends and peak holiday times. Some days I saw nobody at all from leaving the car until returning to it several hours later. This pleasing absence of crowds on the fells is most marked in winter time, except that when you *do* meet people on the tops in winter during weekdays they are likely to be in fairly large parties—mostly young people on outdoor pursuits courses which seem to be proliferating most noticeably. Only two of the walks proved, in any way, trying—the easy round of the Dodds, because I happened to be wearing an old pair of ill-fitting boots, and the Mosedale Horseshoe, through dehydration, since it was walked on one of the hottest and most stifling days of the year. One of the best days—and one of the wettest—was spent on the Scafells. You remember days of bad weather, thick mist, or other difficulties or discomfort long after the memories of a host of fine, sunny days have become blurred together. A compass was needed on only three of the walks—and these were among the best days.

The most northerly of the Lakeland two-thousands is High Pike in the Caldbeck fells; the most southerly, one of the summits of Walna Scar; the furthest east, Grey Crag above Longsleddale; and the farthest west, Iron Crag, south of Ennerdale Water. Some of the easiest summits are in the Grisedale Pike and Grasmoor area where the excellent going, mostly on peat and heather tracks dramatically poised above spectacular drops, enables you to tick off the tops at some speed. The loneliest country lies on the fringes of the district—the 'back' of Skiddaw, and the fells farthest to the east and west—while the craggiest, most dramatic and, therefore, most stimulating country is around the Scafells and the Pillar range. But all the Lake District is rewarding—even if you are standing on Grey Crag on a poor day, looking towards the Shap Fells road, and, far beyond, the greater glory of the Pennine chain, the valley of the Kent, and the silvered horizon of Morecambe Bay.

Walking the two-thousands is, of course, merely an excuse to justify the traverse of all the highest land in the district. By ticking off the tops you ensure you don't miss any of it; more casual walking might exclude some of the less interesting summits. The main value of the exercise, in my case—apart from the loss of half a stone in weight and a noticeable increase in physical fitness—seemed to be the gift of a new assessment of mountain Lakeland. Although almost all the ground was familiar—much of it exceptionally so—the constantly varying areas of my visits enabled me to study the inter-relationship of all the mountains, and to see them as a whole much more clearly than hitherto. By walking and viewing the fells in all directions, and going into different areas every two or three days, it was possible to appreciate the whole lay-out of the district and to see mountains and ridges, not as individual sections, but as clearly-linked parts of all the fell country. For the first time, because I had never been over all the mountains in so short a time before, I was seeing Lakeland as one wonderful area, and not as a dozen enticing bits. For the first time it all fitted together, like some vast, coloured jig-saw puzzle. Before these walks I could readily identify all the mountains of Lakeland from the south and from some other familiar directions. After I had revisited the two-thousands I could recognize and name all the mountains from any angle, north, south, east or west, although, through lack of use, this new facility might later fade away.

But another great gain was the realization that there was still a great deal of Lakeland I had yet to discover. For example, sitting on the top of Pillar Rock—my last two-thousander—I realized that the southern slopes of the Buttermere fells, overlooking Ennerdale's conifer carpet, were largely unknown to me. I had traversed the tops—High Crag, High Stile, Red Pike, Starling Dodd and Great Borne—many times, been into all the northern corries, and climbed on all the crags, but the south-facing sides of these fells still remained *terra incognita*. And there are many other corners of Lakeland where I have been over all the tops but not explored all the slopes and every ravine and gill. To traverse all the mountain summits in Lakeland does not imply, by any means, that you know all the mountains—still less, Lakeland itself. You have merely made a small start and only when you have done this do you fully realize how little you really know. Indeed, merely by linking the summits you are, in very many cases, missing the best of the mountains. You can, for instance, collect all the summits to the north of Skiddaw and not see any of the long-deserted mines that are scattered about the whole area, often in most dramatic places. And you could spend a week doing nothing else except exploring these old workings—and still not know the area.

My humble pilgrimage around the two-thousands was undertaken after fifty years' rock-climbing in the area and a lifetime of mountain walking that began in the early 1920s. A better arrangement would have been to have got the two-thousands out of my system first and then to have started on the real exploration of the district, although this sort of Lake District peak-bagging was hardly known in my young days, and rock climbing seemed much more interesting to a youngster. But newcomers to the district, or to fell-walking, could do much worse than first collect the two-thousands and, thereby, acquire the feeling of the district, its size and shape and how the mountains are linked together. Then they can ascend the mountains by all the better routes, explore lesser-known ways, and gradually extend their knowledge and affection for the whole area.

And now I return to the theme mentioned at the beginning of the chapter—the virtually inexhaustible nature of the mountain challenges and delights of Lakeland. You have done all the two-thousands, let us say, been up and down all the mountains by the usual tracks and, if you are also a climber, done all the routes within your ability. What is there left to do? Well, for a start, you can do them all again in winter for which you will need the right equipment and knowledge, and, in this way, you can enter into a completely new realm of mountain enjoyment, with different, more dramatic, scenery and new, more stimulating, challenges. Under snow and ice a modest fell can become almost an alpine giant, and, surely, high sunlit snows with far horizons bring the height of exhilaration to the mountain wanderer. Snow and ice climbing, in the gullies, is a specialist sport outside the scope of the ordinary walker and I have briefly referred to this in the chapter on Helvellyn. Many of my finest days in the hills are spent in this way, but the walker, provided he is sensibly equipped and shod and carries an ice-axe which he knows how to use, can still taste the joys of snow-capped hills, without the need to hang on by his eyebrows or his alpine hammer.

But most people, of course, come to the Lakeland fells in the much longer summer days and the more experienced of these, satiated with the familiar routes but anxious to extend their knowledge of the hills, can still find unlimited scope. First of all, they can forget the accepted routes up the fells and devise new ones of their own, disdaining tracks. Almost every mountain in the district can be tackled in this way and, even though you may be less than a quarter of a mile away from a well-trodden route, you get the feeling of being in 'new' country. And navigation, particularly in mist or bad weather, can often present an interesting challenge. Another ploy is to circle a mountain instead of going over the top, sticking, perhaps to a particular contour—say, 2,000 feet. I've done this on several of our fells including Bowfell, which can be quite a challenge, Grasmoor, Coniston Old Man, Scafell Pike, Greyfriars—surprisingly long—Crinkle Crags and some others. This exercise need not be so trying to the ankles as you might imagine for you can select natural traverse lines across the fellsides and, if you are a climber, across the crags and outcrops. These traverses always open up unfamiliar, often quite spectacular, country and the fascination lies in selecting the most interesting line, seeking out or avoiding the most difficult places, according to your ability or experience.

Major expeditions might include walking right across the district, east to west, north to south, or along any particular line of your choice. There can be many permutations of this and a refinement is either to draw a line with a ruler across the map and then walk along it, steering by compass, or to keep to a particular grid line. Two men did one of these 'grid line' walks across Lakeland in the 1960s, selecting grid 09 on the one-inch Ordnance Survey map as being the only horizontal traverse to provide a dry crossing. Lakes and tarns provide impassable barriers—unless you are prepared to swim—to most east-west crossings, but, by slightly bending your rules, you can devise other routes. These two took two days on their grid-line crossing, for they stuck exactly to the map and had to ascend and descend something like 13,000 feet, but strong walkers selecting a less demanding route can cross the district in a day. Sometimes, I have merely steered a compass course from a base to a distant summit, trying to hold to the course fairly exactly, and this can often provide an interesting day among out-of-the-way scenery. One such line is the ascent of Scafell Pike from Hardknott Pass—north-east up Mosedale and straight on, through the crags and outcrops, across the Great Moss and up Little Narrowcove to the top. Night walks, too, can have their fascinations. Moonlight and stars can sometimes make the use of torches unnecessary but they should always be carried. If you plan to watch the dawn from a mountain summit arrange to reach there at the right time; arrival at the cairn an hour or two early can involve a long, cold wait. A traverse of the fells at night, with or without the magic of a perfect dawn, provides unexpected pleasures—the feeling of deep silence and solitude, the rare impact of tiny night sounds, the sight of awesome depths, the sense, in cold moonlight, of walking through a lunar landscape, and the picture, from the heights, of the beginning of a new day as the first lights show in the valleys before the dawn. And, always the feeling, as you trot down to the dale in the early morning sunlight, with the shadows at an unfamiliar angle, that you have stolen an extra day.

A favourite pastime is beck scrambling or climbing. You

merely select a rocky ravine or beck and get up it the best way you can. There are scores of suitable becks and you can't select them from the map for, sometimes, even the thinnest, most innocuously-looking blue wriggle can provide a worthwhile expedition. Of course, you are liable to get wet—sometimes very wet—but this is part of the game. Sometimes you have to climb up waterfalls or you may avoid them by routes up the side walls. A few of the becks or gills, of course, require a fairly high climbing technique—Piers Gill on Scafell Pike is one example—but in many of them you can adjust the route to your standard, either climbing the hard places or avoiding them. The fascination of beck scrambling is that, again, you are in 'new', sometimes exciting, country, with different scenery at the top of each pitch or round every corner. It is almost a separate sport, neither climbing nor walking, but a mixture of both, with the waterfalls and the pools providing a great deal of varied enjoyment for the reasonably active person. The fell walker not wishing to scramble can also enjoy a good day by devising a tarn walk—trying to visit as many tarns as possible. There are nearly 500 of them in the Lakeland fells, so the scope is enormous. A day over Glaramara, Allen Crags and Seathwaite Fell, seeking out all the tarns, can provide an introduction and then, by studying the 1:25,000 map, you can select more demanding days.

For the retired or elderly climber, or one, like me, past his best, mountaineering routes provide considerable enjoyment and, often, quite a challenge. A mountaineering route might be described as a way up a mountain using rock as much as possible but avoiding the challenge of really steep or difficult places. There are many of these in Scotland, suitable for mountaineers of experience but not fell walkers, but not so many in the Lake District. Still, they can be found, and I have discovered much enjoyment in seeking out some of them. You can, for instance, climb up to Pillar Rock from the River Liza, linking up the small crags and outcrops, while Red Pike throws down a similar challenge into upper Mosedale. The Scafell Pike area abounds with possibilities and other mountains worthy of exploration in this way include Crinkle Crags, Hart Crag, Fairfield, Nethermost Pike, Red Screes, Great How Crags, Blencathra, Wetherlam and Great Carrs. Or you can go up Harter Fell from the head of Haweswater, using rock nearly all the way, or scramble up the length of Dungeon Gill, climbing all the pitches as they come and then finishing up the easy, upper crags of Harrison Stickle.

So there'll always be interesting things to do in the Lakeland fells, when you are tired of joining the weekend processions on the familiar routes. Seek out, for instance, all the 'little mountains'—the fells that fail to reach 2,000 feet but, so often, prove much more interesting than their modest elevations would suggest. Or you could start a photographic collection of all the summit cairns; many quite attractive new ones have appeared in the last few years.

It is possible that the recital of modest mountain walks that follows might serve to encourage the elderly walker. You can find people of forty who tell you they are too old for walking, which seems absurd and a little sad. One of my companions on some of the walks is over seventy years of age and still rock-climbing to a high standard, while other mountain friends are approaching eighty, and some, even older. None of the scores of climbers and walkers that I know have stopped going into the mountains simply because they have reached a considerable age. They have merely adjusted their activities to accommodate their gradually declining standards. Elderly rock climbers have become active fell walkers; elderly walkers have merely sought out rather less arduous days. All of them still go into the hills—even though they may now keep to the lower fells, or walk up the valleys, or fish the fell becks and tarns. How many people have walked up every mountain dale to its head, including all the little side valleys?

Earlier, I referred to my great good fortune as a resident of the Lake District, able to see the hills every day and walk them when I chose. Brought up in the district I learned to love the hills from an early age and, certainly, after my wife and family, they have been the great joy of my life. And, when the fells and rocks become too demanding, and, perhaps, even the upland valleys something of a strain, I hope I will be content just to look out at the hills and still gain comfort and inspiration from the sight of so much unmatched splendour. Each day, in sunlight or storm, cloud-shadowed or clear, snow-capped or wreathed in mist, the hills are different—a changing panorama of soaring uplands that, like great music, can lift a man from depression to exultation. A magical wonderland of beauty and adventure that will always be there.

# 2. The Northern Fells

The northern fells of Lakeland, dominated by the bulky massifs of Skiddaw and Blencathra, are isolated from the rest of our mountain heritage by the wide, semi-circular moat of Bassenthwaite Lake, the Keswick plain and the curve of the Glenderamackin river. Through this strip of lowland country is threaded the line of the controversial A66—a modern creation of smoothly sweeping highway and striding bridges that runs, in places, across the lower slopes of the fells—and to reach the northern heights you have to cross the road and the traffic. Immediately, with most of Lakeland behind you, there is the feeling that you are entering a different sort of country—still part of the fells and dales but a separate area where the mountains are smoother and more bulky than the rugged or pointed peaks to the south.

And this is, indeed, a different sort of Lakeland—a huge circular area of rounded hills, often with sharply defined ridges, with the wasteland of Skiddaw Forest set right in the middle. Mostly, the mountains are of Skiddaw slates—our oldest rock—which break down into shale to produce the smoothly rounded shapes, the grass and the miles of heather. Skiddaw Forest, incongruously, is completely without trees—except for a planted windbreak around the remote cluster of cottages known as Skiddaw House*—and few walkers penetrate its heart. Skiddaw House, once tenanted by shepherds, must be one of the loneliest places in England. Some years after Pearson Dalton, the last shepherd, retired in 1969 at the age of seventy-five, part of the cottages was taken over by the Border Bothies Association for use by young people taking part in outdoor activities, while the western half of the buildings became the outdoor centre of a local school. But, despite this new interest in the area, these fells to the north of Skiddaw remain among the least-visited of English

* I have written about Skiddaw House and Pearson Dalton, once the shepherd there, in my *Still the Real Lakeland* (Robert Hale 1970).

hills—places where you can generally count on having mountains to yourself, even on summer weekends. And yet, many years ago, the more northerly of these fells were the scene of considerable mining activity and, many centuries before then, ancient people, probably early British, built a remarkable hill fort on one of the summits, Carrock Fell, for what purpose we cannot say. So that, at one time, many people lived and worked in these lonely fells but today, despite the tourist invasion that has had little impact on the most northerly hills, they are probably lonelier and less frequented than they have ever been.

Skiddaw and Blencathra, however, the twin ramparts that mount guard over the Forest and the waves of grassy summits to the north, are by no means lonely or little-visited mountains. Most visitors to the Lake District know them—either their shapes, a well-loved backcloth against the northern sky, or their well-trodden slopes. Skiddaw was the first 'tourist mountain' in the district and Blencathra, with its splendid mountain wall to the south and fine ridges soaring to its summit plateau, has several claims to be regarded as one of Lakeland's most rewarding mountains for the walker. People have been walking up Skiddaw for the view for at least 200 years and, although it is one of the tiny handful of three-thousanders in the district, you are probably more likely to meet grandfathers and toddlers on its summit than on any other mountain. Every July young people run up and down its slopes in competition—ten miles, there and back, from Fitz Park to the main summit—and the distance has been done in a little over an hour. Some years ago I offered a special prize, in this annual race, to the first person to complete the ascent and descent within one hour, but to date (March 1978) this has not been achieved, although I've little doubt it will be some day. Keswick folk have a particular affection for Skiddaw and most of them must have been to the top, at some time in their lives. Certainly, it is the easiest three-thousander in England to ascend.

Blencathra, 'the hill of the devils', is a more striking-looking mountain when viewed from the main road through Lakeland—a saddled dome, buttressed by rocky ridges separated by steep, rocky ravines. Ruskin went up one of these ridges 100 years ago and wrote afterwards: "The finest thing I've yet seen . . . several bits of real crag work and a fine view at the top over the great plain of Penrith on one side and the Cumberland hills, as a chain, on the other." Climbers will find little 'crag work' there today but, for walkers, there is plenty of fresh air and exhilaration. Going pretty hard you can get on to the summit plateau in one hour from Threlkeld and look out, northwards, over the 'back o' Skiddaw' country. This is the beautiful, desolate country John Peel and his little Galloway knew so well—a gigantic sheep pasture of rolling grass and heather fells threaded by slow-moving becks, with few walls or fences. Now that most of the miners have left it seems a sad, rather derelict countryside in places but, on the right sort of day, with a fresh breeze blowing and the cloud shadows chasing across the deserted hillsides, it can be grand walking country—if you want to be alone with the sheep, the birds and your thoughts. And, in these days when the over-crowded hills of central Lakeland are 'wick wi' foak', this sort of quietude may be well worth seeking out.

## Blencathra and Neighbours

After our longest winter for years spring seemed to have reached the Lake District at last when I set off on Sunday, 1st May 1977 on the first of my summit-collecting expeditions. The Windermere water skiers were out in Waterhead Bay, people were walking about the Keswick streets in their shirt sleeves, there was rich new greenery on the trees and in the hedgerows, the cherry and almond blossom were in bloom, and birds sang merrily. And yet, a couple of hours later on the top of Blencathra, I was in the middle of a thunderstorm with curtains of driving hail sweeping across the fell, lightning rending the heavens, and a great black cloud over the mountains blotting out everything but the next few yards of sodden turf. Minutes before I could see right across a sun-kissed Lakeland but, for an hour, battered by a cold wind from the east and lashed by driving rain and hail, I was forced to seek out my summits by compass and saw hardly anything until I was down by the Glenderamackin Beck on my way home round the skirts of Blencathra. Of course, these sudden weather transformations in the Lakeland fells are common enough and serve to underline the truism that conditions in the valleys can never be taken as a reliable indication of the weather on the tops. You should be prepared for any sort of weather in the mountains—even on a sunny, cloudless day in May.

Why I chose the northern fells for the first trip in the series I can't remember but, probably, I didn't know where I was going until I was well on the way. This is my usual practice when going fell-walking—leaving the decision about destination to the whim of the moment, prompted perhaps by nothing more than the sight of sunlight on distant fells or by the realization that it had been some time since I was last on, say, the Scafells or the Buttermere fells. Rock-climbing or ski-ing days are usually different, for then we usually arrange in advance where we are going. But fell-walking days—especially when I am alone—are rarely planned. Far better, I find, to be guided at the moment by the weather or by any sudden wish to explore some little-visited corner, and then let the day and one's inclinations and energy take over. Sometimes, indeed, the choice of a route, selected while quietly motoring northwards, may be finalized by the recollection that, at the end of the walk, there happens to be a good inn where they sell beer brewed from the wood.

I think on this particular Blencathra day I might have been anxious to see how the A66 'improvements' were going along for I remember spending some time in driving along and studying the open sections, so that it was after two o'clock in the afternoon before I left Threlkeld for the tops. My reaction at the time was that the Keswick by-pass and some of the other controversial works were an unforgivable intrusion across the face of northern Lakeland—a national heritage vastly altered for local expediency—but I felt bound to agree that the County Council, within their unfortunate brief, seemed at least to have made a neat job of the new roads. There should never have been such a bold highway across the lower slops of Latrigg but, after Whitehall had made their lamentable decision, the road engineers went about their task with some taste and sympathy. The bridges, for example, are necessarily obtrusive but, at least, are slim and well designed, and the landscaping has been carefully carried out. Early that May the bulldozers were at work on the next eastern section of the highway to make it the shortest possible distance between the motorway and the heart of Lakeland—as if reducing mileage and increasing speed were the only things that mattered. I remember hoping at the time that the engineers would be as fastidious over the other sections as they had been with the by-pass but, for many, the new highway will always be a monument to the gross lack of care that central government can accord its finest national park.

This short day gave me my first six summits—two on Blencathra (the summit and Knowe Crags), two on Bowscale Fell and two on Bannerdale Crags. Despite the thunderstorm buffeting on top it turned out to be one of the easiest of the twenty-seven trips in the series. Blencathra is one of the most spectacular mountains in Lakeland—a steep wall more than three miles long split by some of the finest ravines in the district, with wonderful airy ridges in between. I've no doubt you could devise nearly a score of routes to the top—up all the ridges and ravines with many variations at the side—and each time I go to Blencathra I try to seek out a different way. On this occasion I started up the Hall's Fell ridge—the most direct and one of the finest routes to the summit—and then, remembering that my last ascent had been this way, traversed off the ridge to the right, across the face of the buttress, and then across the next buttress of Doddick Fell. This brought me into the ravine of Scaley Beck which is not perhaps the finest of the group but is impressive enough—a merry, tumbling beck rising steeply through the heather between high ridges towards the rough summit wall. The next ravine to the left, Doddick Gill, provides a craggier, more interesting approach, but I had decided to include Sharp Edge in my route and Scaley Beck would lead that way more directly. And some distance up the ravine I found a little rock platform beside a waterfall and here, in the sunshine with the clamour of the beck for music, enjoyed a late lunch.

To reach Sharp Edge from here meant scrambling up to the summit of Scales Fell and then descending easily to Scales Beck that flows out of Scales Tarn—hardly the usual route to the Edge but, then, I tend to avoid well-tracked places where I can. Only in this way can you learn more about the fells. But there was nothing 'new' to discover that day except that Scales Tarn was more glasslike than I have ever seen it—except when sheeted with ice. There was not the slightest ripple on the surface and the summit crags were exactly mirrored in the water. This is the tarn that some writers have described as 'black', 'forbidding', 'rarely seeing the sun' or 'one of the coldest tarns in Lakeland' but that day it was a magical, sunlit pool in the mountains, as welcoming as an oasis in the desert. Looking up at the mountain wall, perhaps 1,000 feet above, I could see snow hanging in patches from the summit ridge like an ornate lace collar, while the sheep seemed to be clinging to the steep, rocky slopes like the sea birds on St Bee's Head. Instead of taking the track I scrambled up the rock buttresses of Sharp Edge and remembered that this was probably the place where the very first rock-climbing photograph in the Lake District was taken. The picture was taken, of course, by the ubiquitous Abraham brothers of Keswick in about 1890 or earlier and shows two of them, as youngsters, disobeying all the modern rules of rope-craft but no doubt enjoying themselves. They are joined together by a short length of clothes-line and moving together on steep, unstable rock. George Abraham later captioned the picture, wisely, as 'How not to climb'.

From the Edge it was an easy scramble to the summit of Blencathra—this can be quite a tricky place in winter snow and ice—followed by the stroll to the second top of Knowe Crags, perhaps a mile away, and the return to the highest point, Hall's Fell. It was warm and balmy in the sunshine on top but I could see dark clouds massing to the east and knew that a storm was imminent. Southwards, however, the views were still sunny and clear and it was easy to pick out the snow cornices on Helvellyn and the snow gullies on Great End—plenty of snow there to last, possibly, throughout May. As it happened, I got no snow climbing in Lakeland that month—being involved with my peak-bagging—although a fortnight later I was in snow showers on Bowfell and towards the end of the month was snow climbing on Ben Nevis in the sort of superb conditions more usually found in February. Five minutes later, after basking in the sunshine on the top of Blencathra, I was in the middle of the sudden thunderstorm as I trotted down the side of Foule Crag towards the Glenderamackin col. I steered north by compass for Bowscale Fell, the driving hail and marshy ground making the trip more unpleasant than invigorating, and was pretty wet by the time I reached the cairn. This is the least interesting approach to Bowscale Fell which is far better ascended from Mosedale to the east or direct from the River Caldew in the north. In this way much more of the flavour of the mountain—the pleasant east ridge, the rampart of Tarn Crags and the romantic hanging tarn of Bowscale—can be savoured. But when you are merely picking up summits you often miss the best features of the mountains, so that, by completing the 2,000 footers of Lakeland, you certainly cannot claim to have explored the fells, or anything like it. Very much more remains to be seen and experienced.

But the rigours of my self-imposed exercise necessitated

traversing to a neighbouring 2,000-feet top of Bowscale Fell and then, contouring round the remote and little-known valley of Bannerdale, the two listed tops on Bannerdale Crags were collected. It then only remained to drop down the scree to the Glenderamackin Beck and follow well-used tracks, for the first time that day, towards the skirts of Blencathra and the way back to Threlkeld and a welcome pint of beer. The clouds lifted as I came down from the tops and the rain ceased It was a lovely May evening as I drove home through St John's in the Vale.

These lonely valleys above Mungrisdale and at the back of Souther Fell—where the 'phantom army' was seen by the dalesfolk more than 200 years ago—are among the least known parts of the Lake District. Mostly these remote dales are fairly featureless but the mile-long line of cliffs on Bannerdale Crags is dark and impressive and well worth exploring. These are the sort of places where you can find complete solitude in the fells but it is a desolate, almost sad, loneliness for you remember the miners who used to work there—miles from any habitation and almost cut off by the steeply soaring fells from the sunshine. Now there is nothing there but the ravens and the sheep. Curiously, the area was far better known by tourists a hundred years ago for Bowscale Tarn, caught in a hanging valley below the northern crags of Bowscale Fell, was a particularly favourite place for walkers and picnickers. The tarn has an old legend about two immortal fish that lived in its depths and after Wordsworth had written a poem about it the place became a fashionable place of pilgrimage. Victorian walkers trudged up a well-graded track to the tarn and looked, unavailingly, for the fish, but today the track has almost disappeared, few people go there and Bowscale Tarn with its surrounding fells is just a remote area of Lakeland, unknown to most of its visitors.

## The Skiddaw Massif

In more than fifty years of mountain wandering I don't think I've been up Skiddaw more than ten times—perhaps an average of one visit every five years or so. The mountain is the fourth highest in the district, perhaps the oldest, geologically, in the country and, with its outliers, a much bigger mountain mass than the whole of the Scafell range, but its immediate appeal to the climber or hard fell-walker is limited. There are no cliffs, except for the fine combe of Dead Crags, low down on its northern flank, its slopes are steep but grassy, and the ascents are long but easy. Almost certainly Skiddaw was the first mountain in the Lake District to be ascended for the view or just for the fun of it, people were riding ponies up it nearly 200 years ago, Bren gun carriers and tanks crunched about its slopes during the last war, and motorcars have, regrettably, been driven to the summit. All this—along with the probability in summer that the mountain will be alive with trippers—tends to discourage the mountaineer seeking some sort of challenge or, at least, solitude, so that Skiddaw is neglected by many mountain folk. They make, perhaps, a token ascent by a well-tracked route and then leave the mountain alone, reserving their energies for fells that seem more rewarding.

But Skiddaw *does* have its appeal—its superb views over northern Lakeland, the solitude of its northern slopes, the complexity of its satellite peaks and radiating valleys, the invigorating scenery around Dash Falls, the outlook over the little-visited northern fells and the feeling, as you survey the Scottish Lowlands on a clear day, that you are on the top of England. Perhaps more country can be seen from Skiddaw's stony summit than from any other place south of the Border, and here was where they lighted the fire that 'roused the burghers of Carlisle'. Perhaps nobody boasts about going up Skiddaw, but Keswick folk are rightly proud of their mountain, and if you seek out its hidden ways and untracked places this hoary, old fell amply repays exploration. Skiddaw is a mountain that grows on you. There's much more to it than the familiar back-cloth to Keswick and the wide track that runs some distance across its upper slopes.

My peak-bagging visit to Skiddaw and its satellites was in the middle of June—a very windy day with cloud on the summit but, otherwise, splendid sunlit views. The last time I had been on the mountain was several years before when two of us went up and down at night in a drizzle of rain during a round of the Lakeland three-thousands to mark my sixtieth birthday. On that occasion, of course, we saw nothing except an occasional circle of wet slate and grass illuminated by the torch, and the summit—where we only stopped long enough to jot down the time—seemed a particularly wet, miserable and inhospitable place. But this time I hoped for better things.

There are six 2,000-foot summits on Skiddaw and its lesser heights—including Lonscale Fell—which seemed a fairly leisurely round, for the intention was to leave the nine summits in the 'back o' Skiddaw' group to another day. No doubt the whole of the fifteen tops could be covered in one round but this would be a particularly strenuous day and it seemed better to do the others from Mungrisdale. Besides, I wanted time to look around and perhaps do a little exploration in the more northerly fells which I hadn't visited for very many years. So I started from Keswick and cheated, right from the start, by driving to the top of Gale Road and walking from there. This cuts out the Latrigg ascent and about 800 feet of height but conscience was salved by the reflection that it was the first time I had done this and that, anyway, one was only bagging summits.

The track up to and beyond the site of the former Halfway House refreshment hut—which I well remember—is rather steep and tiring so it was completed as quickly as possible. Far better, I find, to keep going on steep places; stopping and re-starting destroys the rhythm. Leaving the main Skiddaw track I went up to the gate and the sheep pen and carried on easily, by the side of the wall, to the summit of Lonscale Fell—my first top of the day. The southern view was superb—the long skyline of the Lakeland fells from High Street to the Grasmoor fells, with the winding length of Borrowdale in the centre reaching out to the highest mountains in England. One could also see right through the central trough of the district—along Thirlmere and over Dunmail Raise to the fells around Windermere. Skiddaw was still in cloud but Blencathra was clear. A tiny patch of snow still clung to the upper slopes of Great Dodd.

Easily, then, down from the summit to rejoin the Skiddaw highway and then up to the twin cairns on Skiddaw Little Man. Most people going over Skiddaw avoid Little Man and thereby fail to see one of the most remarkable views in Lakeland—indeed, Alfred Wainwright, the guide-book writer, seems to regard this as the very best view of the heart of the district, and he could be right. You look straight down steep slopes to Applethwaite and the wide vale of Keswick, with Derwentwater laid out like a map and the highest central mountains from the Langdales to Great Gable stretched out along the horizon. Borrowdale, with its crowded woodlands, runs through the centre of the picture and, if the lighting is right, Keswick itself looks like a fairy-tale town—surely one of the most beautifully sited towns in England. I have written elsewhere of the splendour of the view from the lovely Applethwaite road and the slopes above the hamlet*; this is the same view, as seen from 2,000 feet higher and, therefore, vastly more extensive and spectacular.

From Little Man it is a straightforward descent and ascent to Skiddaw itself but, first, the subsidiary summits of Carl Side and Long Side had to be collected. To do this it seemed best to cross the steep scree slope of Broad End and this went surprisingly easy. The untracked screes looked loose and unpleasant and I thought it might take me some time to pick my way across but, in the event, they proved quite stable—slates lie flat and firm, unlike more rounded stones—and the crossing was quick, simple and interesting.

Carl Side and Long Side are lesser summits on the south-western flank of Skiddaw which, from the Keswick to Bassenthwaite road, seem to merge into the parent mountain but, in fact, are separated from the stony, summit slopes by the trough of Southerndale, one of the least-visited of the valleys of northern Lakeland. There is a small tarn on Carlside col and thence a simple stroll to the grassy summit which commands a splendid view to the south. The summit of Long Side was only half a mile away and the two tops were collected within minutes. From Carl Side I looked down on the heather-covered summit of Carsleddam and thought about going there but since this would have meant a considerable descent and subsequent ascent—and the little peak, although strangely attractive, is not a two-thousander—the digression was abandoned. It is at times like this that the mere peak-bagger collecting the two-thousands in Lakeland or the 'Munros' in Scotland feels—or rather should feel—rather ashamed of himself. Peak-baggers, eschewing interesting tops merely because they don't happen to reach a certain height are lesser mortals than real freemen of the hills. I felt suitably chastened but consoled myself with the thought that there were still some miles to go and Skiddaw had still to be collected.

From both Carl Side and Long Side you look down on the massed conifers of Dodd Wood and perhaps idly wonder how many thousand trees the Forestry Commission had planted there. This is not the most enlightened area of afforestation in Lakeland—the Commission has been far less regimented in its

* *The Roof of England* (Robert Hale, 1968).

planting in later forests—but it must be admitted that the forest roads provide interesting approaches to the heights in unusual surroundings. Long Side is the more attractive of the two summits—an airy belvedere of heather and bilberry with glorious views down into Southerndale and across the West Cumberland plain to the Solway and the Galloway hills. Prominent in the foreground is the peak of Ullock Pike with the fine ridge that makes probably the best route for the ascent of Skiddaw. From below, Ullock Pike looks a particularly fine peak but Long Side is slightly higher and there is not sufficient drop between the two to merit the Pike's inclusion as a separate two-thousander. Long Side is therefore taken as the summit of Ullock Pike although, strictly speaking, Long Side is the name of the flank of the fell overlooking Bassenthwaite Lake, the summit itself—splendidly situated though it is—having no name, so far as I am aware.

There was one feature of the view from Long Side I had not seen before—the sight of the controversial section of the new road along the shore of Bassenthwaite Lake. I could see the white scar of the road works, the darker section of ruler-straight new road and the lines of speeding traffic. It shouldn't look offensive from this height, once the roadworks have been tidied up, but I remember the long arguments and rows and realize that the routing of this section will not please everybody. No doubt, in time, the new lake-shore section will have its attractions for memories are short, but this bit of the map will have to be redrawn.

Leaving Long Side with some reluctance, for it must be one of the most rewarding viewpoints in northern Lakeland, I returned to the Carlside col and began the almost 800 feet of steep ascent to reach the south summit of Skiddaw. On the way up I met two young men, making their first visit to the mountain, who asked whether it was, in fact, the Isle of Man they could see across the Irish Sea. I told them it was and also pointed out the Galloway hills and Criffel across the Solway. The distant views were remarkably clear that day but, a few minutes later, we were in quite thick cloud on the south summit, with nothing to be seen except a few yards of stone and turf. The two young men thought they had reached the summit of Skiddaw but I told them the main top was nearly half a mile away and accompanied them there, afterwards walking on to the north top, but there was still no view. Thinking back on my visits to Skiddaw I believe I have only once seen the view from the summit, and that was many years ago.

My day was nearly finished but there was still the rounded outlier of Sale How, more than a mile away to the east, to visit. To do this I contoured easily across the screes, taking a compass bearing through the cloud, and then, below the mist, ran down grassy slopes to the dip near Stile Gill and then on to the summit. Sale How has no interesting feature so a descent was made down its eastern slopes for a better view of Skiddaw House, the lonely collection of deserted shepherds' buildings far below, and the bulk of Great Calva on the opposite side of the valley. Some time later I would be collecting Great Calva and the 'back o' Skiddaw' fells and it was interesting to study the lie of the land. Then back up the slopes to the ridge between Skiddaw and Lonscale Fell where I had a sudden doubt. Had I, in fact, been to the summit of Lonscale Fell earlier in the day? Was the east peak, which I had not visited, higher than the cairn on the featureless mound that had been my first top of the day? There was only one way to be sure—to go up there again.

So a second visit was paid to Lonscale Fell where a walk on to the east peak made it perfectly plain that, in fact, the first top had indeed been the true summit. But it was a worthwhile digression for I was able to scramble about on the summit tower of the east peak, explore the craggy slopes and look across the Glenderaterra Beck to the surging slopes of Blencathra. The east face of Lonscale Fell is, by far, its best side, and the ascent by the north-east buttress an interesting scramble. At the end of the day a descent was made straight down the steep heather slopes of the fell to the ravine of Whit Beck, avoiding the tourist route for Skiddaw. Straight ahead was the long line of the Dodds and the Helvellyn range and, to the right, the crumpled ram's horn shape of Causey Pike showing black against the sun sinking in the west. It had been a straightforward round over and around a much-visited mountain, made more interesting by its diversions and by the reward of particularly fine views. Skiddaw and its satellites form a worthy massif—no matter what some people say.

### The 'Back o' Skiddaw'

One of the last rounds in the series was the collection of the nine lonely summits in the 'back o' Skiddaw' country—an area quite unlike any other part of the Lake District and a blank on the map to most mountain folk. Here is a wild, untracked countryside of heather-draped fells, long-deserted mines and unusually distant views. As expected, nobody was seen all day until the return to the starting point—even in the distance—and nothing moved except the clouds and the quietly grazing sheep. There is a spaciousness about these views—mostly of the sky, flattened moorlands and vastly stretching plains—that, except for the distant sea, reminds one of the broad acres of Yorkshire. My day of high winds, sudden showers and scurrying clouds demanded careful compass work at times but the absence of tracks, cairns and litter was welcome after weeks in the over-used fells of central Lakeland. Even the sheep, standing their ground or trotting up for a close inspection, seemed unaccustomed to, or, perhaps, anxious for, human company.

I motored, past the skirts of Souther Fell and Bowscale Fell, to the hamlet of Mosedale by the River Caldew and then took the mines road to Carrock Mine, perhaps two miles up the valley. Carrock Mine is best known for its output of tungsten or wolfram, a rare metal not found elsewhere in Lakeland, but on that day the workings were hidden by thick cloud and curtains of driving rain that made the prospect of fell-walking not very attractive. But I didn't want to waste the day, having driven more than thirty miles, and set off into the mist and rain hoping for an improvement later. And I was to be rewarded for, in a quarter of an hour, the heavy rain ceased and, although there were showers and low cloud later, the weather was never so bad as at the start and, several times, the sun peeped out. Initially, I steered a compass course north-east for the summit of Carrock Fell across tussocky grass and small outcrops of rock, reaching the ruins of the ancient fort on top in exactly three-quarters of an hour from the car, at precisely noon—and in welcome sunshine, with a keen drying wind. I don't often time myself in the hills but I did that day, and the figures may be interesting to some. The first summit, as I have said, was reached at noon and the last, the ninth, Great Calva, at exactly 4 p.m. And the total time, from the car and back, was five and a half hours although I had expected to take seven hours. But the walking, although mostly trackless, was easy and one always goes quicker alone. With a companion and the likelihood of conversation, however limited, each unconsciously adjusts his pace to the other's, with resultant slower speeds. It is pleasant and often rewarding to have a likeable companion in the hills but not always, I find, if you are in a hurry.

Nobody knows the age of the ruins of this ancient hill fort on the summit of Carrock Fell, although it is thought to be early British, and we can only guess at its original purpose. There are signs of gateways at the four main points of the compass but who lived up here at more than 2,000 feet above sea-level, and why, we don't know. Certainly it is a fine viewpoint—across the wide valley of the Eden to the Pennines, north-west to the Solway Firth and Criffel in the Scottish lowlands, and south-west to Pillar and Great Gable. There is also a glimpse of Bowscale Tarn, high up on the slopes of Bowscale Fell on the opposite side of the Caldew. I remembered previous visits to the summit, years before, when we had been climbing the rough gabbro rocks of the mountain. It was on one of these outcrops, incongruously, that I first drove a piton into Lakeland rock—rather ashamedly, at the time, although since then pitons have been driven into most of the Lakeland crags. Modern experts will find it difficult to believe that a piton should be required on one of these modest routes but, although I can't remember the climb or whether we were trying a first ascent, I remember it seemed very necessary at the time. Probably I was off-form.

Carrock Fell, which is said to carry more varieties of rock upon its slopes than any other hill in Lakeland, is a splendid little mountain—of continued interest to geologists, mineralogists, archaeologists, photographers, bird-watchers and rock-climbers, besides ordinary fell-walkers. There are also acres of heather and bilberry, scattered traces, here and there, of forgotten civilizations, and plenty of refuges for foxes. And, scattered about the fell—in addition to Carrock Mine—are the remains of other, long-abandoned workings.

My next summit was High Pike, two miles away, the most northerly two-thousander in Lakeland. It was approached over trackless, tussocky heather and grass—apart from a section of tractor ruts—first over Miton Hill and then right-handed to the summit, everywhere very wet and boggy. Here, overlooking the Border country, on the northern fringe of Lakeland and the national park, is an unusually decorated summit. Besides the sprawling cairn, there is the Ordnance Survey column, a beacon site, the ruins of a keeper's cottage and a memorial seat. Years ago there was actually a wrought-iron garden seat on the summit—2,157 feet above sea-level—but, more recently, this has been replaced by the memorial seat built of slate slabs with an inscription to a young man, 'who loved all these fells'. And he was a good judge for High Pike, another mountain gouged out by many ancient mines, is a splendid viewpoint from which to look out at the Carlisle plain, the West Cumbrian coast, the Eden valley, the northern Pennines and the Scottish Border hills. Chris Bonington, the Everest climber, lives on the northern slopes of the hill and, during the planning of his expeditions to distant mountains, often walks over the summit to do some thinking and get a little fresh air. And I sat down on the seat, had my sandwiches, and looked at the clouds that were now settling down on the tops to the west that were the next to be traversed.

The two summits of Great Lingy Hill—uninteresting mounds most profusely covered in heather—were easily collected and then came the descent to Roughton Gill before the ascent to Great Sca Fell. To get a sight of these disused mines in quite dramatic scenery I climbed some distance down the gill but soon decided this was a place worthy of more leisured exploration when I had more time. It is an interesting area of caves, old mine levels, shattered crags and waterfalls but the clouds had now come down and it was raining again, so a compass course was laid for the summit of Great Sca Fell and the walk continued up rather dreary grass slopes to the summit.

Alfred Wainwright, the guide-book writer, is a friend of mine but I never take his wonderful little guides into the hills. In my view, these guide-books are for study at home—preferably *after* you have explored a particular area—and not as replacements for map and compass. To follow them blindly, almost yard by yard—as many people appear to do—seems to me to destroy some of the sense of adventure and exploration that can still be found, especially in bad weather, in the hills. I have argued this out with Mr Wainwright more than once and we have agreed to differ, each of us, I think, appreciating the other's point of view. Undoubtedly, Mr Wainwright is primarily writing for those who do not know the fells intimately; were the guides intended for more experienced walkers, he would probably agree with my point of view. But when I say I *never* take his guide-books into the hills I am not quite correct for I *did* have his relevant book with me on this occasion—the only time I have ever done so. Only one minor summit, Coomb Height, was unknown to me but it was many years since I had been over some of the tops and the guide was taken for interest, rather than for direction. And, remembering something he had written about Great Sca Fell, I nearly went wrong.

'Great Sca Fell', states the Northern Fells guide, with authority, 'has no cairn', so that when on what I decided, by direction and distance, must be the summit I stumbled on a cairn I wondered whether I had gone astray. Great Sca Fell is a grassy moorland of a summit—as different a mountain from the great Scafell as you could find—so that, in the thick cloud, I had to be certain of the exact summit, so as to fix the correct bearings for the later tops to be visited. So I walked some distance northwards and downhill towards the direction of Brae Fell and then, puzzled, returned to the cairn. It certainly seemed to be on the highest point, although, in the cloud, it was difficult to be sure. Wainwright, they said, was never wrong but, in the end, I decided that, this time, he was, and set a compass course from the cairn for Little Sca Fell which, according to the oracle, 'has a cairn and an unusual wind-shelter'. And, in a few minutes, I was on the summit of Little Sca Fell—for there was the shelter—and, a few moments later, the clouds lifted and all was revealed. I told Alfred Wainwright about this later and he enjoyed the joke. But, he explained, his guide-book had been written fifteen years before and, since then, new cairns had been springing up all over the place. It was always happening, he said—new features on the fells that altered his original findings. There had certainly been no cairn there in 1962 and, of course, I'm quite sure he was right.

As I have said, the clouds suddenly lifted on the summit of Little Sca Fell with its curious wind-shelter, and the rain stopped. Nobody could describe this little hill surrounded by smooth, grassy heights, as an exciting place but that day, with the mists lifting all round the horizon and shafts of sunlight illuminating many distant places, it seemed to have a special appeal—an appeal quite different from that of any other Lakeland summit that I can recall. Southwards towards the real Lake District there was little of interest to be seen, except a glimpse of Bowfell and the Crinkles nearly twenty miles away, but northwards, the view over the vast Cumberland plain to the Solway and the mountains across the Border, was curiously invigorating. After the cloud and rain the moors and fells looked newly washed, the Solway, almost Mediterranean blue, sparkled in the sunshine, and there was a feeling of spaciousness rarely experienced in the Lakeland hills. Except for the distant waters it might have been a view across the broad acres of Yorkshire—mostly sea and sky, with valleys and ridges reaching to remote horizons, houses and woodlands in the hollows, plenty of fresh air and a fine, gusty wind.

Knott was the next summit—the highest of the day, but only 2,329 feet, and a long bulky fell, with high sheep pastures, deep ravines and nothing much in the way of tracks. It was an easy walk and from the sprawling summit there were close-up views of the 'back' of Blencathra and Skiddaw and the crags of Lonscale Fell—a scene not often viewed by Lake District walkers. The more shapely summit of Great Calva, which was to be my last top, could be seen almost due south but, before going there I had to pick up the insignificant top of Coomb Height—the two-thousander I had never visited before. This meant a tramp of about a mile and a half to the east across grass and bogland and a return to the depression between Knott and Great Calva. There was no sense of achievement about picking up this spur of the main summit that, in fifty years of wandering about the fells of Lakeland, I had managed to miss—only a slight annoyance about having to make this digression just because a grassy mound happened to top the 2,000 feet contour by 58 feet.

Great Calva dominates the waste of Skiddaw Forest, where there are almost no trees. The mountain is a symmetrical pyramid—well seen from the main road through Lakeland in the gap between the bulky masses of Skiddaw and Blencathra—but was almost unknown to most mountain folk until the 1920s when Eustace Thomas included its summit in his record-breaking round of the Lakeland fells within twenty-four hours. Nowadays, all people attempting the round include this remote summit and Great Calva is now perhaps better known to fell-walkers than it ever used to be. Previously, it was mostly shepherds who knew its heather slopes but, now, the last shepherd has left the area. I came down by the fence through the heather to a tributary of the Caldew and looked leftwards to Skiddaw House set in its wind-break of trees—perhaps the loneliest residence in England. Then, easily along the track in the evening sunshine to my car near Carrock Mine. Not one person had been seen on the fells all day but here, around the mine, were dozens of people—picnicking families with their children and about a score of geologists, each with a hammer in hand. Perhaps it was a geologists' meet, there were so many of them, and they had obviously had an interesting day chipping about round the mine, for they were chatting together most enthusiastically. And I, too, had had an interesting day, with surprisingly easy going, considering the amount of ground covered—no excitements, but many wonderfully rewarding views of country that is part of Lakeland but so different from the more popular areas. It was pleasant to have revisited these lonely summits at the 'back o' Skiddaw' and to have had them to myself on such an invigorating day. Within a few hours I had seen the familiar Lakeland fells from an unfamiliar angle, looked across into Scotland and been reminded of ancient local industries and even older forgotten civilizations.

# 3. The North Western Fells

There are only nineteen summits over 2,000 feet in height in that area of the Lake District commonly known as the north-western fells—the attractive segment within the boundaries of the Rivers Derwent and Cocker or, more familiarly, the Borrowdale and Buttermere valleys. This seemed too brief a section for the purposes of this book so, to swell the total, I have included the long, exhilarating High Stile ridge with its several summits—loosely, the Buttermere fells—under the heading the North Western Fells which, if you look at the map, is reasonably accurate. My arbitrary westwards boundary is thus shifted from Buttermere to Ennerdale—the other side of the long line of summits stretching from Honister Hause to the farthest end of the planted forests. This brings the sum of summits in this section to thirty which may bring rather more balance to the book.

All this area is splendid walking country—among the most satisfying within the national park. The ridges are easy for the most part and quite long walks may be covered at a good speed—sometimes on springy turf or peat. After the initial steep ascent to a ridge the walker can usually continue, with little further effort, over several linked summits and experience the joy of traversing a switchback skyline with impressive depths below. This, I think, is the special attraction of this area—the following of easy tracks, except in a few places, above steep crags and rocky combes. Almost everywhere the plunging slopes on either hand are steep, sometimes spectacularly so, although the walk over the summits may be little more than a promenade. And so you stride along in comfort, admiring the views of the highest peaks and the long valleys, sometimes jewelled with lakes, and feeling—as you are—on top of everything. Sometimes you can pick out the Isle of Man or the Scottish Lowland hills and there may well be views of Pillar Rock or Scafell Crag lighted by the evening sun or perhaps, far to the east, the snow-capped summits of the Northern Pennines. The vast afforestation in Ennerdale and Whinlatter may strike a discordant note for some but although those of us who remember the first of these valleys before the conifers were planted may sigh for the former wildness of the dale, the forests—especially those in the Lorton Fells—can, with their little-known glades and rides, have their own intimate appeal.

Of the dales between these heights Newlands, stretching south into the heart of the fells, has always had a great attraction for me—its links with the old miners of hundreds of years ago, its quietude and serenity, and its pastoral peace on a summer's evening. Buttermere is one of the most rewarding valleys in the Lake District, with its trio of shapely lakes and its ramparts of mountains and crags, and is still less spoiled by modern usage than many of the other dales. I recall many holidays spent, as a youngster, at Richardson's farm at Gatesgarth and the atmosphere seems largely unchanged today. And the sunlit crags in Birkness Combe where I spent many of my early climbing days are among the friendliest and most welcoming in the district. Perhaps they have a special nostalgic appeal for others as well. Many years ago I encountered three elderly mountaineers on these crags—revisiting climbs they had pioneered fifty years earlier.

Besides the walks detailed in this section many others can be recommended. One of these is the horseshoe round of all the summits on either flank of the Buttermere side of Honister Pass. It is better to start and finish this round in Buttermere village; otherwise, starting from Honister Hause, you have the ascent from the valley, in the middle of your walk, of either Robinson or Red Pike, depending on whether you are doing a clockwise or anti-clockwise round. I once did this round of eight summits, starting and finishing on the pass, on a day that turned into quite an adventure, described elsewhere.* More recently, I contrived an unusual ascent of Robinson from the top of the pass, keeping to rock almost all the way. The Grasmoor fells present many opportunities for shorter horseshoe rounds than the rather spidery circuit described in the following pages. One of the best of these is the circuit of Gasgale Gill, starting up the steep front of Grasmoor above Lanthwaite Green with a scrambling or rock-climbing route, continuing to Coledale Hause and then finishing over Hopegill Head and Whiteside. While the horseshoe round of Coledale

* *The Roof of England.*

Beck from Braithwaite, embracing Grisedale Pike and the Causey Pike ridge from Eel Crag is one of the classic circuits of Lakeland. The little Ard Crags ridge, north of Newlands Hause, is also well worth doing and the descent of Robinson by way of High Snab Bank can make a fine finish to a round of these fells.

The Borrowdale and Buttermere fells were first explored by my brother and I at holiday times and now, half a century later, they still retain something of that holiday atmosphere, although not to the same extent as Wasdale Head. We used to stay at farms and cottages and the dales folk became our friends. There were no climbing huts or organized camp sites in the early days and tourism was nothing like the industry it is today, although the four-in-hands were still going over Honister Pass forty years ago. We had oil lamps in our bedrooms and ate tremendous meals in huge, warm farmhouse kitchens. Mrs Edmonson's pies at Seathwaite, made from Herdwick mutton, slowly cooked for many hours, were the most succulent I have ever tasted. Taking the Borrowdale bus from the square at Keswick was always the start of new adventure, long awaited, and the return, in the evenings, on Buttermere holidays, to the lamp-lit front room at Gatesgarth Farm, papered with notices of sheep sales, an always memorable occasion. We were fortunate, indeed, to have known these lovely dales before the motorcar menace and before the rash of car-parks, official camp sites, public conveniences, litter-bins and grossly-eroded footpaths.

## The Newlands Round

My first outing in the Lakeland hills after a week's snow climbing in Scotland was an easy round of the shapely Newlands fells on a perfect day in early June. The comparison between the two experiences—separated by less than a week—could hardly have been more marked. Wonderful days of climbing steep snow slopes or balancing along narrow snow ridges on and around Ben Nevis, and then this equally wonderful day ambling along sunlit heather tracks in the homely Newland fells with distant patches on the Scafells the only snow to be seen. Alpine scenery, winter techniques and range after range of snow-capped hills reaching out to far horizons, one week: the next, the compact variety of familiar fells, the cuckoo singing in the woods and the fragrance of evening woodsmoke. But all the hills are worthwhile and familiarity with one's little homeland fells will never breed contempt—or even mere acceptance. At the right time, a perch on High Spy can be as rewarding—although in a completely different way—as the north face of Ben Nevis.

This pleasant Lakeland day was merely the circumnavigation of the upper Vale of Newlands from Little Town and the collection of six easy summits in the Derwent fells. About forty years ago I remember coming down into Newlands one evening after a similar sort of day and being so impressed by the peace and quietude of the dale that I resolved, there and then, that if I lived long enough to reach retirement age this was where I would make my home. Today, long since retired—for authors writing about lovely places are not thought to work—I still have the same affection for this delectable corner of Lakeland, although my roots have long been established elsewhere in the district.

The weather on this mid-week day in early June could hardly have been better—warm and cloudless with rather hazy morning views changing later to vistas of remarkable clarity and colour. There were spring colours on the trees as I motored north, past a brimming Thirlmere, and later the quiet of the leafy lanes around Newlands, with sheep dogs asleep in the morning sunshine, and a cuckoo singing somewhere below Scope End. From the start I went straight up over Knott End and through High Crags and Bull Crag on to Maiden Moor, selecting a rock-climbing or scrambling route that proved very satisfying. Sometimes, coming to a place that seemed too steep or too holdless for a lone climber, I had to retreat and find another way but I managed to keep on rock nearly all the way. Such unconventional ascents are not recommended for the ordinary walker but the climber, in reasonable form, can get a great deal of pleasure by picking out simple rock routes up craggy slopes, and eschewing the well-marked tracks. Bilberries were growing in great profusion below and among the crags—it looked like being a good year for them—but, unfortunately, the fruit was not quite ripe. I thought of coming back for the picking in a month or so but never managed it. From the top of the crags I looked down on the roofs of the hamlet of Little Town—looking, for all the world, like a cardboard model of Toy Town.

The first 2,000-foot summit further along the ridge is labelled Nitting Haws on Falkingham's list but this is hardly correct. Nitting Haws is really the crag above Dalt Wood in Borrowdale, about half a mile east and much lower than the summit ridge. Actually, this first summit has no name, although Blea Crag might be an approximation. Somewhere along the Narrow Moor track I fell in with a young American teacher, on her first visit to Lakeland. She had been up Catbells with a guided party and then, not admiring the leader's rather truculent manner, and with a commendable display of independence, had left them for a walk on her own. Her enthusiasm for the views of Borrowdale and the high fells was refeshing but, perhaps, a trifle exaggerated. "We've nothing like this in America;" she said, although I suspect her knowledge of the uplands of that vast continent was rather limited. But she only went as far as the Blea Crag cairn where she proposed to sketch and then find her way down to Borrowdale, hopefully avoiding her abandoned party.

After naming all the distant summits for her—she jotted them down in a notebook—the walk was continued along the top of Eel Crags to the well-built cairn on High Spy which had recently sprouted a second, fairy-like erection, too delicate to withstand the winter gales to come. This is a splendid viewpoint for the highest hills in England and I studied the distant snow patches on Scafell Pike and Great End, trying to decide whether they were still large enough for climbing or skiing, and finally concluding they were not. A thin, blue haze hung over these distant hills, so that they seemed more like a colour-washed backcloth than sculptured, bulky mountains. But the sprawling houses and hotels of Keswick, the unruffled surface of Derwentwater and the wooded length of Borrowdale glowed and glinted in the sunlight, and motorcars slowly edged their way up the dale towards the mountain wall.

It was not until the late 1940s that the buttresses of Eel Crags were first properly explored by climbers. Some time before then I remember asking Jim Birkett, one of the boldest pioneers of Lakeland climbing, whether he thought these cliffs might yield good routes but he considered them too broken and undemanding to be worthwhile. But he was later proved wrong—a rare thing for this man with an expert's eye for a challenging route—for some of the climbing on Eel Crags is delightful and, in places, of quite a high standard. Continuing down the edge of these crags to Dalehead Tarn I had a chance to study the cliffs, floodlit by the slanting afternoon sunshine, and to remember many pleasant days on the firm, grey rocks of Miner's Crag, the most southerly of the buttresses. Prominent in the view was the abrupt front of Honister Crag on Fleetwith Pike which vaguely reminded me of the side of Glencoe where I had been a week earlier. In a little, rowan-shaded pool in a ravine below the tarn a young man and a girl were enjoying an early summer bathe, but it looked too cold for me. A July bathe—and I had several—would be soon enough. Instead, I found a natural rock seat in a little outcrop above the tarn and had my lunch.

Then, up the steep slopes of Dale Head—an unrelenting ascent of 900 feet—to the dramatically-sited cairn. This is one of the mountain cairns of Lakeland that is regularly wrecked by vandals but the latest structure looked firm and shapely and, for good measure, there was a second well-built cairn close by. During my revisitation of the two thousands that summer I noticed many new or rebuilt cairns on the summits—some of them almost works of art and, clearly, the result of a great deal of devoted labour. There are certainly wreckers about but, in compensation, plenty of people who retain affection for these summit monuments—many of considerable antiquity—and are prepared to do something about it. We could do with far fewer cairns on the paths—about one-tenth of the present number would probably be adequate—but summit cairns, with their special significance, are different, many being old friends that were there when the oldest of us first went into the hills, and some even dating back to days before recorded history. From the summit I looked down the lovely length of Newlands and the mile-long front of Eel Crags and, turning round, could see most of Lakeland, from Skiddaw to the Langdales and Pillar to Helvellyn, with a peep at the Pennines, far away to the north-east.

Nearly every Lake District walker knows the magnificent ridge route from Dale Head to Robinson with crags to the right and Buttermere unfolding far below to the left. It is an easy, airy route that can be covered at speed and this day I had it all to myself. Some visitors are curious about 'Robinson' as the name of a Lake District mountain. Climbers among them might wonder if the fell had been so named after John Wilson Robinson, the pioneer cragsman and statesman farmer who lived at Lorton ten miles away, but, in fact, the name crept into Lakeland nomenclature long before men first began to climb rocks—or even mountains—for fun. One quoted derivation is that the mountain was originally called Robecon at the time of the Normans and was used as a look-out station but this is unlikely. The very earliest guide-books to the district do not name the fell—my 1799 edition of Thomas West describes it, curiously, as "a vast, rocky mountain" with "a thousand gaping chasms"—but, almost certainly, it took its name from one Richard Robinson who bought much of the land in the area about the time of Henry VIII or Edward VI. The property passed to the Stanleys in the middle of the sixteenth century but Robinson's Fell—later abbreviated—kept its name. For me, the name has a homely, local ring about it. There are seven columns of Robinsons in the Cumbria telephone directory and it would be difficult to find a much more localized surname. One can only be grateful that Richard Robinson was not called Longbottom or ffinch-ffarington. There was only one man on top of Robinson on my round—he asked the way down to Newlands Hause—and then I was retracing my steps back to Hindscarth, deliberately by-passed on my westwards walk. The two summits of Hindscarth were soon collected and I sat by the north cairn to eat some mint cake and savour the view. By now the lighting of the fells had changed completely, for the earlier haze had melted away and the mountains were sharply sculptured in the sunshine, with the crags partly shadowed, and the scree, grass and heather making a superb colour picture. The sideways view of the Grasmoor fells, in particular, looked strangely dramatic, despite their smooth upper slopes, and the side-lighting of the succession of ridges made them appear even more exhilarating than they actually are when followed along the well-worn summit tracks.

But the north ridge of Hindscarth, down which I now trotted to the cliffs of Scope End and, eventually, the car, provides, on the right sort of day—and this was just such a day—one of the finest descents from the high fells of Lakeland. The tracks wind attractively through the heather, and the views down into the valleys on either side are surprisingly colourful. First, the dark green of the bracken, then the bright green—almost yellow—of the bilberry, and, finally, the warm green of the grass—a coloured carpet stretching for miles. To the left, the rarely-visited upland valley of Little Dale, threaded by a ravine and leaping waterfalls, and, to the right, the Vale of Newlands where, hundreds of years ago, the Germans were winning their gold. You could see the old zigzag mine tracks and pick out the spoil-heaps and some of the shafts and levels. Opposite rose the buttresses of Eel Crags and I could trace most of the climbing routes, now full in the evening sunlight. A magical valley this, both to look down into and to traverse, but whether the German miners thought so is doubtful. Certainly, the dale has hardly been scratched by the mining and remains one of the really delectable corners of Lakeland.

The evening sun threw the crags on the Causey Pike ridge into high relief, scattered woodlands flecked the sunlit floor of the dale and the sounds were an orchestra of tinkling becks, the cries of the lambs, the clatter of pails in the dairies, and the barking of farm dogs. I had heard the cuckoo in the morning and there he was again—this time somewhere in the wooded crags of Maiden Moor. It had been an easy day, in unspoiled country, following the sun around the sky. To me the Derwent fells are among the friendliest in the district and the Vale of Newlands one of the most restful settings for the end of a perfect day.

## Around Coledale Hause

You can hear the noise of the traffic racing along the 'improved' A66 highway from quite high up on the slopes of Grisedale Pike—the whine of the lorries and the shriek of those low-powered, over-revved motorcycles that increasingly disturb the peace and quiet of country lanes nowadays. To this clamour as I set off from Braithwaite up the Pike at the beginning of a round of thirteen summits in the Grasmoor fells was added the harsh whir of a chain saw in operation at one of the farms and, now and again, the throbbing of unseen aircraft high above the fells. A noisy start, I thought, to what turned out later to be a quiet, lonely day along easy, switchback ridges where the miles could be rattled off at speed. And the early cacophony was the only discordant note on a lovely day in mid-June, with the fells bathed in sunlight and a cool wind on the tops to keep one refreshed.

The shapely cone of Grisedale Pike is a familiar feature of the north-western fells—especially striking under snow—and the ascent from Braithwaite is well-known to most Lakeland walkers. It starts very steeply from the foot of Whinlatter Pass and I generally go as hard as I can up the first eroded groove to test my 'form' for the day. If I arrive undistressed at the easy ground higher up I assume I am reasonably fit for a fairly hard day; if legs and lungs protest I fear I am getting decrepit. But, generally, one improves after a shaky start and, on most walks, I take the first half-hour fairly easily, increasing speed as the day goes on and, on the best days, finishing at the run. This day, having done twenty-two summits during the previous week, I felt fit enough and, indeed, the seven hours round went as comfortably as any of the walks. The distance was about eighteen miles, which is by no means a long day, but these fells between Whinlatter Pass and Newlands Hause provide some of the easiest and most rewarding walking country in Lakeland—impressive views, but easy on the feet for the ridges are well-tracked and mostly over turf or peat. The mountain sides are often steep and craggy but their sky-lines are simple and, almost everywhere, can be taken at the trot.

First, up through the heather on to Sleet How and then up the stony *arête* to the summit where I passed two people resting who thought it "a steep climb". There were two other people having their lunch on the lee side of the summit—they asked me where I was going and seemed awed by the length of my proposed round; they proposed to go on to Hopegill Head and then call it a day. I met one other man on Grasmoor some time later and these were the only people I saw all day. So much for the crowded fells of Lakeland in June, although this happened to be a Friday. No doubt there were many more people up there on the next two days.

From the summit and the subsidiary 2,300 top which was my second summit I looked down into the vast Whinlatter forests to the north. When I first walked these fells there was nothing like this spread of afforestation above the pass, and no forest at all in Ennerdale, now covered with a dark carpet of conifers. We used to look down from the top of Pillar Rock on a completely bare dale, wild and desolate, and I seem to remember they were only starting the Whinlatter forests. These tightly packed plantations were planted long before the much more enlightened afforestation techniques of today and look far too uniform from many angles. But, down in the forests, there is a great deal of unexplored beauty, well worth seeking out. There are ways up Grisedale Pike through the forests from Thornthwaite and High Lorton that can take the walker into little-known country with its own special woodland charm.

The walk along the edge of Hobcarton Crag to the summit of Hopegill Head is one of the highlights of this round of the Grasmoor fells. Here is a slender rocky peak poised above the great crumbling cliff of Hobcarton Crag—the only home in England of that rare plant, the red alpine catchfly. The crag is about 500 feet high and perhaps half a mile wide—one of the largest cliffs in Lakeland without recognized rock climbs, for the disintegrating Skiddaw slate has no attraction for the climber. Draped over the cliffs are acres of bilberry, in such bright green summer profusion that the rotting towers can look, to those with fertile imagination, not unlike some old, stranded hulk, hanging in seaweed. The crag is owned by the National Trust—partly to preserve the rare plant and partly to limit the extent of the afforestation to the north and east. I have never found the alpine catchfly in its habitat—my botanical knowledge is limited—but I know approximately where it grows. After reading about the plant in one of my books a correspondent who happened to be a keen botanist wrote asking for its location and I gave him some rough guidance. A few weeks later he wrote saying he had found the plant and giving me precise information about where it might be found but I have never bothered to seek it out. The tiny summit is popular with the ravens and, on warm summer days, with the swifts that swoop and swerve over your head in the currents of air surging up and out of the gullies.

The next summit was Ladyside Pike, about half a mile away to the north along the fine ridge that leads down to High Lorton. Many years ago this little peak used to be called Lady's Seat; I don't know why the name was changed. There is a pleasant descent across easy rock slabs and then a short walk to the top with fine views of the forest and the Lorton fells. To avoid the return to Hopegill Head—which I had to make later, in any case—I traversed across the rocky north face of the mountain to reach the Whiteside ridge—an interesting bit of scrambling and route-finding. The ridge itself is an exhilarating high-level traverse—especially in winter—with dramatic views to the left into the fine ravine of Gasgale Gill and across the rocky gorge to the great bulk of Grasmoor and the cliffs of Dove Crags. As you progress westwards along the ridge, first to the east summit of Whiteside and then to the main top, the views of the Loweswater Fells gradually improve until, eventually, you are looking down on to the coastal plain of West Cumbria, stretching out to the sea. To get the very best view I went on westwards for nearly a quarter of a mile to look down on Crummock Water and Loweswater and across the little fells to Cockermouth, the Solway Firth and the Lowland hills of Scotland. A really spacious panorama—much more extensive than that seen from the central Lakeland fells.

But this fine ridge was only one of the several excursions I had to make that day along the imaginary spokes of a wheel, centred perhaps on Coledale Hause, so back I went, retracing my steps, to the summit of Hopegill Head—there is no feasible short cut—and then down, over Sand Hill, to the hause. This high mountain pass between Lanthwaite Green in Buttermere and Braithwaite is the key to ascents, all round the compass, of Grisedale Pike, Hopegill Head, Grasmoor, Eel Crags and the Causey Pike ridge—an almost unique staging-post in the hills, comparable in some ways, perhaps, with Esk Hause. There are two ways to the summit of Grasmoor from here. You may trudge southwards to the top of the track between the hause and Buttermere and then up the long grassy slopes to the cairn or, with much more enjoyment, walk westwards and more directly to the summit along the edge of Dove Crags. This latter is the way I took, peering down the crags as I went and, now and again, looking north to Grisedale Pike, Hopegill Head and the Whiteside ridge, looking so dramatic above Gasgale Crags. From the sprawling summit cairn where I once found a brand-new walking stick there was the expected fine view of the Scafells and, due south, the long line of the Buttermere Fells that I was to traverse two days later. It looked a long way from Fleetwith Pike to Great Borne but, in the event, it went easily enough.

To reach my next summit of Whiteless Pike I trotted down south-east to rejoin the Buttermere track and then south-west past Thirdgill Head Man, down to Saddle Gate and up to the sharp, little peak. Seen from the shore of Crummock Water, Whiteless Pike appears one of the shapeliest peaks in Lakeland; approached from the 'back', as I was doing, its pyramid appearance was not so sharply defined but its setting, in the afternoon sunshine, seemed perfect. The Pike is a rocky excrescence stuck out on a spur below a far higher backcloth of bulky fells so that, on its summit, you feel in the middle of the mountains rather than perched on their crests. That day it seemed a superb eyrie, with views of the Buttermere valley, seemingly vertically below, the western mountains and, immediately behind me, the great bulk of Grasmoor, looking twice the mountain you see from the east. It seemed a particularly colourful scene that day—the bright green of the bilberry, the darker green of the heather, the grey, blue and brown of the rock and scree, and the grey sheep grazing the steep grass among the crags. I thought it one of the best view-points I had seen that day—the chain of lakes below, the cars crawling up to Newlands Hause, the sunlit cliffs of Pike's Crag just to the left of Scafell Crag and, further to the right, the huge bulk of Pillar, with the Rock showing clearly above the line of the Buttermere fells. The profusion of heather (or ling) and bilberry seen on this walk, and on that in the Newlands fells, is one indication that these are 'slate' fells. These fells of Skiddaw slate erode down to a scree of soil and gravel that gives excellent rooting to both heather and bilberry—perhaps the best and most succulent bilberries in the district. On mountains of volcanic rock, encountered a mile or two further south, the soil is not so amenable to the bilberry but heather can sometimes grow well.

Again I had to retrace my steps along the rocky ridge up to Thirdgill Head Man and then across the grass above the ravine to the flat summit of Wandope—my ninth of the day. From here it was an easy ascent of about 350 feet to the broad, rocky summit of Eel Crag. The way traverses around the cliffs of Addacomb Hole—a remarkable hanging valley—and looks down to the head of Sail Beck that flows down to Buttermere. Eel Crag is called Crag Hill on the Ordnance Survey maps and this is probably the more convenient name since Eel Crags (plural) is the name of the climbing ground in Newlands, not far away. According to the 1:25,000 map Eel Crag is really the cliff at the northern end of the mountain, just above Coledale Hause, but, for as long as I can remember, the mountain itself has been known by this name to both locals and visitors, so I use the more familiar name. The Ordnance Survey also sometimes use Wanlope for Wandope but I have never known it by this name, and they prefer Burtness Combe to Birkness Combe in the Buttermere fells, although climbers have called this place Birkness for a hundred years. Long-established local usage should, I think, be followed in all these and similar cases.

Although the top of Eel Crag is broad and flat the mountain is a fine, bulky peak with a great deal of rock on its slopes, but without any climbing routes. The mountain has several ridges and is really the centre-piece of the Grasmoor fells, Grasmoor itself being really an outlier. Eel Crag is the culminating, and highest, point of the fine Causey Pike ridge which is traversed by thousands of walkers each year. Joined on to the Grisedale Pike ridge the round forms one of the finest horseshoe walks in the district. All I had to do to complete my walk was to traverse the ridge to Causey Pike, picking up my three remaining summits, and then cut through the lower fells down to Braithwaite. This proved an easy walk over very familiar ground—on to Sail, then over Scar Crags and finally on to the rocky perch of Causey Pike. To the right lay, first, the upper reaches of Sail Beck and, then, the length of Rigg Beck, separated from the ridge by a two-miles' long rampart of rock and steep heather slopes, while leftwards lay the Coledale valley, threaded by its mines road. At the head of this dale is the rampart of Force Crag, shaped like a huge dam, and here, in the mines, amid impressive scenery, barytes was being worked at the time of my visit—and may well be still worked there today.

I sat in an armchair of rock above the heather on the summit of Causey Pike and looked back with some satisfaction over much of the way I had come. Perhaps I had first sat up there fifty years before and I remembered taking my children up there in the 1940s—one of the best-loved little peaks in Lakeland. All that now remained was to trot down the three miles or so to Braithwaite and this was done by retracing my steps a little way along the ridge, dropping down to the col between Outerside and Barrow, and then crossing the Coledale Beck on to the mines road. There was a new, green carpet of bracken in Coledale and, looking back, I could see the clouds settling down on the higher fells. The shadows were lengthening as I came down into Braithwaite but the wind had dropped and the smoke rose straight from cottage chimneys. There is an inn at Braithwaite where they sell real ale drawn from the wood and this was where I concluded my perambulations in suitable style. It had hardly been a round—more a series of traverses along diverging ridges—but I had been all round the compass and trodden all the highest of the northwest fells—some of the best walking country in Lakeland.

## The Buttermere Skyline

The traverse of the smooth switchback of what might loosely be called the Buttermere fells—High Crag, High Stile and

Red Pike—is one of the most exhilarating and best-known ridge walks in the Lake District. Viewed from the north or east these are impressive, craggy mountains—rock walls frowning over rough corries and forests—and their summits are linked by the striding ridge. South and west this magnificent trio of tops slopes steeply, but less dramatically, to the Ennerdale forest so that, on the ridge, you are perched high above parallel valleys with the blue necklace of Buttermere, Crummock Water and Loweswater to the north and Ennerdale Water reaching westwards towards the sea. On a rather cloudy but sultry day in June I planned to walk this familiar ridge, adding Fleetwith Pike at the start and finishing with the western continuation of the switchback as far as Great Borne. The walk embraced eleven two-thousanders but the total was unduly swollen by Fleetwith Pike's three listed summits and Great Borne's two. In addition, Haystacks was included—not quite a two-thousander but one of the most splendid little mountains in Lakeland—because it happened to fit in with the round, and is always worth visiting for its own sake.

The summit of Honister Pass seemed a logical starting point but the four-miles' road walk, mostly uphill, back to the car from Buttermere village at the end of a fairly long day, looked unnecessarily trying. I had no compunction about taking the car to the top of the pass but remembering many occasions when I have had to trudge up the western zigzags of the road after a hard day's climbing or walking around Buttermere I decided to avoid tarmacadam if I could this time. So I approached my friend Ted Stacey of Levens and he readily agreed to accompany me on the walk and recruit his wife, Peggy, as relief driver. By this subterfuge we were able to finish our walk at Buttermere. Ted is a strong walker and an excellent companion in the hills. He is also an amateur meteorologist, more capable than most of forecasting the likely weather for the day, and can often suggest areas of Lakeland where the best conditions might be found—a particularly useful facility. On another occasion also—when I did the High Street fells—he cut short a great deal of low-level walking for me by an adroit motoring ploy to which I will refer later in the book.

On our Buttermere fells walk we dispatched our wives on a leisurely walk up Haystacks with instructions to have the car waiting for us outside the Fish Hotel at Buttermere an agreed number of hours later—I forget how many. They kept the tryst almost to the minute and told us they had enjoyed a pleasant, easy day. Meanwhile, we hurried off up the Drum House track to collect the three 'summits' of Fleetwith Pike. If you start from Honister Hause these must be among the easiest two-thousanders in Lakeland; our only difficulty lay in positively identifying all three for there is little variation in height along the summit ridge. One of the summits is the top of Honister Crag — a dramatic viewpoint — and to make sure of the third we kept to the ridge all the way. From the main summit there was a beautiful view of the string of three lakes pointing north-west towards the Vale of Lorton and, southwards, the giants of the central fells. Fleetwith Pike, with its little rocky outcrops and patches of heather, is a pleasant, airy summit and you are conscious all the time of the great north-facing precipice that drops just below your feet. Many years ago two of us did some exploration of these crags and gullies but failed to yield anything worthwhile although, more recently, several difficult routes have been made.

Honister Crag itself, of course, has been one of the main slate quarries of the Lake District for generations and the almost vertical face of the cliff is a labyrinth of tunnels, shafts, cuttings and tramways. Here, men used to work, hanging out from the face on chains or dragging heavy sledges filled with slate down the precipitous galleries. Nowadays, the quarry-men use more sophisticated methods but the tremendous shattered crag, so dramatically poised above the zigzags of the pass, remains a monument to the skill, ingenuity and courage of centuries of Cumbrian quarrymen. Because Honister Crag was being worked long before the oldest of us was born we have always accepted its rived and shattered face as part of the scenery; whether it was quite so dramatically steep — easily recognizable, because of this, from many distant parts of the district — before the quarrymen came, none of us can be sure. But the black crag, despite the operations of the quarry-men — and also, perhaps, because of them — remains one of the most impressive sights of Lakeland.

This day, however, we had no time for exploration but trotted down easily to Dubs Quarry at the head of lonely Warnscale *en route* for Haystacks — an easy ascent of 1,000 feet or so. Haystacks, as I have already indicated, is one of the most rewarding of the smaller hills of Lakeland. Although failing by about 100 feet to reach the 2,000 feet contour this rugged little fell has more crags, rock outcrops and tarns than many much higher mountains and, where the rock doesn't show through, the fellsides are delightfully carpeted with heather and bilberry. You can climb, scramble, bathe or botanize all over little Haystacks and it is no platitude to say there are surprises round every corner. Some of the gullies on the north-facing crags are of considerable severity—Green Crag, in particular, has many fine routes—but there are much easier climbs on the clean, rough outcrops of Little Round How and Great Round How. Among the tarns Blackbeck Tarn and Innominate Tarn are among the finest in the district and there is another tarn, sheltered by a rock ridge, on the very summit. Here we sat for our lunch during which we were questioned by members of a youth party about a missing member, the best way to get down to Honister and Buttermere, and the names of the surrounding fells. Do these people *never* take maps into the fells, we wondered. The views that day were unusually striking. Billowing clouds masked the summits of Great Gable and Pillar but, through one gap in the grey curtain, Pillar Rock peeped out of the gloom and we had time to identify the line of some of the climbs before the mist swirled across the fellside.

Sandwiches consumed, we worked our way down to Scarth Gap, selecting a rock scrambling route some distance from the track, and then trudged up the screes over the rocky ridge of Seat to the grassy hollow at the foot of Gamlin End, the south ridge of High Crag. This bulky front of the mountain, a soaring treadmill of grass and scree, always seems steep and, like most steep places, needs to be attacked with determination. And so we went at it, in bull-at-a-gate fashion, as hard as we could go, straight up the middle without a stop. I've no doubt that fell runners could do it in half the time but we took exactly fifteen minutes from the hollow to the cairn—an ascent of 750 feet.

The two miles walk from High Crag to Red Pike, by way of the intermediate summit of High Stile, is one of the most exhilarating in Lakeland. For the whole of the way you are treading the roof-tree of the ridge with the craggy corries of Birkness Combe and Bleaberry Combe on your right, and, leftwards, the contours dropping steeply to the Ennerdale forest. It is an easy walk but although the highest skyline in England, the Scafells, is stretched across the horizon behind you, there is little temptation to turn round for the succession of crags, plunging beneath your feet as you circle the corries, commands most of your attention. Not often can the walker look down on such a procession of climbing crags and, on fine weekends, he can pick out climbers on the great, grey buttresses. Similarly, the climbers can see the walkers on the ridge—tiny, moving match-sticks working their way round the corries. On this walk I noticed that a tremendous area of rock on Chockstone Buttress in the Grey Crags area of Birkness Combe had crashed down on to the screes. It was a year or two since I had last climbed on these crags and I had not heard about this rock fall which presumably happened when nobody was about—otherwise, the event would have been well-known to climbers. The fall had certainly altered the whole shape of this buttress and must have been a mighty crash. This disintegration of the crags is going on all the time—often the rock is split by the ice in winter and crashes down in the spring. Fortunately, most of the major rock falls seem to occur at night or when climbers are not around. One of the biggest of them occurred on The Screes above Wastwater several years ago and people living miles away heard the thunder of hundreds of tons of rock crashing down the mountain side.

After passing over the separate summit of Chapel Crags we reached the big cairn on Red Pike from which we had to make a rather trying diversion north-east to pick up the summit of Dodd—the little spur that helps to enclose the fine rock pool of Bleaberry Tarn. This meant a height loss of about 500 feet which would have to be immediately regained for we had to return to the ridge. People doing this ridge walk, continuing on to Starling Dodd and Great Borne, rarely bother to pick up this outlying spur but we had to do *all* the 2,000-foot summits on our round, and Dodd, unfortunately, happens to be about fifty feet above this contour. But the diversion at least gave us an opportunity for a closer look at Bleaberry Tarn, one of the finest corrie tarns in the district, which Robert Southey stated, incorrectly, had once been the crater of a volcano. We rattled down the screes in a few minutes, rather dreading the steep slog back, but, in the event, contrived to avoid the return to Red Pike by making an interesting scrambling traverse across the upper rocks of Ling Combe. In this way we cut the corner by perhaps half a mile, avoided a couple of hundred feet of dull ascent, and enjoyed a pleasant bit of route-finding.

Back on the ridge the character of our walk quickly changed from an airy traverse above rocky depths to a very ordinary trudge across heathery moorland—over Little Dodd, on to the

Harter Fell-type cairn on Starling Dodd, and then a further two miles to the twin summits of Great Borne. We ate some mint cake at one of the cairns on this, our last summit of the day, and spent a few minutes looking round the skyline and picking out familiar mountains from a rather unusual angle. The Helvellyn range looked very distant—actually nearly fifteen miles away. During the last hour the weather had been improving. All the clouds had lifted and it was going to be a clear, sunny evening. Knowing the extremely boggy nature of the old track across Mosedale to Floutern Tarn we set a course almost due east for Scale Force but, even so, could not escape a certain amount of bog-trotting. This country to the west of Crummock Water is among the least-known parts of the Lake District and yet, a hundred years ago, was one of the most popular. The great attraction was Scale Force, popularized as the biggest waterfall in Lakeland, and most visitors to Buttermere sought it out. Even in my youth Scale Force was much more popular than it is today and the paths, I seem to remember, were in far better condition. But waterfalls—particularly those out of the way, like this one—are no longer fashionable and the area now has an air of dereliction. You could almost say that Scale Force has become a Victorian relic and the tracks to the fall—which I never thought particularly impressive—are now extremely boggy, neglected and, on this day, fly-ridden. Another sign of the times, like the decline of the old stone walls on the fells, the growth of knick-knack shops in the villages, the high charges for car-parking and the constant drone of aircraft? Scale Force, it seems, is too far away on too messy a journey to tempt the modern motorist, although the Victorians would walk there and back from Scale Hill without thinking twice about it.

For our part, we walked round the corner of Crummock Water and through the fields in the evening sunshine to the end of our walk in Buttermere village to find our wives complaining about the car-parking charges. The atmosphere of the Fish Hotel has changed since my memories of the place forty years ago when we used to drink real ale from glazed earthenware mugs in a tiny parlour and talk about the early climbers. So we motored over Newlands Hause finishing up in an old inn, looking out to the Derwent Fells, where sausages and chips, washed down with a very respectable brew, seemed to put the seal on a rewarding westwards tramp in which the despised motorcar had proved more than usually useful.

# 4. The Western Fells

The area of Lakeland that I have arbitrarily designated the Western Fells embraces the highest and most spectacular mountains in the country. As well as the extensive Scafell range, with four summits exceeding 3,000 feet in height, there are lofty Pillar and its wonderful Rock, shapely Great Gable with its crags, unusually, facing both north and south, and also—curiously, in such a well-loved area—several little-visited summits that were probably better known a thousand years ago. All these mountains and crags were holiday country to me nearly fifty years ago for they could not be reached so easily at weekends by bicycle, train or, later, our first, unreliable mechanical vehicles. We were on the crags and fells around Coniston and Langdale every weekend but only saw the Wasdale hills from a distance and could only explore them, at first, in our summer holidays. Our earliest visits were on foot from Foxfield railway station, carrying tents, and sometimes we used to bed down in the barn at Down-in-the-Dale near Wasdale Head. Later visits were by train to Seascale where, if I was accompanying George Basterfield, my distinguished sponsor, we would be met by the hotel car from Wasdale Head and drive, in style, up the dale. This was because George was a frequent and favoured visitor—he used to take up the fruit and groceries for the hotel—and I used to bask, an unknown youngster, in the aura of his popularity. So these western mountains and crags became my holiday retreat and, after a lifetime, they still have a flavour about them of happy freedom and carefree relaxation. These were the mountains I used to dream about in my nearer homeland fells and even today, when I can get over there in an hour or so, they still retain something of the old holiday atmosphere. The Wasdale hills were the finest country in the world in my youth; today, they are still the best part of the Lake District.

Wasdale Head was the birthplace of mountaineering in this country, and the proximity of the highest and roughest mountains in Lakeland, and the preponderance of crags suitable for climbing, make it easy to see why. Haskett Smith selected the area for his university reading-parties that led to his first pioneering climbs because the dark shading on the map suggested steep, remote country and we are all grateful for his sagacity. Within a short generation Scafell Crag, Pillar Rock, and the Napes ridges and other cliffs had been roughly explored and a new sport had been born. Undoubtedly, Pillar Rock and Scafell Crag are the finest precipices in England. The Rock is a cathedral of a crag, but far bigger than any cathedral in the world, and Scafell Crag is a particularly steep and extensive face of splendid rock. Further, the Scafell and Pillar ranges comprise the roughest mountain sides in the district. The tourist walking the well-tracked routes to the highest summit in England does not see all the rock but it is all there, on both sides of the ridge, to be sought out and explored. These were the roughly-hewn mountains to which the first climbers came, most of them seeking, not rock, but snow-filled gullies. Many of them were Alpine Club members, used to snow and ice climbing, and to them the Lake District fells were places to visit in winter time in the hope of useful snow practice in the gullies. They came, with their long ice-axes, heavily-nailed boots and balaclava helmets, cutting steps up the snow, and even when rock-climbing began to be developed as a largely summer sport they still brought their ice-axes, using them as props, footholds and hooks in the crags and chimneys. Several of the easier climbs were first ascended in snow and the north-facing gullies of Great End became an important winter climbing centre — and still are today.

The great, hanging corries along the north face of the Pillar range provide wonderfully rough country that is still surprisingly little known. The walk along the ridge is splendidly rewarding but only in the coves — Mirklin, Mirk, Windgap and the rest — can you get the full flavour of this wild country above the Liza and the forestry plantations. Again, Great Gable, is regarded by many as the queen of Lakeland mountains, a shapely triangle at the head of the dale, but, from other angles, this is seen to be a broad, bulky fell, almost surrounded by crags and skirted by some of the steepest screes in the district. So there is much more to Great Gable than the Napes Needle, the Westmorland Cairn and the war memorial on its summit. Furthest to the west in this most exciting segment of the fells are the much shyer summits of Seatallan,

Haycock, Middle Fell and Caw Fell which—especially the first and last—are not often traversed by the devotees of Wasdale Head. They were known to primitive peoples hundreds, perhaps thousands, of years before the 'discovery' of the Lake District—you can see their cairns and tumuli—but, today, for many, this is unknown country, although only a few miles from the most popular mountains in the district.

The western fells provide one of the finest horseshoe rounds in Lakeland—the Mosedale Horseshoe—and several other possibilities suggest themselves. One of these is the round of Nether Beck, a glorious necklace of pools and waterfalls, that could take in Yewbarrow, Red Pike, Scoat Fell, Haycock and Middle Fell, including Seatallan if you wish. A much shorter round traverses the heights around Over Beck. There is also the obvious horseshoe round of the Wasdale hills—the Scafells, Great Gable and Kirk Fell—and this can be considerably enlarged by those fit enough to get round a longer circuit. The perfect round, which makes a very long day, includes the whole of the Mosedale Horseshoe, with the addition of Great Gable and the Scafells, including Great End. Perfectionists might also include the Westwater Screes, with their wonderful viewpoints of Whin Rigg and Illgill Head, and, in any case, this fine traverse, far above the length of Wastwater, should be made by all visitors to the district seeking an unusual walk. The return or the approach along the foot of The Screes is not nearly so rough as early guide-book writers made it out to be.

Some noteworthy mountain pools may be sought out in these western hills—the highest tarn in Lakeland, Broadcrag Tarn, the smallest to possess a name, Fox Tarn, one of the prettiest, Lambfoot Dub, and the more remote pools of Scoat Tarn, Low Tarn and Greendale Tarn, each one a rather special gem. Kirk Fell also has its tarns, set between the twin summits, while Burnmoor Tarn is the third largest in the district. And, for bathing on a hot day, there are pools aplenty in which you can wash away all your weariness and resume refreshed your exploration of an uplifted countryside that, despite the grievous erosion of the popular tracks, is still the heart of the shrine.

## The Gables and Kirk Fell

Towards the end of June, having done ninety of my summits, interspersed with a fair amount of snow climbing in Scotland,

I was feeling reasonably fit and remember my day over the Gables as quite an easy one. It was rather a cloudy day, windy on the tops but fine. My companion was Ivan Waller, a strong walker and redoubtable mountaineer, but on this occasion he was resting from some strenuous climbing days and preferred **to allow** me to do some of the scurrying about on my own. Ivan, who probably prefers hard rock-climbing to the mere collection of summits, and who had recently, at the age of seventy, traversed the Cuillin ridge in Skye, is an excellent companion on a walk or climb but we normally have so much to say to each other on our outings that speeds can suffer. Both of us like to argue for the sake of it—it may be about a route, or about each other's ability, or even about such matters as the growth of tourism or the theory of motorways—and the arguments can continue in the most awkward situations. We started off on this occasion, I remember, with an argument about the best way up Grey Knotts from Honister Hause but I won the day, arguing that I couldn't remember having been up the fell from the Drum House, although I'd been up and down the other route many times, and that, since I was collecting the summits that was the way we would go. (But it's probably not the most interesting way.)

So on we went, easily, over Grey Knotts and Brandreth scrambling over rocky outcrops where we could find them, and admiring the views down Ennerdale and the noble outline of Pillar Rock. Reaching the cluster of tiny tarns at Gillercomb Head I announced my intention to collect the summit of Base Brown, perhaps a mile to the east, to which Ivan replied that I was welcome to do so but that he would continue over Green Gable. He would continue at the same pace, he said, and, if I stirred myself, I could catch him up before the summit of Great Gable. This suited me for I felt like a trot so I contoured across the rocky combe to the cairn on Base Brown and then scuttled up the track over Green Gable to Windy Gap. Ivan was just ahead, making up the side of Great Gable and shouted to me to hurry up, earning me some sympathy from some walkers in the gap who concluded I had been lagging behind a hard task master. Of course, we understand one another. Very shortly we were on the familiar summit of Great Gable and moved over to the Westmorland Cairn, out of the wind, for lunch. Perhaps the view from here is too familiar to lovers of the Lakeland fells to require any gilding from me, but the sight of Wasdale Head, set among its patch-work

The ridges of Blencathra

Skiddaw from Bassenthwaite Common

The Scafells from High Stile

Birkness Combe, High Stile

Red Pike, Buttermere from Robinson

Great Gable

Buckbarrow and Middle Fell

Great Gable from near Sprinkling Tarn

Yewbarrow, Red Pike and Kirk Fell from Styhead Pass

Mirk Cove, Ennerdale

The Screes, Wastwater

Pillar Rock, West Face

fields, with the lake and the sea beyond, is always a considerable experience, no matter what the weather. This is the view the Westmorland brothers considered the finest from any mountain in the district, and few people will disagree with them.

Great Gable was, I suppose, my very first 'holiday' mountain, as distinct from the familiar fells around Coniston and Langdale. One of the first of a hundred little adventures was our first climb up Napes Needle—two rather scared youngsters in plimsolls, with 80 feet of hemp rope, cautiously testing the rather sloping, little foothold on the top block. Once safely on top we felt more confident and, on the way down, having heard that two climbers could slightly rock the top block if they co-ordinated their movements, tried to do so—without success. Mostly, my Gable memories are of sun-baked, summer days on the soaring Napes ridges. Some days we would go up and down three or four of them, one after the other, foolishly stripped to the waist, and I remember one sleepless night at the hotel, my skin red raw and aflame, and the kindly Mrs Whiting treating my burning shoulders with calamine lotion. Mr and Mrs Ritson Whiting, the proprietors of the Wastwater Hotel, were always very kind to me—a seemingly improvident youngster—lending me clothing when my own became unwearable, and providing accommodation at the cheapest rates. For years I used a pair of knee-breeches that Mrs Whiting had rather dramatically repaired—with a black patch on one knee and a white one on the other. It was on Great Gable that I led my first very severe—Eagle's Nest Direct, with George Basterfield, as second, patiently describing every move. Later that day he lowered a rope down Innominate Crack on Kern Knotts so that I could climb it. Another day, in another party, I had the mortification of being almost inextricably jammed within the confines of Smuggler's Chimney on the other side of the mountain. But all these Gable days were youthful, carefree holidays, with no worries except how to do the next move, and all ended with the run down the screes or Gavel Neese at the end of the day, with Wastwater, far below, stretching out to the coast, and the sun gilding the upper rocks of Scafell Crag.

Some climbers had just finished one of the routes on the Napes on my visit with Ivan and we discussed climbs and techniques with them for some time before dropping down to Beck Head. A surprising number of people fail to hit off this route from the summit in thick mist, finding themselves on steep awkward screes well south of the pass; I have made the same mistake myself. The solution is to keep well to the right, along the top of Gable Crag. This day, however, there was no problem for the views were clear and we could see down the whole conifer-carpeted length of Ennerdale and across the dale to the cliffs of Scafell Crag. All I intended to do was finish down Moses Trod and back to the car but Ivan argued that, in addition, I ought to collect the two summits of Kirk Fell. "But," I countered, "I want to include Kirk Fell in my round of the Mosedale Horseshoe"—but Ivan, as usual, had the answer to that. "Do Kirk Fell now," he said, "and when you come to do the Horseshoe you'll be grateful to me that I saved you from doing it then". "But I always do Kirk Fell when I do the Horseshoe—it's cheating if you don't," I argued, but Ivan would not relent and went on to describe, with vivid detail, my future traverse of the Horseshoe, on a stifling hot day, with my tongue hanging out, and faced, at the end, with the steep pull on to Kirk Fell. And so, eventually, I gave in and it was agreed that I would go, as hard as I liked, on to Kirk Fell and that he would follow, at his leisure, meeting me somewhere on my return.

This is what I did, finding myself in unaccustomed good form and trotting most of the way—but the bold Ivan did not follow and the next time we met he was sitting waiting for me half-way up Gable Crag. He had met some friends, he explained, and they had chatted so long he had not thought it worthwhile to follow. So I had Kirk Fell to myself, admiring the distant view of the Isle of Man and, on my return, the bold, rocky front of Great Gable. This is one of the very best views of Gable and well worth the scramble from Beck Head. I remembered an occasion many years ago when four of us, all experienced mountaineers, lost ourselves on the mountain after a day's climbing on Boat Howe. We decided to go over the summit and down to Beck Head but, in thick cloud, missed our direction and wandered all over the mountain, each of us leading in turn, until the mists parted and we found ourselves looking down the screes at Wasdale Head, with a weary trudge ahead of us up the pass. As it happened, I had cause to be grateful to Ivan for persuading me to fit in Kirk Fell that day. For when I *did* come to go round the Horseshoe the day turned out to be one of the hottest and most enervating of the summer, and the lack of water—as he had jokingly forecast – quite a problem, as I will later relate.

And so we came down, on this really quite easy day, round the familiar contours of Moses Trod and made our way back to the car. There were the usual wonderful views of Ennerdale and the Rock, the western dales, and the crags and colours of little Haystacks. It seemed too early to drive home so we did a bit of modest exploring on Honister Crag, scrambling about the quarries, and tracing the climb on Honister Wall just across the head of the dale. And then we went round to Sandbed Gill in St John's in the Vale and had a look at that – it makes a pleasant, varied climb on a bad day – and finished up in a certain hostelry where I seem to remember we got involved in discussions about peregrines. All sorts of things make up a good Lakeland day, and this was another of them – only seven summits, but in a superb area, and plenty of variety.

## Seatallan and Outliers

Many years ago and long before he became the best long-distance fell runner in the country Joss Naylor, the Wasdale sheep farmer, finished first in the Lake District mountain trial – but had to be disqualified. By mistake, he had missed out one of the check-points – the summit of Seatallan – and, when questioned about it afterwards, confessed, with commendable candour, that, in fact, he'd never been on this particular mountain in his life. Since Joss happens to live nearer the summit of Seatallan than anybody else – only two miles away, as the crow flies – and was born only four miles from the mountain this seemed rather strange at the time. I've no doubt he's since made up this gap in his knowledge of the Lakeland fells but the story perhaps underlines the comparative obscurity of shy Seatallan.

It must be true to say that many mountain walkers who believe they know the Lake District quite well have never been up Seatallan, and some of them may not even have heard of it. Seatallan is, in fact, one of the least-known mountains in Lakeland although it is one of the Wasdale hills, within the very shrine of the district, facing the Scafells across the lake, and not far from Pillar and Great Gable. Perhaps it is because the mountain *is* so near to the finest hills in the country that it is so neglected. Thousands of people, hurrying on to the greater delights of Scafell or Gable, pass it by without a glance and Seatallan, hidden from most valley views by Middle Fell, successfully escapes the hordes and, generally, even devoted pilgrims.

Almost certainly, Seatallan was far better known in ancient days—hundreds of years before the first tourists 'discovered' the Lakeland fells. For the huge cairn on its summit is believed to have been placed there by the early British inhabitants and archaeologists say the heap of stones could well be thousands of years old. Incongruously, the only other feature on the otherwise grassy summit is an Ordnance Survey column—the ubiquitous official stamp of civilization.

The round of the two-thousanders to the north of Wastwater, including Seatallan, was made on a very hot day towards the end of June—three days after our traverse of the Buttermere fells. Only five summits were collected but they included, besides lonely Seatallan, the remote height of Caw Fell which is even more lonely. Caw Fell lies far west of the great cliffs of Pillar and is joined on to that splendid range, but is as unlike it in character as is chalk to cheese. Very few people bother to walk across Caw Fell which is about as remote from habitation as you can get in Lakeland. It is a vast, sprawling mountain stretching across many square miles, with several summits and many separate valleys on its flanks but little else. There are forestry plantations on its distant, lower slopes and, to the west, many evidences of the primitive people who used to live on these remote moors in the days before recorded history. This is, perhaps, the one feature of Caw Fell that distinguishes it from a mere mass of uplifted land—its links with an ancient past. Those who are interested, if they have sufficient energy, would, I'm sure, be able to find, in a long day, ancient circles, cairns, tumuli and other relics of our earliest times but the average mountain walker may not want to be bothered. Maps record some of the sites but many remain unrecorded—lost for ever.

One of these sites on Stockdale Moor, on the skirts of Caw Fell, even has a name on the one-inch map—the intriguing-sounding Sampson's Bratfull. Archaeologists say this was an ancient burial place, but the popular local derivation has always been that this was where some ancient giant dropped his brat—or apron—of stones as he hurried across the moor.

I knew these fells of old, slightly but not intimately, so that there was less excuse for my going wrong than for Joss Naylor. But, even so, I very nearly *did* go wrong—through carelessness. My intention was to go up Seatallan first, from the lovely valley of Nether Beck that debouches on to the northern shore of Wastwater. The mountain is not visible from this valley but I knew its general direction and, without bothering to consult my map, scrambled up the waterfalls of a rocky ravine in order to gain the ridge by an interesting route. The waterfalls looked attractive on such a scorching day but the climbing proved unsatisfactory—loose and unpleasant. Arrived on the ridge I turned left for my peak but, seeing Greendale Tarn far below to my right, after going part of the way, quickly realized I was making for Middle Fell instead of Seatallan. If you look at the map you will see that if I had taken the second ravine instead of the first for my scramble I would have been on the correct line. So easy to make these stupid mistakes if you don't use your map on unfamiliar ground; over-confidence can be a costly failing.

There was no need for me to go on to Middle Fell on this particular round—the summit is 92 feet below the 2,000-foot contour—but I remembered the wonderful view from its summit so decided to include the top, adding an extra two miles to my walk. And I was glad I did so. From the rocky summit of Middle Fell, perched high above Wastwater, you look, seemingly vertically downwards, along the whole length of England's deepest lake. On the other side of the valley was the rocky rampart of The Screes, to the left, the great precipice of Scafell Crag and, further to the left, the bold dome of Great Gable. Very few mountain views in Lakeland are more dramatic. I munched my sandwiches by the cairn while I tried to pick out the line of the gully climbs on the mountain wall across the lake. Thence followed the long trudge down the fell and over Seatallan and then a contouring around the headwaters of the tortuous River Bleng to the great wastes of Caw Fell. There was nobody about—there never is, in these parts—and I left my rucksack at the cairn so that I could pick up the mandatory summit of Iron Crag, a remote outlier that reaches out towards Ennerdale. There are three miles, there and back, between Caw Fell and Iron Crag, the day was getting even hotter, and by the time I had returned for my rucksack I was getting just a little tired of these remote hills that have about them more of the atmosphere of the Yorkshire dales than of the Lake District. But the very remoteness and the views of the West Cumbrian plain had a certain charm; that, and the knowledge that I might never be in these parts again since this is not the sort of country I normally seek out.

After all, you can't leave your rucksack for an hour on the top of every Lakeland fell and know it will still be there when you return. Not long ago a pair of my best woollen winter climbing gloves—left at the shelter on Helvellyn by mistake—was appropriated within ten minutes of my departure, and I had to buy a new pair the next day.

So I turned my back on the western fringe of Lakeland—Iron Crag is the most westerly two-thousander in the district—and set off, with a more springy step, towards the better country of Little Gowder Crag, Haycock and Scoat Fell—the high road to the glories of Pillar. For just five minutes on the summit of Haycock there was no sound of aircraft or anything else—a still, evening silence in the sunshine that was vastly rewarding. I looked across at Black Crag—to be traversed in my Mosedale Horseshoe round about ten days later—and turned round to see the evening sunlight gilding the upper rocks of Scafell Crag. Ennerdale Water stretched out towards the sunset and the sea—I had seen the cooling towers of Windscale from Iron Crag—and, far below, the conifers marched up the dale. Then, back down Nether Beck at the trot towards Wasdale, with the pools and the waterfalls getting bigger and better with every half-mile. Scoat Tarn, to the left, a quiet, blue pool set among green grass and grey rocks, suggested a bathe but I was too lazy to go across and rather short of time. Three miles further down the beck I met the only people I had seen all day—three youths bathing in one of the Nether Beck pools. It was cold, they said, so I wasn't tempted.

On a perfect summer's evening I came down to Wastwater to see the sunshine lighting up the whole length of The Screes and the grey cliffs of Pike's Crag. The lake was calm with hardly a ripple on the surface and there was one white sail on the water—a little yacht slowly gliding across the blue. It had been a lovely day in lonely country with only the sheep and the ravens for company. The sunshine glowed on the new bracken and as I came down past Joss Naylor's farm there were the cries of lambs. Only the drive back home over the passes remained and on Wrynose the sheep were already bedding down for the night on the tarmac—cooler for them, it is said, on a hot night, than the fellside grass.

**The Mosedale Horseshoe**

There are half a dozen Mosedales in the Lake District—perhaps not surprising since the name means 'valley with a bog'—but only one Mosedale Horseshoe. As most energetic visitors to the Lake District know, the term 'horseshoe' is used to describe a round of the fells surrounding a particular valley, starting and finishing at the same place. There are many of these horseshoe rounds, since the spokes-in-a-wheel configuration of the fells and dales lends itself to these upland circumnavigations, and such mountain walks are among the most rewarding ways of enjoying the heights. You are going all round the compass, with constantly changing views, never treading the same ground twice, and keeping on the tops all day. Sometimes you can so arrange your round that you are walking into the sun most of the way round—if you prefer this to having the sun on the back of your neck all day.

The Mosedale Horseshoe—the circuit of the finest of the Mosedales, the splendid dale that reaches north-west from Wasdale towards the Pillar range—is one of the most enjoyable rounds in Lakeland and, perhaps, after the Fairfield Horseshoe, the best-known. There was even a television play about it a few years ago although the characters, I seem to remember, failed to get round. Indifferent or irresolute walkers tackling the circuit in half-hearted fashion also have a habit of retreating to base before they have managed the full round, for the walk is fairly lengthy and can be quite strenuous for those not fully fit.

The usual way to do the walk is to start with the ascent of the rocky crest of Yewbarrow and finish with the traverse of the western summit of Kirk Fell. You end the day with the steep run down the scree and grass of Kirk Fell which lands you straight into the back bar of the hotel—a most suitable conclusion. The hotel is plainly in view from the top of your last mountain—a mile and a half away and about 2,500 feet lower down—and the time for your descent is dependent upon the measure of your need for sustenance. During hot weather some very fast descents can be made. But many people doing the round miss out Kirk Fell altogether—the 850 feet of the steep ascent from Black Sail sometimes proves a little too demanding towards the end of a fairly tiring day—and, as a result, don't really complete the horseshoe. They also have to do without the break-neck descent for the beer which, at the time, generally seems to make the extra exertion well worth while.

But when I did the Mosedale Horseshoe during my collection of the two-thousands I not only did the walk the 'wrong' way round but missed out Kirk Fell as well, thereby invalidating the trip as a genuine round. My excuses were that I had done the Horseshoe correctly on many previous occasions, was merely bagging a few more of my summits, and had been over the twin tops of Kirk Fell about ten days before. You will remember that my companion on that occasion, Ivan Waller, had persuaded me to include these summits in my modest round of the Gables, adding that I would have cause to be grateful to him for his suggestion if my Mosedale day turned out to be very hot. As it happened the day, early in July, was one of the hottest of the year, with shade temperatures well into the eighties, and not enough wind on the summits to blow out a match. For this reason I decided to do the round this time in an anti-clockwise direction, having worked it out that by this means I would be facing the sun most of the time, instead of having it on the back of my neck, which I like to avoid if possible. The few people I saw during the day seemed to be going the proper way round—or part of it—and were staggering about with handkerchiefs tied on their heads and obviously feeling the heat. For once I seemed to have made a sensible choice, and more than once, I silently blessed Ivan for his advice.

The last time I had been round the Pillar summits in this direction must have been nearly twenty years earlier when I was regularly climbing on Pillar Rock. After our climbs we used to trudge up to the top of Pillar mountain and then continue the round, in the evening sunset, over Scoat Fell and Red Pike, descending to Wasdale Head by way of the Dore Head screes. This used to be the finest scree run in the district for rapid, easy descent but, over the years, the beautiful, loose surface of sliding stones has been swept away by constant use, transforming Dore Head nowadays into a very poor imitation of its former pre-eminence as an escalator. But, in any case, on my present round, the short-cut of the Dore Head screes was not available for I had to collect the summits of Stirrup Crag and Yewbarrow, further round the Horseshoe.

Secretly, without even admitting it to myself, I think another reason why I went this way round might have been to avoid the extra two miles of road walking which the ascent of

Yewbarrow from Bowderdale can involve. This is the most exhilarating start to the Horseshoe—especially if you climb over the little cliff of Bell Rib, which is not a walker's route, on the way—and gives the true flavour to the round, but road walking on a mountain walk merits avoidance where possible. I had been round this way several times and, more than once, had started by going straight up the side of Yewbarrow from Wasdale Head—a grievously-steep slope of sliding screes and rocks cunningly concealed in heather and bracken. This is the way I intended to come down this time—straight to the hotel and the car—but as a route of ascent it leaves much to be desired. I remember Alan Heaton, the former holder of the Lake District twenty-four hours fell record with sixty summits traversed, once jokingly telling me that when he had reached the summit of Yewbarrow by this route at the start of some of his record attempts he used to feel he was half-way round.

So I set off up Black Sail from Wasdale Head on this very hot day with the high fells shimmering in the haze, and the becks almost dry. Not only was it oppressively hot but there was no breeze of any kind so that Wastwater in the morning sunshine was really like a giant mirror, cliché or not, with the highest mountains in England, in all their summer colours, exactly reflected in the unrippled calm. Sheep lay, apparently exhausted, in the shade of stone walls winding over the fells or sheltered from the burning heat among the bracken on the steep slopes of Kirk Fell, and reaching the dwindling trickles of Gatherstone Beck on the way to Black Sail was like arrival at an oasis in the desert. This, due to forgetfulness, which I will explain later, was to be my last and only drink during the round, although I didn't know it at the time. Stripped to the waist, as is my wont on mountain walks in summer, and with my rucksack only half its winter weight, the perspiration nevertheless ran down off my nose in an almost united stream and I could feel the pounds oozing out of me.

The rigours of my peak-bagging game meant I had to collect the little summit of Looking Stead which is off the track—I had taken the short cut to the ridge avoiding the summit of the pass—and, later, had to pass over three summits of Scoat Fell and the fine, little peak of Steeple which need not all be included in the Horseshoe round. There was still not a breath of wind on Pillar mountain—nearly 3,000 feet above sea-level—and all the surrounding fells were suffused in heat haze. The first walkers encountered during the round—I saw half a dozen all day—passed in the opposite direction, looking distinctly dispirited. It was hardly a day for running but they were barely moving. We croaked something to each other about it being hot and crawled on into the haze. The northern crags along the ridge dipped steeply down to the Liza and the straight lines of the Ennerdale afforestation, far below, looked an affront to nature. I could hear a chain-saw being used in the forest but this was the only sound. Sandwiches were consumed on a rock outcrop overlooking one of the wild corries but there was nothing to drink.

Walking over to the northern edge I looked down on the top of Pillar Rock, perhaps 500 feet below and wondered whether anybody was climbing there. (As it happened three friends of mine who I chanced to meet later in the bar at the Wastwater Hotel were doing the very severe route of Grooved Wall, a splendid climb on the north face of Low Man. Partly sheltered from the sun they had escaped the worst of the heat, but seemed to be needing their drinks, nevertheless.) Few people go this way—over the summit of Pillar—to climb on the Rock. The most favoured way from Wasdale is by the magnificent high-level route from near Looking Stead, passing Robinson's Cairn on the way. Sometimes we have gone to the Rock through Wind Gap, the high col west of the summit of the mountain, but this is better, although rough, as a route of descent.

Later, from the rocky summit of Steeple, I could see thin becks tumbling down the fellside and hear the sound of distant waters far beneath but this didn't help my thirst. I looked across at the climbs on Black Crag and decided it would have been a better day for climbing than for walking. Ennerdale Water, shaped rather like a spoon, looked immeasurably inviting but lay four rough miles away and nearly 3,000 feet lower down. I reached the cairn on the main summit of Scoat Fell—the only mountain summit cairn that I can think of that is built on top of a wall—and turned south along the Horseshoe towards the next summit of Red Pike. Not far from the track from Scoat Fell to Red Pike—unmarked on the one-inch map but clearly indicated on the 1:25,000 map—there is a spring that never fails, even on the hottest day. I had used this spring many years before and should have remembered it—but didn't. At the time I was trying to decide whether or not it was worthwhile to drop down to Scoat Tarn for a drink and a bathe, but the necessary loss of several hundred feet of height, and subsequent re-ascent, persuaded me against this—and the inner debate perhaps made me forget the spring.

And so on to the splendid, rocky mountain of Red Pike—one of my favourites. There is an attractive mountaineering route, on rock nearly all the way, from the head of Mosedale to the summit and I traced some of it as I sat perched on the tops, with my legs hanging over the cliff. What a wonderful viewpoint this is, with the curious shape of Great Gable—looking, from this angle, something like an atomic explosion—the mass of Kirk Fell, and the dramatic sight of the great cliffs of Scafell, caught by the late afternoon sunlight. The swifts were swooping and darting about the summit, riding on rising zephyrs that I could not feel, and, a little further on, I sat in The Chair—the comfortable eyrie that many mountain folk will know.

Rested, I trotted down to Dore Head, looked sadly at the ruined scree slope, and then scrambled steeply up the rocks of Stirrup Crag and on, across peaty moorland, to my final summit of Yewbarrow—my tenth top of the day. By now much of the heat haze had melted away and the mountains stood up all round in sharp clarity, with the evening shadows sculpturing the crags. Almost every yard of my round could be seen, looking back, and I was glad, thirst excepted, that it had gone so easily. Far below Mosedale slumbered in the shadows and Wasdale Head, the heart and shrine of Lakeland, beckoned attractively. Straight, then, down the screes, getting a decent run here and there, and then the plunge through the boulders in the heather and across the old, familiar bridge that I have known for more than fifty years, into the shady bar. Stupidly, I could hardly croak out my order for I was more dehydrated than I had been for a long time. The friends who had been climbing on Pillar Rock came in and, eventually, my voice returned. "What a waste of a good day, plodding round the Horseshoe, instead of climbing," argued my friends, and I had to confess I was a peak-bagger for the summer.

Only the evening drive over the passes remained of a memorable day in which many familiar scenes had again been enjoyed and many old memories recalled. Little, I decided—except the Ennerdale forests—had changed in fifty years. And the Mosedale Horseshoe—even if you miss out Kirk Fell and go the 'wrong' way round—must always be one of the best walks in Lakeland.

## The Scafells Ridge

Francis Falkingham lists thirteen summits in the Scafell group but these include Esk Pike and Rossett Pike which fall more naturally within the Bowfell round. However, due to my bad planning—or, rather, complete lack of it—I had failed to tick off these outlying summits during a traverse of Crinkle Crags and Bowfell in May and so had to fit them in while collecting the Scafells. It seemed reasonable to collect Rossett Pike and Esk Pike from Langdale but the Scafell round would include the descent to Slight Side and this would involve a further descent and ascent to get back to the start. So I decided to divide the Scafell summits and outlying tops into two, collecting some from Langdale and the remainder from Wasdale Head. Had I thought about it earlier I could easily have included the two Pikes in my Bowfell day, and then collected all the remaining eleven Scafells in one go. This I would commend to others, and the round could also present several interesting alternatives.

My companion for the first day in the Scafells was my son, Robin, who is a competent mountaineer but has been involved, for many years now, in Rugby Union in Scotland, as player and administrator, so that his mountain activities have suffered. At the age of eighteen years he had accompanied me on a traverse of the Cuillin Ridge in Skye and, over the years, he and I had done a lot of climbing and mountain walking together—much of it in appalling weather in Scotland. Robin has a particularly well-developed sense of direction in mountain country and can also read the contours and small print on a map without a magnifying glass—an achievement that is beginning to escape me—so is a useful companion. As a youth, in the cause of fitness, he used to carry the rope and, often, my rucksack but, unfortunately, he doesn't see the need for this nowadays.

This first Scafell day turned out to be one of the wettest of all my days among the two-thousanders, the clouds hanging depressingly low over the dales for most of the walk—the usual weather, in fact, when Robin and I go out together. We splashed along Mickleden to the sheepfold, from which we gloomily surveyed the lower reaches of Rossett Gill—the upper reaches were concealed in grey cloud. Off and on, I have been toiling up Rossett Gill for fifty years but familiarity had not increased the attractiveness of the place and, this day, it seemed the old, wearisome plod. I prefer, when ascending, to keep to the side of the steep, stony ravine but, in descent, it is a good plan to use the former pony track which sweeps away to the west and can be trotted down in comfort. Steep, unattractive slopes are best taken direct—if only to get the business over as quickly as possible. This is what we did this time and on our return we ran down the pony track. We were, of course, pretty wet through by this time. In a lifetime of mountaineering I have never really solved the problem of keeping dry. You can buy all sorts of garments for keeping out the rain but the excessive condensation they produce makes you just as wet in the end. Years ago, during wet weather in summer, I used to strip to the waist, putting all my clothes in the rucksack, but nowadays I find even summer rain rather too chilling to the body when high in the hills. Sometimes, as a compromise, I wear a very light cagoule next to the skin but, after a time, the interior of the garment becomes just as wet, through condensation, as the exterior, and you merely achieve a cold, sticky clamminess. Probably the best plan, I find, for coping with wet weather in the mountains in summer is to wear the thinnest possible woollen sweater next to the skin, with a lightweight cagoule on top. In this way, although your sweater becomes wet or damp through condensation, you avoid becoming too chilled—but may be much too warm. On these occasions a small towel is a useful item for the rucksack.

Some people wear so-called weather-proof over-trousers but I have always found these too warm, too prone to condensation and far too much of a nuisance, pulling them on and off. So I just get wet through below the waist in summer—and wetter still if I am also wearing the average cagoule, for the water drains off these on to the legs and knees. Of course, the unpleasantness of getting wet through in the fells only lasts during the build-up period. Once you are really wet through—provided you keep moving—the misery is over, and you feel warm and cosy. All these remarks apply only to summer expeditions in the hills. In winter, the problems are much different and more serious. I then take a couple of thin sweaters, anorak and wind-proof cagoule and also wear a woollen shirt and gaiters. For snow climbing, when one can sometimes remain stationary on sunless, north faces for quite long periods, I have an old pair of 'long-johns' and, of course, proper woollen mittens and gloves. At all costs, in winter time, you must maintain body temperature and cold winds are the principal danger. Cotton or nylon underclothes and shirts are not good enough.

The almost universal reliance by people going into the fells nowadays—especially parties of young people—on lightweight, wind-proof cagoules as an all-purpose garment, seems to me to be very much overdone. Many of these people seem to wear cagoules all the time—often on top of a great deal of other clothing, even in summer time—and then wonder why they are so tired, enervated or generally hot and bothered and sticky. Far better to wear an absolute minimum of clothing for the ascent, especially in summer. Stripping to the waist in warm weather is often the answer, with the cagoule used against the wind on the tops, or—subject to its marked deficiencies—against the rain.

I was wearing a very thin sweater next to the skin with a cagoule on top on this Scafell trip and was very warm and wet for most of the time. Of course, when we stopped for lunch, we put on extra clothes against the wind, but many people seem to keep on the same clothes all day. Emerging at the top of the gill we strolled across to our first summit, Rossett Pike, which can be a particularly fine viewpoint. From the Mickleden cairn on a clear day there is a tremendous prospect of the whole length of the dale and the ramparts of the Langdale Pikes, but this time we could only see a few yards along the ridge. It was pouring with rain and pretty dreary but there was a young man sitting by the cairn, without anorak, cagoule or headgear. We wished him good-day and left him there—perhaps waiting for the view, which might have come about four hours later.

Down we squelched to Angle Tarn, by the shores of which I once spent an even wetter night, awakening in the morning to find the tent completely surrounded by water. We then took the easy track to the high and very ancient pass of Ore Gap which was in thick cloud and took a compass bearing for the traverse of Esk Pike and down to Esk Hause. Esk Pike is the tenth highest mountain in Lakeland, or thereabouts, but was not given the dignity of a name on the one-inch map of the Ordnance Survey until, I think, 1964. Up to then it had to be content with a dot in the centre of a ring contour, and the figure, in feet, of its quite impressive height—2,903. At one time I've no doubt the mountain was merely regarded as a spur of Bowfell, despite the drop of several hundred feet to the red earth of Ore Gap, and it was not until 1870 that it was given its individual name—by a geologist named Ward who was working on a survey. Ore Gap was used by the stone-axe makers of Langdale thousands of years ago and by the iron-smelters of olden days bringing the ore out of Eskdale, but the mountain on its southern flank has only had a name for a hundred years. You can still see where the bright red vein of hematite runs down the Eskdale side.

We found the rocky summit of Esk Pike—it lies some way to the east of the track to Esk Hause—and then trotted down to a little cluster of rocks, just above the Hause, and out of the wind, where we eat our sandwiches. This, of course, is the true Esk Hause—the high pass between Eskdale and Borrowdale—and not to be confused with the popular 'Esk Hause' of the tourists—the much-used highway between Langdale and Wasdale which is 100 feet lower and perhaps 300 yards away to the north-east. We could just see the incorrectly-named 'Esk Hause' through the thinning cloud but the summits were all hidden in the wet, grey blanket.

Our next summit was Great End and this, also, had to be sought out by compass for not many walkers, bound for Scafell Pike, the highest mountain in England, bother to turn aside from the over-cairned track to top the bold northerly end of the range, and the way is not clear in mist. We peeped down the gullies, with their memories of many winter climbs, but there was nothing to be seen except streaming walls dropping into boiling cauldrons of cloud, so we retraced our steps to the grievously-eroded highway. For the climber, these gullies present the most direct route to Scafell Pike from Borrowdale by way of Grains Gill and I have often found hard-packed snow in them on the hottest of June days. Just before we left Great End we had the first of our two magical revelations of the day—the only two occasions when the mists parted, if only for a moment. We looked south to the Scafells, draped in thick cloud, and then, turning round, looked briefly to the north. Suddenly the mists parted and, through the hole, we could see the great bulk of Great Gable across the trough of Wasdale with the Napes Needle showing quite plainly. But the wonderful view only lasted for seconds; in a moment the gap was refilled with cloud and everything looked as dreary as before.

We found the summit of Ill Crag (North)—not far from the track—and then went on to our first three-thousander of the day—Ill Crag (3,040 feet). This is one of the noblest mountains in Lakeland but again, not many of the Scafell Pike pilgrims make the necessary diversion, finding the walk to the Pike, from any base, a sufficiently long day. The true splendour of the mountain is really only appreciated from the wild, upper reaches of Eskdale—a bold cliff of crags and scree presenting many opportunities for mountaineering routes rarely explored. We found a scrambling route to the rocky top and then traversed across the main plateau to the next three-thousander of Broad Crag—3,054 feet. This has been described as the roughest summit in the Lake District since it is protected by a sea of piled boulders and outcrops that could lose you time if you were racing. Once when I was making the round of the seven Lake District three-thousanders within a day I took the trouble to reconnoitre a route on and off this summit, so as to save time, but, on this latest visit, I had forgotten my quick route and we just scrambled up the rocks in a direct line. Somewhere along the ridge I caught a glimpse through the mist, underneath the cliffs of Great End, of the lovely little pool of Lambfoot Dub, which is shaped, exactly, like a lamb's foot. But there was nothing else to be seen.

Since I had planned to collect the summits of Scafell Pike and Scafell on a later walk we had no need to continue south-west from Broad Crag col, but still had to find the rather remote summits of Rough Crag and Pen which lie to the south-east of the Pike. We could have reached these from the Pike but this seemed a duplication of effort so we decided to take a more direct line and launched ourselves down the screes into Little Narrowcove. (I have always thought that the correct name for this steep, rocky gateway to the ridge should be Little Arrowcove, for the Eskdale farmers know it as 'La'al Arra', but the Ordnance Survey prefer their spelling and we must accept it.) We left our rucksacks in a coign of rocks in this finest of Lakeland corries—experiencing some difficulty in finding them later—and scrambled on to Rough Crag and then on to the magnificent little peak of Pen.

Perhaps Pen is the least-visited summit in the Lake District. Unmarked on the one-inch map it is clearly shown on the larger maps—incongruously, within half a mile of the highest and most popular summit in England, Scafell Pike. People go up the Pike every day—many hundreds of them some days in summer—but I doubt whether more than a handful go on to Pen in a year, and probably only the most determined peak-baggers even know of its existence. Appropriately, no tracks point the way and although the little, knobbly summit is graced by a neat cairn there are no disfiguring beer-can rings, orange peel or sandwich wrappings to indicate the previous presence of civilized man. Only a handful of grazing sheep were there this wet and misty day on the tiny patch of turf among the rocks and the usual pair of ravens circling overhead. The name sounds Welsh and means, in fact, 'hill top' in that language but how it came to be applied to a Lake District peak I cannot say. Fortunately, keeping away the hordes, it is separated from the Pike by some of the steepest and roughest ground in the district so its obscurity is likely to remain. Only people used to rough scrambling and anxious to seek out unusual places will trouble to find this shy summit.

My first acquaintance with Pen, many years ago, came following a day's climbing on Esk Buttress, marked Dow Crag on the map—the splendid crag some distance below the summit—when the top merely provided a convenient resting place after coping with problems of verticality. But on this last visit we were amply recompensed for our 700-foot descent from the Broad Crag col and the scramble to the top by our second revelation of the day. Just at the right moment the clouds briefly parted again and we could see the tumbled wilderness of upper Eskdale far below and, looking round, the dark crags just underneath the very roof of England. Across the narrow combe we saw the black precipice of Ill Crag and, right at the head of the dale, the saddle of Esk Hause. A most dramatic picture from our remote eyrie, and the sight of Esk Hause made us wonder whether it would be better to descend Little Narrowcove into Eskdale and then ascend the col for our route home. But, in the end, we decided against this and, after finding our rucksacks—hidden in what seemed the wrong pile of rocks—scrambled steeply up the rocks and scree to the Ill Crag col, thus winning back our lost 700 feet. This may not be the easiest way to tick off Rough Crag and Pen but it suited us all right, for we were in good form and on the lookout for rough rock. It had been an exhilarating diversion and transformed what might have been rather a pedestrian day into a memorable one.

Back to the familiar Scafell Pike track we trotted, down to Angle Tarn and back to Rossett Gill. The rain had nearly stopped and the clouds were lifting. We could even see the Langdale Pikes. Down the gill by the wide sweep of the old pony track we raced, back to the sheepfold and then, more sedately, along the wonderful turf of Mickleden to the car.

The rocks on Gimmer Crag seemed to be drying out a little but there was nobody up there, although later we spotted a lone climber on Oak Tree Wall, Raven Crag. Not very far away real ale is available for the faithful, so we imbibed and dried our clothes. Watery sunlight briefly flooded the dale as we drove slowly past the intake fields to join the main traffic stream for home.

## The Roof of England

Five days after our collection of the Scafell outliers—and the day after my scamperings up and down the fells at the 'back' of Skiddaw—I returned to the highest land in England to tick off the remaining five summits. This time my companion was Ivan Waller and we went up from Wasdale Head. Our journey to Wasdale over Wrynose and Hardknott passes took longer than expected—due to the extraordinary incompetence of several drivers encountered on the way. These passes seem to attract indifferent motorists during the summer months—many of them clearly unable to cope safely and confidently with the steep, winding roads. We were held up several times—once for about a quarter of an hour—by complicated manoeuvres ahead of us on the sharp bends, and constantly had to reverse down the zigzags to accommodate nervous or inadequate drivers. One of the problems on these passes is that many drivers do not follow the elementary rule that descending traffic should give way to vehicles struggling up the hills. In the alpine countries where very much higher and more complicated routes have to be negotiated this important rule is almost always obeyed—otherwise, there would be many more accidents and tragedies than there are on these often hair-raising passes. Most motorists met abroad seem to take it for granted that descending vehicles should pull to the side and stop when meeting ascending traffic. But, in the Lake District, many drivers—obviously unused to this sort of motoring—press on downhill regardless, leaving the possibly-inexperienced ascending drivers to do the best they can—probably stalling, and then finding themselves unable to restart. I can't understand why the County Council don't have signs at the foot of these passes, explaining this rule. The present proliferation of road signs in the Lake District is greatly to be deplored but these signs on the passes seem to be needed. Many other signs should be scrapped. Besides being outrageously unsightly, scores of them only lead to unnecessary confusion.

So, with all this shilly-shallying on the passes, it was quite late when we left Wasdale Head and we pressed on into the fells with some haste. The day was misty and damp, with thick, low cloud on the mountains—it was my fifth outing in a row with poorish weather although this day we had little rain. Lingmell was to be our first summit—a mountain that only fails to achieve greater distinction because it is really a spur of Scafell Pike, separated by a depression of less than 300 feet. But its north-east face is one of the craggiest mountain walls in the district and these cliffs are split by the most dramatic ravine in the whole of Lakeland—the great cleft of Piers Gill. From the Fell and Rock Climbing Club's hut at Brackenclose we went straight up the steep western shoulder of the mountain and along the grassy plateau to the summit without a stop. From the particularly shapely summit cairn—regularly demolished by vandals but intact on this occasion—there is, in clear weather, a remarkable view of Great Gable, seen across the bowl of Wasdale. The splendid southern front of Gable, with its crags and scree seems very close, as if viewed through a telephoto lens, and you can easily pick out Napes Needle and other climbs. There is, also, in the opposite direction, a dramatic view of Scafell Crag and Mickledore but, on this July day, we could see nothing through the mist. We peeped down into the tremendous gulf of Piers Gill and then trotted down to the Lingmell col for a late lunch but, finding it too cold and windy there, trudged a few hundred feet up the Scafell Pike track to seek out a more sheltered corner. The cloud was now thick but the path to the untidy, eroded summit is unmistakable and we were soon there—the highest of the two-thousanders at 3,206 feet. As all mountain folk know, Scafell Pike used to be 3,210 feet—the easiest possible height to remember—but, a few years ago, the Ordnance Survey recalculated their heights and the Pike, like several other Lakeland mountains, had to suffer a certain amount of decapitation.

Scafell Pike is a fine mountain—possibly the finest, as well as the highest, in the country—but the summit has always seemed an ugly place to me. The huge, circular cairn, with steps leading to the top, is partially ruined and invariably littered with the remains of meals or their wrappings, beer cans and other impedimenta. Set into one side of the cairn is a tablet commemorating the gift of the summit to the nation as a war memorial for the Lake District by the third Lord Leconfield in 1920. Close by is the triangulation column of the Ordnance Survey and all round the summit the stones have been heaped into shelters and wind-breaks, where more rubbish can generally be found. The whole summit area is a wilderness of stones, across which tracks have been scratched and eroded in confusing multiplicity. Indeed, there are so many tracks over the boulders in all directions that the highest point in England can be an easy place in which to get lost in bad weather. No matter how well you think you know the summit a compass can often prove a blessing in thick mist. Many indignities have been heaped on the summit of Scafell Pike—unveilings, bonfires, pyrotechnics, flag-flying, concerts, meetings and, once, the dumping there of an enormous, red iron bedstead—so that, when there is no view, the place has little charm. There's nearly always somebody up there at any daylight hour and, on this rather damp, depressing day there was the usual cluster of people on and around the summit cairn, looking appropriately proud that they were nearer the skies than 50 million other English folk.

There was no need for us to linger up there, with nothing to see except a few hundred yards of boulders, so we turned right for Mickledore and, after the usual arguments about the route, due to the confusion of tracks, hit off the ridge by the stretcher-box. To reach Scafell from Scafell Pike the direct route makes the ascent of Broad Stand—an easy rock-climb. This is not a route for inexperienced walkers—indeed for walkers at all, for it is technically a rock-climb—and yet, every year, walkers get stuck there and, very occasionally, killed. Indeed, in the summer of 1977 the Lake District Special Planning Board warned ordinary walkers, especially youth parties, to keep away from Broad Stand, Lord's Rake—an alternative route up the side of Scafell Crag—and Jack's Rake on Pavey Ark. They explained, correctly, that two of these were climbing routes and that all three were badly eroded and dangerous, as a result, to inexperienced people. Over the years, there have been fatalities in all three places. The only safe route for walkers from Mickledore, they suggested, was by way of Fox Tarn, reached by a descent from Mickledore on the Eskdale side. But, with something like 100 years of rock-climbing between us, we didn't feel tied by the Planning Board's strictures and clambered up the wet rocks to Broad Stand. Even so, Ivan, who was still climbing to a very high standard, never likes Broad Stand unroped and I remember when we did the Lakeland three-thousands together, insisted on our going up and down Lord's Rake, to my great disgust. And, on this latest July day, Broad Stand proved unpleasant enough for the holds on the short, vertical pitch were very greasy in vibram-soled boots. There was a lone walker there, surveying the pitch, but after some advice from us—and, no doubt, after watching our inelegant scrambling—he departed to find an easier way. I suppose I must have been up and down the place a score of times but it always proves awkward under bad conditions. Once, many years ago, I was coming down the pitch alone after a fairly long, hot day when I suddenly took cramp in both legs and could neither get up nor down, no matter how hard I struggled. I had no salt tablets with me—but always take them now, in hot weather—so I sat down and ate a cheese sandwich. And, remarkably, after about ten minutes, my legs straightened themselves out and I was able to descend with ease, the cramp having completely disappeared. What would have happened without the cheese sandwich I don't know.

On, then, through the mist, on this viewless day, to the summit of Scafell—the mountain summit that H. M. Kelly, pioneer of some of the hardest rock-climbs on Scafell Crag, claimed he had never visited until years after his exploits, when solicitous friends took him there. Again, there were people crouching round the cairn in the dampness—the first time, I think, I have ever met people on the actual summit of Scafell which does not attract the hordes like the Pike. Again, we passed on for there was still nothing to see—and two more summits still to collect. After leaving the summit I wondered whether we should have gone on to the top of Scafell Pinnacle. This is not one of Francis Falkingham's summits, but perhaps it should be, for it is well separated from the summit of the mountain by the cleft of Jordan Gap and would be the only one of the two-thousanders—apart from Pillar Rock—only attainable by climbing. It is reached by a moderate, little climb that both Ivan and I know well but, since I was only supposed to be doing Falkingham's list, and, in any case, climbing it would involve going back on our tracks, we decided to press on. Regrettably, we had seen little or nothing of Scafell Crag—the boldest cliff in England.

Our last two summits were Cam Spout Crag and Slight Side, both of them on the long, south ridge of Scafell. The way was easy and straightforward, with no need to consult the compass. Half-way along the ridge the clouds lifted for a moment and we had a magnificent view, as through a gap in a curtain, at the curves of the River Esk far below and the black cliffs of East Buttress and Cam Spout Crag. Slight Side is an airy, rocky viewpoint and some way below the summit, on our way back to Wasdale Head, we finally came beneath the clouds and could see Wastwater reaching out towards the sea. On the descent we had a slight disagreement about the best route, Ivan suggesting a bee-line for Hardrigg Gill and the Burnmoor track whereas I preferred a traverse along the contours to Green How and then a quick run down. In the end I deferred to my companion but, afterwards, we both agreed that the Green How route might have been better and slightly shorter—not that it would have made much difference. There were many memories for me on this side of Scafell—a place I haven't visited a great deal in recent years. I remembered, for instance, my brother and I going up this way in the late 1920s to watch the sunrise from Scafell and I also recalled the day, even earlier, when we walked over to Wasdale from a camp in Eskdale for our very first view, from the highest point on the Burnmoor track, of the Wasdale hills—the most exciting view, we thought then, we had ever seen.

There was a heavy shower of rain as we trotted down to Brackenclose, but not enough to damp our spirits. It had been a rewarding day, despite the weather, among our highest mountains, and the five summits collected left me with only one still to do—Pillar Rock, which I had deliberately left to the end, as a fitting finish. I remember, too, I was pleased with my boots, a new combination of socks having achieved a comfort for the feet that I had been seeking for months. The boots still let in water but I had a newer, more water-resistant pair for the winter. For a change, we eschewed the Wastwater Hotel and sought and found welcome hospitality among friends at The Woolpack in Eskdale before our drive home over the passes.

## Pillar Rock

Pillar Rock, the most magnificent precipice in the Lake District, is the one two-thousander in the list that can only be reached by rock-climbing. Because of this I had deliberately left it to the last, as the most dramatic conclusion to a rather pedestrian exercise. Ivan Waller and I went up there one lovely day towards the end of July—leaving me the rest of the year for my neglected climbing, gardening and house decorating and, I hoped, plenty of skiing and snow climbing before the end. There was no celebration on top—not even a handshake. After all, Bill Tilman seemed almost ashamed of himself for having shaken hands with Odell on the top of Nanda Devi.

It is more than 150 years since Pillar Rock was first climbed—by an Ennerdale man, John Atkinson, on 9th July 1826. Before that it had been deemed inaccessible. By 1850 there had only been six ascents of the Rock and by 1875 about fifty but thousands of people have reached the summit since then, and there are now about eighty routes—some of them extremely severe—to the top. A precipice that used to be regarded with awe throughout the district is now a playground. But Pillar Rock, fortunately for some of us, has never achieved the popularity of the Langdale or Gable crags for it is still a comparatively remote climbing ground, only reached by long or steep walking—not welcomed by some modern cragsmen. Indeed, in many visits, I have never encountered more than a handful of people on the crag and, more than once, have had the whole of the Rock to myself. Perhaps the only occasions when the cliff was really crowded were on Easter Sunday 1926, when the centenary of the first ascent was suitably celebrated and a July day fifty years later—and on days following—when the 150th anniversary was commemorated, by, among others, several ladies in bonnets and long skirts.

I think my first acquaintance with Pillar Rock was in about 1930 with an ascent of the North Climb but I can't recall who were my companions. Not long afterwards I went up there again with two distinguished climbers—George Basterfield and C. F. Holland—on a particularly nasty day of driving rain and thick cloud. This was the occasion when, resting on the summit of Black Sail on our way to the crag, we were accosted by a man with a bicycle on his back who appeared dramatically out of the mist and asked us the way to Whitehaven! On another day in the early 1930s I was taken up my first very severe on the crag—the splendid North West climb—by another famous climber, G. S. Sansom—the man who partnered Herford on the first ascent of Central Buttress on Scafell. I have never done any of the really hard climbs on

Pillar Rock, and probably only about twenty of the easier ones.

On the other hand—until this ascent when collecting the two-thousands—I thought I had *reached* the Rock by every route. There had been approaches from Wasdale by way of the High-Level Route, Wind Gap or Pillar Mountain, from Buttermere and Ennerdale by a variety of ways, and even a route from distant Borrowdale, under Gable and Kirk Fell crags. But, on this visit in July 1977 we managed to select an approach route new to both of us—from Ennerdale by way of High Beck and White Pike—and found it an excellent way. For those visiting Pillar Rock for the first time the High-Level Route from Black Sail is very well worth doing—an interesting approach along an ingenious track and, then, suddenly, the dramatic sight of the Rock from Robinson's Cairn. This was the way I took a friend of mine for his first climbs on the Rock a few weeks later and he was suitably impressed. One of the most demanding approach routes is that from Buttermere for this involves the ascent of Scarth Gap and then the descent to Ennerdale, but the subsequent climb to the Rock, first through the forest and then up to the Waterfall, gives the best overall picture of the precipice, towering far above as you work your way up the fellside. Some years ago those of us who belonged to a certain climbing club had special permission to take our cars some distance along the Ennerdale forest road which shortened the approach route considerably. This facility has now been amended, allowing a limited number of climbers in general to drive only as far as Gillerthwaite Farm—about one and a half miles short of the previous terminus. Only two specially designated vehicles a day are allowed to use the road in this way, and permission has to be obtained by writing or telephone. This is a big help if you are approaching the Rock from the west. It is not nearly so convenient as the previous arrangement, but, then, this was restricted to certain climbing club members.

This sunny July day we drove round by Keswick to Ennerdale collecting our road pass at Pardshaw on the way. We felt a trifle privileged, if not embarrassed, near Bowness Knott where we continued on through the gate, past the parked cars, but soon we had to leave our car at the youth hostel and walk along the forest road. The original plan had been to climb the Rock by a suitably modest route such as New West or North Climb but, unpacking the equipment, one of us said to the other—I can't remember which one of us it was—"What's the point in taking all this gear? After all, we're only supposed to be peak-bagging." The other agreed, and so we dumped the rope and all the gear back in the car and tramped on—not climbers now but walkers, although we hoped we were also mountaineers. I blame the heat for the change of plan. It would certainly have been very warm, lugging all the equipment up the mountainside, but, really, I think we were just lazy. But it was very pleasant plodding steadily up the mountain with light sacks and stripped to the waist.

Of course we had a little difficulty finding the correct ride through the plantations but soon found ourselves on the open fellside near High Beck and followed a line of fence posts, beyond an old wall, to the broken rocks below White Pike, an outlier of Pillar. This is really a splendid route up the fell with fine views of Wind Gap straight ahead, Black Crag to the right and, further right, the commanding pinnacle of Steeple. We were making for the screes below the west face of High Man—the most impressive face of Pillar Rock—and argued about the best line we should take. One of us wanted to go over White Pike, the other preferred a traverse much lower down, so, in the end, we compromised and took a line in between which landed us exactly where we wanted to arrive. There were two climbers on Rib and Slab and we watched them working their way up the splendid, steep rock for some time, before launching ourselves on our easy way to the summit of Low Man and thence to the top of the Rock. This is only a moderate scramble for unroped climbers but by no means a route for walkers. As we were taking to the rocks we were approached by a middle-aged walker who had been photographing the climbers. He asked us the name of our route and we told him, the Old West—it was probably the route by which Pillar Rock was first climbed. Did we think he could go up that way, he next asked, and we gently advised him against it when he said he'd only done 'a bit of scrambling'. He decided, however, to follow us but when he had done a few feet, confessed he didn't like it very much, and retreated, wisely, down the fellside. Even the easiest routes on Pillar Rock should be completely avoided by ordinary walkers. It is very easy on any of them to get into very difficult situations and the exposure is considerable everywhere—exceedingly so, in many places. In addition, the Rock is one of the slimiest crags in the Lake District in indifferent weather and several inexperienced people have slipped to their deaths from the cliff.

We went up the ascending traverse to the cairn of Low Man and then up the little cracks and chimneys to the summit and the end of my pilgrimage. Many years ago there used to be a tin box at the cairn for recording names but this disappeared long ago. Soon after we arrived, the two Rib and Slab climbers appeared over the edge and we went down together. They were two young Yorkshiremen on their first visit to the crag and, as is customary with mountaineers the world over, we compared notes. Asked to recommend another good route the two old-stagers suggested the North West and were delighted to see them later coping with this fine climb in excellent style. Meanwhile, we all went down the old, familiar Slab and Notch, meeting an old climbing friend, Tony Greenbank, scrambling about near Jordan Gap which meant another long chat and even, I seem to remember, a spate of photography. And then, back round the foot of the Rock and down the fell-side towards the road and the car.

By a leaping beck near the foot of the Rock we had some food and surveyed the countryside. It was a perfect early evening, the west face of the Rock aglow in the sunshine, the becks splashing merrily down the fellside, the lake and the conifers far below, and the long line of the Buttermere fells showing boldly across the dale. All the mountains we could see I had recently revisited but it occurred to me how little I knew about some of their slopes. The summit line of the Buttermere fells, for instance, was very familiar and also all their northern corries but those southern slopes, above the forest, were almost unknown country. How true it is that you can spend a lifetime exploring the Lakeland fells and still find corners where you have never been. The north-west corner of the Rock reared, in dark silhouette, against the evening sun and, right on the edge, we could see the two Yorkshiremen inching their way up the cliff. They would soon be climbing into the sunshine and we hoped they enjoyed the climb.

# 5. The Southern Fells

The real southern fells of Lakeland stretch in a long, undulating ridge, perhaps fifteen miles long, from Wrynose Pass south-west to Black Combe on the edge of the sea. This line of high land is only broken when it drops down to the woodland of the Duddon and its complete traverse, preferably northwards towards the heart of the fells, is suggested as a rewarding trip for those who can arrange transport at each end. Except for the much lower Furness and Woodland fells and the pleasant limestone heights to the west of Kendal, the Wrynose to Black Combe skyline provides the only mountain country in the southern segment of the Lake District. Everything else worthwhile lies north of the passes of Hardknott and Wrynose or within the wonderful mountain country of the sadly deposed county of Westmorland.

But only the Coniston fells and their neighbouring outliers of Harter Fell and Walna Scar provide summits above 2,000 feet—Black Combe, a splendid, bulky upland, fails to reach the magic figure by a mere 30 feet—and, therefore, to achieve some proportion, my Southern Fells section has had to be extended. The fells on both sides of upper Langdale, only separated from the Coniston fells by the trough of Wrynose, could obviously be fairly included and, in addition, I have included the circuit of Glaramara, Allen Crags and Seathwaite Fell. These hills, although approximately contiguous with the Bowfell ridge, are hardly southern fells but they are hardly western fells either. Their inclusion, however, does maintain a certain balance in the book and, after all, these geographical divisions are merely included for convenience. There are no official southern fells of Lakeland, but the forty-three summits traversed in the following chapters are merely *my* southern fells. Wainwright includes most of them in his pictorial guide to the southern fells—including the Glaramara round—but places the summits on the northern side of Langdale in his central fells. This may be more accurate but, dealing only with summits above 2,000 feet, I have had no need to include a central fells section.

My southern hills, with the exception of the Glaramara tops, embrace the first mountains of my youth. As I have related elsewhere my very first boyhood hills were Stickle Pike, above the Duddon, and Black Combe, and the Coniston and Langdale fells followed soon afterwards*. The main attraction, from the age of seventeen, was rock-climbing with hill walking merely an incidental pleasure. Dow Crag, Gimmer Crag, Pavey Ark, Bowfell Buttress and other steep places were known in some intimacy before all the neighbouring summits were really familiar. The highest mountains—Scafell, Great Gable, Bowfell, Pillar and the rest—were traversed but, mostly, to and from the crags. Skiddaw, with no rock-climbing on its broad fellsides, was not 'discovered' until much later, and Helvellyn was a place to go in winter for the snow.

From my boyhood home in Furness I could see Black Combe every day and, from the top of a road about one mile away, the Coniston fells stood clear on the horizon. It was a two-hours' bicycle ride to Coniston and, later, something over half an hour on a New Hudson motorcycle. Sometimes we went by train—mostly, the early morning 'workmen's' train which was cheaper—and, later still, our first second-hand cars brought the hills even nearer. Invariably, our base was our own hut—near Coniston Old Hall, on the shores of the lake—and we were on the crags every weekend, summer and winter, except when the weather was appalling when we went walking in the hills. Quite often, we would walk to Langdale from Coniston by the way of Fell Foot, and this was the way we went to Scafell and Great Gable. The last mile from Yewdale to Coniston, on the return journey, after a strenuous day, had sometimes to be taken at the trot to catch the last train—long years before they closed the line.

Inevitably, for me, the Coniston and Langdale fells are the hills of youthful adventure. Here, we taught ourselves to climb—there were no outdoor-pursuits centres in those days—using the primitive equipment of those days, and here we went exploring the old mine-shafts or scrambled up the magnificent ravines in Oxendale, or practised step-cutting in the snow gullies on Bowfell and Crinkle Crags. Here we did our early tarn bathing and, several times, we skated on Goats Water and Stickle Tarn. The first time we went over High

* *Inside the Real Lakeland* (Guardian Press 1961).

Raise was in the snow and I saw my first skiers here—in the early 1930s—but it was to be more than ten years later before I first tried out the sport—on clumsy, wooden skis, without edges, roughly fixed on to ordinary climbing boots. But, despite the familiarity of these homeland fells, the old atmosphere is still there. The break-neck run down the screes from Gimmer Crag for a much-needed drink can still be enjoyed, despite now creaky knees, and the smell of the woodsmoke as you come down to Coniston from Dow Crag in the evening is still the same.

The finest horseshoe round in the area is the circumnavigation of Langdale—the Pikes, Bowfell and the Crinkles, with the continuation over Cold Pike and Pike o' Bilsco. In the rounds later described this was divided because I had to include High Raise and Ullscarf, but the real Langdale Horseshoe makes an ideal day. The familiar round of the Coniston fells is particularly rewarding and, once height has been gained, a surprisingly easy day. While the Glaramara-Allen Crags-Seathwaite Fell circuit—missing out the outliers of Cam Crag and Tongue Head which I had to include—is a classic walk.

In the chapter on the Langdale fells I briefly discuss the situation of High Raise as the approximate centre of the Lake District fells. Further substance to this claim may be given by drawing diagonals on the map from the most northerly two-thousander, High Pike, to the most southerly, Walna Scar, and from the most westerly, Iron Crag, to the most easterly, Grey Crag. These diagonals will be found to meet near the summit of High Raise. Of course, this does not establish that High Raise is, indeed, the central mountain in Lakeland but there must be few, if any, fells in the district from which a more comprehensive panorama may be viewed. Almost all the mountains within the national park may be seen from the broad summit ridge, as well as Morecambe Bay, the Solway Firth, Ingleborough and the Northern Pennines. High Raise is also the highest summit on the central watershed of the fells. As a mountain it may lack dramatic shape, crags or character; as a high-level central promenade for the Lake District it is unequalled.

## Above Wrynose Pass

My first trip of the series into the southern fells was something of a disaster. I had intended collecting Crinkle Crags and Bowfell with all their outliers, making a day's total of thirteen summits, but in the event, only did a miserable four. If I had done any proper planning before embarking on the two-thousanders I should have included Esk Pike and Rossett Pike in this round, making fifteen tops in all, but, as explained earlier, I was a bit casual about the whole thing and, as a result, had to fit these two in with the Scafells. However, on this rather dull day in early May I only had these thirteen summits in mind and no doubts about being able to complete them with ease. It should be made clear at the start that this round was nothing like as ambitious as it might sound for, in arriving at his total of thirteen summits, Falkingham had counted—quite accurately—five for Crinkle Crags and three for Bowfell, so that, really the trip was no more than a fairly leisurely stroll. But, even so, I failed miserably.

It was, in fact, a motoring disaster—brought about, no doubt, as a punishment for my decision to start and finish on the summit of Wrynose Pass. Purists might regard this as cheating—cutting out 1,000 feet of ascent by the use of the car—but I have never had much compunction about seizing chances like this on the rare occasions they are offered. However, on this occasion, I was hoist with my own petard. I stupidly locked the ignition key inside the car boot. Why it happened I can't say—I'd never done it before, or since—but it meant that I was stranded on top of the pass, on a rather raw, windy morning, without any means of moving the car, either then or later. Of course, expert mechanics may tell you it's quite an easy matter to start a motorcar without an ignition key, but I'm no mechanic, let alone an expert one. I made various feeble attempts to open the boot or to reach it through the rear seats without success, and couldn't think of anything else to do. Of course, I had a spare key but this was at home twenty miles away. Furthermore, I knew my wife was out so it was no use ringing her, even if I could get to a telephone, and, even if I could get home somehow, I didn't think I could get in my own house, since I had no door key with me.

It was getting a little chilly hanging about on the top of the pass with nowhere to go. There was only one other vehicle up there—the place is normally crowded—and, luckily, a driver with it. He turned out to be a driver from an outdoor-pursuits centre at Coniston, waiting for the arrival of an instructor who was attending to some pupils camping up the fell, near Red

Tarn, and he was most helpful. When the instructor came down, he said, they could take me down the pass to a telephone and, eventually, this is what they very kindly did. They dropped me off at Clappersgate, near Ambleside, where old friends of mine, Sid and Jamie Cross, reside, and, fortunately for me, they were at home. Sid listened to my sorry tale with more sympathy than I deserved, and then, while Jamie provided coffee, telephoned to an expert to discover how I could best get my vehicle in motion again. But it was no use; neither Sid nor I could understand the technicalities and he eventually decided, with great kindness, to abandon his house-decorating and drive me home to find my other key—if I could get in. Jamie, however, with womanly perception, immediately saw a way of getting me home and keeping Sid to his painting. He should lend me his car—and this he readily agreed to do. So I drove home, and discovered my wife had fortunately left the door key in the hidden place, picked up my spare ignition key and drove back to Clappersgate for lunch. I will always remember this ready kindness from these trusted old friends.

Lunch over, they drove me back over the pass where I rescued the ignition key and locked the car. I had had to leave it unlocked for a couple of hours or more but nothing had been stolen. On another occasion, when I came down to the pass after a walk, I saw that the window of a parked car had been smashed and the occupants—an elderly couple—told me afterwards that their money and valuables, left inside while they were walking the fells, had been stolen. By then, on this May day, it was too late to do my proposed round but I thought four of the nearer outliers might be fitted in, and Sid and Jamie accompanied me. Forty-five years earlier Sid Cross and I often used to meet when climbing on Dow Crag and elsewhere but we hadn't been on the fells together for many years. It was therefore a great pleasure to have their company this day—even on a modest walk.

Our little round was Cold Pike, Red How (or Little Stand), the southern extension of the Crinkles, Great Knott, above Browney Gill, and Pike o' Stickle. Sid is a distinguished climber and mountain rescue leader but, curiously, did not know the wonderful corner of Gaitkins between Cold Pike and Little Stand, which is one of my favourite places in the Lake District. Here are splendid, little crags of rough, clean rock, lovely tarns and a completely unspoiled atmosphere of mountain serenity. We did a quick exploration of the crags on Gaitkins and Little Stand—there are dozens of attractive, mostly undemanding, routes—and resolved to come back some day with a rope and sort them out. Then, over Stonesty Pike, on to Great Knott, up Pike o' Blisco from Red Tarn and down the fellside back to the cars. Pike o'Blisco is a splendid, little mountain, with an attractive summit of grey rocks set among heather and mosses. The fell is buttressed by several crags and the views from the top, of Bowfell and Crinkle Crags, are particularly impressive. One of the features of Pike o' Blisco is its fine, columnar cairn—one of the Lake District summit cairns that is occasionally decapitated by thoughtless vandals. This day, however, it seemed reasonably intact—a carefully-built pile that can be easily seen from the floor of Langdale. The views down into Langdale and across to the Pikes were wonderfully revealing and it was particularly pleasant to be sharing them with Sid and Jamie, who, for many years, were the popular hosts of the Old Dungeon Ghyll Hotel, at the foot of the crags. From the start of the Crinkles we had also looked across at the crags of Scafell but the mists were hanging over Mickledore, and no detail could be seen. But this was mostly a talking day—or, rather, afternoon. When you are revisiting familiar scenes with old mountain friends there is a great deal to say, and time passes easily and quickly. We never noticed the ascents, being far too busy chatting and exchanging experiences. This was a short, but memorable day—not on account of my stupid negligence, although occasioned by it, but because of the companionship of old friends. Mountain friendships, I decided, long ago, are the best of all.

## Crinkles to Bowfell

My remaining nine summits in the Bowfell area were collected in a very easy round a few days later. Again, I went round from the Three Shires Stone on Wrynose Pass although a more determined mountaineer would have started from Langdale. Eskdale or Cockley Beck. My excuse this time would be that I left home rather late. This approach from the pass is very sedate—well suited to any elderly motorist—but can be made rather more rewarding by first traversing Cold Pike, Little Stand and Stonesty Pike. But I merely went by the well-tracked route past Red Tarn and the shoulder of Great Knott.

The exhilaration of this approach is the sudden transition from gentle walking over grass and peat to the rock scrambles over the Crinkles. Undoubtedly, this line of turreted summits provides one of the best ridge walks in the country—especially in winter. All the way along there are peeps down craggy buttresses into the fine Oxendale ravines on one side and into the wild country of upper Eskdale and Lingcove Beck on the other. There are no climbing routes on these quite impressive buttresses facing Langdale, but any amount of interesting scrambling, and the steep scree gullies in between—notably, the fine cleft of Mickle Door—can provide useful snow climbing practice in winter. From the ridge there are, in reasonable weather, magnificent views of the Scafell range, the long valleys of the Duddon and the Esk winding to the sea and, in the other direction, the whole length of Great Langdale.

Walking the ridge, on the way up to the second Crinkle from the south, you come to Wainwright's 'bad step'. When we used to go this way forty or fifty years ago we never realized there was a 'bad step', taking it all easily in our stride, but Mr Wainwright, the guide-book writer, is an expert in finding these places. He even found one on Low Pike above Ambleside. Half a page is devoted to the Crinkle Crags 'bad step' in one of his guides and the place is described as "the most difficult obstacle met on any of the regular walkers' paths in Lakeland". I suppose it depends on what you mean by 'walker'. Any ordinarily active walker should find no difficulty with it whatever—a couple of rock steps—but I must admit I have seen many people making more than a meal of it. Perhaps if it hadn't been labelled it wouldn't seem quite so awesome to the timid.

You can avoid some of the summits of the Crinkles if you like but in my peak-bagging traverse I had, of course, to collect all five and also the separate summit of Shelter Crags, furthest to the north. It was a delightful walk, with constantly changing views, and no risk of going astray, but, in thick cloud and, perhaps, falling snow, it is easy enough to go wrong for the route is a pleasantly winding one. On a more recent visit, in bad weather, I left the snow-covered ridge to go down Long Top to the Lingcove Beck, and some walkers, bound for Three Tarns, followed my foot prints by mistake, until I explained where I was going. A compass may be needed under these conditions.

Three Tarns—there are really five of them—is reached after Shelter Crags—a pleasant, often windy, haven just below the rocky upthrust of Bowfell, more than 600 feet higher. This ascent of Bowfell from Three Tarns is, I think, the only bit of mountain country over which I always time myself. Over the years, it has become a sort of personal test of fitness. If I do it in reasonable time, I am in satisfactory condition; if I take longer, I am unfit or sickening for something. Twenty minutes is the average time for plodding, without a stop. My best time is seventeen minutes. Runners, of course, could do it more quickly. A much more interesting route for climbers up this slope is to take to the splendid, rough rocks on the right that provide quite an exhilarating staircase.

I forget my time on this occasion for as soon as I reached the summit cairn I found my companion of a few days earlier, Sid Cross, perched up there with several other friends—an encounter that put such matters out of my mind. We sat up there chatting, in a miniature snowstorm, and then they went down another way while I wandered off to collect the two other Bowfell summits—the top of Bowfell Buttress and the top of Hanging Knotts. Bowfell is one of the most readily recognized summits in the district—a perfect cone, the shape a child draws of a mountain, from most directions, or a small cone stuck on the end of a rocky ridge in other views. Except to the west the extensive summit ridge is completely surrounded by crags—Bowfell Links, Flat Crags, Hard Crags, Bowfell Buttress and Hanging Knotts—and there is a square half-mile, nearly 3,000 feet above sea-level, of some complexity in bad weather. I should be familiar enough with Bowfell, having been up there on dozens of occasions, but one day I got myself lost for a time. It was a very wet, misty day and I was surprised to find another walker on the little, rocky summit in such weather, and even more surprised to discover he was an old acquaintance. We left the summit together, parting a few hundred feet lower down—he to go down by way of Ore Gap, myself down to Three Tarns. Ten minutes later, not recognizing the ground, I consulted my compass and found I was going down towards Ore Gap—the opposite direction to that intended. Returning to the summit area I encountered my friend again—he, also, had taken the opposite direction and found himself making for Three Tarns. We both felt ashamed of ourselves.

The errors had not been due to compass reading, but to our

mutual belief that we didn't need to consult them, thinking we knew every inch of the ground. It is quite remarkable how easy it is to go astray through over-confidence or carelessness. I do it often. Some guide-books will tell you that there is magnetic rock on Bowfell so that compasses are unreliable, but we couldn't claim this excuse for we hadn't used them — until we found we were going wrong. In any case, the facts — discovered in a survey by the Brathay Exploration Group many years ago — are that minor variations of up to three degrees may be experienced at a number of points between Crinkle Crags and Esk Pike — but only if you hold your compass close to the rock. But on the north-west side of Ore Gap it is possible to get deviations of up to 170 degrees on some rocks, so that compasses used in this way — actually placed on the rock — could send you in the opposite direction to that you are seeking. All you have to do, therefore, in the Bowfell summit area, to avoid going astray in bad weather is to make sure you don't place your compass on or near the rocks — and, in my case, to use the compass and not rely on — in my case, at least — an obviously unreliable sense of direction.

On this summit-collecting day in May I retraced my steps over Crinkle Crags, although avoiding some of the summits, to get back to the car. This is perhaps the only disadvantage of the easy approach from Wrynose Pass — you normally have to return the same way. To avoid this I have resorted to several expedients over the years including a roundabout traverse of the rough ground above Lingcove Beck, and a strenuous crossing of the even rougher ground well to the east of the summit ridge. This second avoiding tactic can involve you in a fair amount of climbing and scrambling across the rock buttresses — hardly a walker's route, but quite enjoyable — or a tiring scramble into and out of the ravines that cross the route, notably Crinkle Gill, Isaac Gill and Browney Gill, before you reach the steep track out of Langdale to Red Tarn. You have to be very keen on avoiding the return over Crinkle Crags if you select this last route which is much more exasperating than it looks from near Three Tarns.

These splendid Oxendale ravines are, of course, among the most attractive features of the skirts of Crinkle Crags, and the descent of Hell Gill, by way of Whorneyside Force, can provide an exciting route back to Langdale — but only for those with climbing experience. More interesting ways off Bowfell include the descent of the gully at the left-hand side of Bowfell

Buttress—looking up—or of the Great Slab on Flat Crags, and then by the so-called Climbers' Traverse. Bowfell Buttress is the familiar scene of many, happy climbing days and the scree-gully, filled with snow, is a route I have often used in winter to reach the summit. Sometimes the snow cornice becomes a near-vertical wall and I can remember some days when we have hauled ourselves over this and out of the cold, shadowed gully into the sparkling sunlit snows of the summit ridge. A particularly fast way off Bowfell, avoiding the over-trodden tracks of The Band, is to descend the grassy slopes of Green Tongue, at the run, straight down into Mickleden. There is also quite an interesting, rocky route from Bowfell Buttress to the top of Rossett Gill, the descent of which can be largely avoided by the use of the old pony track to the south, while a rather longer route can bring you down to the east of Angle Tarn. An even longer circuit is to descend by way of Ore Gap. There are routes, therefore, in profusion on to Bowfell and off the mountain without using the stereotyped route by way of The Band which seems boggier and more eroded at every visit.

As I have stated, there was a snow shower when I was on Bowfell on this rather dull day in mid-May but only patches of snow on the ground and very little to be seen on the highest tops. A few days later I left for some winter climbing in the Ben Nevis area and ran into some of the hottest weather I've ever known in Scotland, with shade temperatures well into the 80s. Even so, the snow was as plentiful as is usual in February and the Ben Nevis cliffs completely plastered—an alpine scene of exciting grandeur, although the snow was too soft for the best climbs. But for more than a week I was in this winter wonderland returning in the evenings to a chalet where it was sometimes almost too hot for bedclothes. But one evening, returning after a long day in the high snows, there came what seemed like the ultimate tragedy at the time. So hot had it been in the glen and so heavy the demand for refreshment that the inn had run out of beer. It seemed wise to get back to the Lake District and resume my interrupted tour of the two-thousanders. They never let things like that happen in Cumbria.

### Harter Fell

In the distant days of my youth we came to know the shoulder of Eskdale's Harter Fell with some intimacy but, for several years, never bothered to scramble to the wonderful, rocky summit. Harter Fell—or, rather, its western shoulder—was, for us, merely part of our route from the railway at Foxfield or Broughton to Wasdale Head and all we were concerned about was getting there as quickly as possible. We were nearly always laden with tent and blankets—we had no sleeping bags in those days—and the walk through Broughton Mills, over the shoulder of Stickle Pike and down to the Duddon, up through the woods to Grass-guards and on to Eskdale and Burnmoor, seemed a long way. But it was much better, both economically and aesthetically, than the longer train journey to Seascale and the long road walk thereafter. I can't remember when I first went to the top of Harter Fell—it was probably on an evening walk from Eskdale—but it must have been a revelation—the cluster of rocky summits, the remarkable view of the Scafell range and the much nearer picture, almost as if from an aeroplane, of the squat, square shape of Hardknott Fort, just over a mile away to the north. Harter Fell is, unquestionably, one of the finest of the smaller mountains in Lakeland—a perfect picture-postcard of a fell, with its surrounding woodlands, its higher belts of bracken and heather, and its little crags and outcrops of grey, welcoming rock.

Our early visits to Harter Fell took place before the mountain became the centre of the Hardknott National Forest. Planting of the eastern and southern slopes below the 1,500-foot contour began in 1936 and, as a result, the fell has been transformed—but, fortunately, not spoiled. This has been sympathetic afforestation—much more enlightened than in Ennerdale and Whinlatter—for the Forestry Commission have tried to avoid regimented lines of conifers, and have interspersed deciduous trees and evergreens among the spruces and firs. Freedom to wander at will over the mountain is, however, restricted by the thick woodlands and the forest fence but many ancient tracks have been retained and new ones provided, and most routes to the summit are unaffected. But the Harter Fell of today is a different mountain from the one we used to know—more colourful and varied in some ways, but a wild, untouched corner of Lakeland made into a commercial proposition. We can only feel grateful that the Forestry Commission agreed, this time, to plant the area with good taste, and even affection.

But fitting in this lovely, little mountain into some horseshoe round of the two-thousands and even tacking its ascent on to something else presents obvious problems—especially if you have left its collection, as I had done, to the final stages of the exercise. For Harter Fell stands proudly alone between the Duddon and the Esk, with the Bowfell and the Coniston groups, already traversed, the nearest mountains of the requisite height. A more resolute planner than I might have included it in some ambitious Scafell round but, finding it still unassailed half-way through July, I seemed to have no option other than to collect it on its own. The answer seemed a short evening walk and, discovering that this need only involve a three-miles' stroll, there and back, and an ascent of less than 1,000 feet, my wife agreed to accompany me. This is not to suggest that my wife is not a good mountain walker—she can manage mountains like Ben Nevis but is content to leave me to my Lake District gallivantings when at home. A much more worthy ascent of the fell would have been from Eskdale—an especially rewarding trip—but perhaps we were both lazy, we didn't leave home until after five o'clock and it was very hot. Certainly, the tarmac was melting near the top of Hardknott Pass where we left the car.

From here the walk to the summit was without incident, although rather boggy, and the evening views, of course, superb, with cloud shadows across the sunlit fells and the Roman fort as clear as if portrayed on a map. We could, for instance, plainly see the soldiers' exercise ground to the east of the fort—not nearly so easily spotted from the site itself. I scrambled up to the three separate, rocky summits and then busied myself with finding some moderate climbing problems on the splendid, rough rocks while my wife dozed in the sunshine. For climbers this rather dull approach to the summit of Harter Fell can be made more challenging by the ascent, *en route,* of Demming Crag, a broad sweep of steep slabs that provides several routes of varied interest. This evening, however, we merely strolled back to Hardknott across the fragrant fellside and then descended the passes to the tourist-packed streets of Ambleside. In one of these steep lanes is the cool parlour of the Golden Rule Inn, purveyors of real ale, and here we concluded the evening with the distinct feeling, on my part, that we hardly deserved such a reward.

**The Langdale Pikes**

The best-known skyline in Lakeland is the battlemented profile of the Langdale Pikes. They rise in turreted splendour from the level floor of one of the most perfect valleys in England—a line of rocky summits, floodlit by the evening sun, in the shape of a crouching lion guarding the dale. Only little hills, perhaps, but they *look* like mountains and almost every visitor to the district knows their shape—the central, craggy crown of Harrison Stickle with the dark cliff of Pavey Ark as its right shoulder and, further to the left, the steep, rocky thumb of Pike o' Stickle. Between the two Stickles is the soaring sweep of Gimmer Crag—one of the best climbers' playgounds in the district—but the tourist may not notice this bold cliff that hardly breaks the skyline and tends to merge into the fellside. To him, Pike o' Stickle looks the exciting peak but, in fact, there is little climbing to speak of on these rocks. Gimmer, though—steep, smooth and impressively exposed—is criss-crossed with routes of every degree of severity and thronged with climbers every summer weekend.

Early in June I did the familiar round of these heights, together with the less dramatic summits of High Raise and Sergeant Man, and the more distant top of Ullscarf, the other side of Greenup Edge, which seemed to fit fairly easily into the walk. It was rather a breezy day, with cloud shadows racing across the fells and intermittent sunshine lighting up the crags in turn—a good walking day, just three days before the Queen's Jubilee. There are many ways up Harrison Stickle, the highest of the Langdale Pikes, but my favourite, and the one I selected on this occasion, is the direct approach up the ravine of Dungeon Ghyll and then straight up the summit crags to the cairn. John Ruskin went to Dungeon Ghyll about 100 years ago and found "the loveliest rock scenery, chased with silver waterfalls, that I ever set foot or heart upon"—but he didn't go right up the ravine. The tourists' Dungeon Ghyll—and Ruskin's—is the lower fall which is certainly an impressive place but too redolent of picture postcards and coach tours, and too often thronged with people in high heels or carrying umbrellas, to tempt one to tarry for long. But, quickly leaving the grannies and the toddlers below, the more determined traveller enters the main ravine—a winding, upland mile of remarkably varied and even exciting scenery. Here, by the higher falls—and there are several of them, all much more photogenic than the popular one down below—he can escape the crowds and the orange peel and discover a rare corner of Lakeland. There are other similarly wild places in, for instance, Oxendale, further up the valley, but none quite so near to motorcars and other signs of civilization like juke boxes. The transition, therefore, from the commonplace to the sublime is remarkable. (Keen eyed readers will have noticed my spelling of Dungeon Ghyll. This is a deliberate mistake, and, I hope, the only occasion in this book where I have spelled the word 'ghyll'. The correct spelling is 'gill'—from the Old Norse—and scores of becks and ravines in the Lake District properly have this spelling but the Ordnance Survey use 'Dungeon Ghyll', the two hotels have the same name, and this unfortunate usage has been so long established that it would be merely pedantic to change it now. Authorities claim that 'ghyll' is a poetic affectation; the Victorians thought it looked pretty and, perhaps, romantically Welsh.)

The ascent of Harrison Stickle by this route—the ravine and the crags—may be a scramble or a climb, according to one's choice. You can scramble up the ravine, avoiding the waterfalls and the rocks, or you can seek them out, varying your route, in places, dependent upon the volume of water coming down and your standard of performance. The final crag, below the summit, is, I suppose, rock climbing of a sort but, here again, you can make it as hard or as easy as you like. Many years ago I got my Border Collie, Sambo, up these rocks in a rope sling so it can't be too demanding. Sometimes we have gone up the ravine trying to keep in or above the beck all the way—a quick way to get wet through but an interesting ascent in summer when the water's not too cold. On this particular June morning I wanted as much scrambling and climbing as I could get, without getting wet, and managed to find a fairly dry but invigorating route. The scenery was wild and impressive, one waterfall dropping vertically into a perfect pool, cradled by birches and rowans, making a superb colour photograph. I normally avoid the last waterfall in the ravine—an awkward climb—when going this way for it is really off-route. Instead, as on this occasion, I go straight up the fellside, making a bee-line for the summit. The easiest way up the crags of Harrison Stickle is by way of a gully or wide, twisting chimney but I chose a slightly harder route up the rocks further to the right and, eventually, pulled myself up to the cairn.

Falkingham's next summit was Pike o' Stickle and I wandered across to it by way of the top of Loft Crag—the Pike buttressed by the magnificent precipice of Gimmer Crag. On the way to the easy summit rocks of Pike o' Stickle I crossed the top of the scree gully where scores of stone axe-heads, dating back for up to 4,000 years, have been found. One of them is in use as a paper-weight in my study. Hereabouts was the site of Lakeland's main stone-axe 'factory', the axes being taken over the passes by primitive salesmen for sale and distribution in many parts of the country. A little way down the scree is a man-made cave, hewn out of the rock, and it seems likely that this could have been the place where they trimmed and polished the axes. Probably most of the axes found on the scree were rejects, but the one I have looks practical enough, with one side chipped out for holding in the hand. It is a sobering thought that this chunk of green slate on my desk was hammered into shape by a Stone Age man probably 2,000 years before the birth of Christ.

From the airy peak of Pike o' Stickle I looked across to the north-west face of Gimmer Crag and saw two climbers half-way up the splendid route known to all rock men simply as The Crack. So far that day they were the only people I had seen since leaving the car. Across the dale were the ramparts of Crinkle Crags and Bowfell, darkly shadowed against the sky. Moving north-east across Harrison Combe I steered for the two summits of Thunacar Knott by a slightly roundabout route avoiding the bog and easily ticked these off. Thunacar Knott is the least impressive of the Langdale Pikes, and, indeed, must be one of the least impressive mountains anywhere. For some reason the boundary between the former counties of Cumberland and Westmorland used to take a sharp turn on the summit but this was the only feature of the fell—and now that has gone, leaving no more than a rounded mound to pass for a peak. In view of the featureless nature of Thunacar Knott it is therefore unfortunate that Francis Falkingham should have found *two* summits there—and none on Pavey Ark—but his magnifying-glass was accurate enough. The Knott *does* have two two-thousand feet summits and Pavey Ark, only a quarter of a mile away, has none, for the ground rises steadily, but almost imperceptively, from the summit of Langdale's largest cliff to the relative wasteland of the Knott. Even so, if only out of sympathy for Pavey Ark, I had to go over there to look down the precipice at Stickle Tarn and recall many happy days spent on the face and in its gullies.

Pavey Ark is a wonderful hanging garden of a crag—formerly regarded as a rather old-fashioned climbing ground but, in recent years, coming into its own as a major crag with many hard routes. The crag is traversed by the remarkable diagonal rift of Jack's Rake—first climbed about 100 years ago—and this provides an easy, scrambling ascent of the cliff. Technically, this route is a rock climb—although a very easy one—but is regularly used by non-climbers who, on occasions, have got themselves into difficulty. In places, the Rake is quite exposed and a slip, caused by bad weather, strong winds, or inexperience, could be serious. Fatalities, indeed, have occurred. In recent years the Rake has become increasingly eroded and loose and, in the summer of 1977, the Lake District Special Planning Board, on the advice of its full-time wardens, warned walkers, especially school parties, against using the route.

Returning to Thunacar Knott I walked northwards over easy grass slopes to the summit of High Raise—at 2,500 feet above sea-level my highest summit of the day. High Raise is regarded by many as the central mountain of the Lake District, although Armboth Fell or even Ullscarf may also have claims. It is hardly an impressive mountain, the summit plateau being no more than a vast sheep walk, but, as a promenade from which to view almost the whole panorama of Lakeland, High Raise is almost unexcelled. It can be said to rise in a series of rocky steps all the way from Grasmere, with attractive tarns on several ledges, and drops down, on the other side, to Langstrath in long, uninteresting slopes, contouring gently southwards to the rocky front of the Langdale Pikes. From the summit, on a clear day, you can identify sixty or more mountains grouped all around the skyline—except where Morecambe Bay intrudes—but you feel far removed from most of them because of the dipping slopes all round and the surrounding, deep-cut valleys. There is no feeling of being crowded on High Raise by the circle of heights but, rather, an impression of spaciousness with the mountains filling the horizon but hardly the foreground. On a sunny summer's evening, with long shadows across the turf and the larks singing, this is a very special place—especially when the fell is quiet and deserted. But sometimes in winter, with the clouds down, half a gale blowing and untracked snows stretching in all directions it can be a challenging summit plateau, with ways off far from obvious, and good compass work often essential.

On my visit this early June day the distant views were clear and I could see most of the Lakeland mountains, Morecambe Bay, the Solway Firth and Ingleborough far to the south-east. The Esk Hause track could easily be picked out and there seemed sufficient snow in Central Gully, Great End, for climbing. No snow at all on Bowfell but two small patches still remaining on Esk Pike. The sun was catching the curious slope of the Great Slab on Flat Crags, Bowfell, giving it a strange, magical appearance. When I was a youth we used to know High Raise as High White Stones—to distinguish the fell from the other High Raises of Lakeland—but this is only the name of the stony summit area. There is also a Low White Stones, a little nearer to Greenup Edge. I trotted down this way to the pass—the sun had dried out the boggy ground, making the going much easier than usual—and rattled along the two and a half miles of easy ground to the summit of Ullscarf. This is quite a craggy mountain to the south and east but dreary along its summit ridge. Not many people walk over Ullscarf and it was therefore quite a surprise to see three young men sitting by the cairn—all of whom I knew slightly. They were working their way down into Borrowdale by a roundabout route.

My round meant that I had to return over the High Raise plateau but I made the route rather more interesting by contouring around Green Comb high above Wythburn valley, across Greenhow Crags and then over the shoulder of High Raise to my last summit, Sergeant Man. The valley of the Wyth Burn is one of the least-visited dales in Lakeland but you traverse it if you are making the round of the three-thousands, and everybody who has done this will remember the place for its bogs. I don't think I've ever been up or down the dale without getting my feet wet through—sometimes to the knees. This day, however, I was merely looking down into the dale and discovered a beauty there I had not noticed before. You couldn't see the bogs but just the pools and the tarns, and that day—three days before the Queen's Jubilee—these sheets of water were a surprising royal blue, glinting in the sunlight. Green Comb itself, a peaceful, green haven sheltered from the wind, seemed a very welcoming place and I decided that I must have been unjust to the Wythburn valley in the past. Across the dale, on the slopes of Steel Fell, another tarn sparkled in the sunlight. This is the tarn, on the former Cumberland and Westmorland boundary, unnamed on the maps and even unmarked until recent years, that some of my friends jokingly call 'Griffin's Tarn' because of my efforts towards its official recognition.

Sergeant Man once again proved a dramatic viewpoint. The great cliff of Pavey Ark stood out boldly, black against the sunset, and, at its foot, Stickle Tarn seemed to dance in the sunlight. Around the skyline the more distant fells had taken on their evening blue mantle and, far below, the last of the walkers and climbers were rattling down the screes by Mill Gill to their cars. I remember I trotted nearly all the way back to Langdale—down to the tarn, round the back of Tarn Crag, and then down the familiar zigzags to the hotel. The bar was gaily decked with flags for the Jubilee, but they were making a levy of five-pence for the beer glasses, explaining they had lost at least forty glasses at Easter and didn't want to risk further loss during the coming celebrations. But it didn't seem important. My modest round of seven summits had gone very well and the day, although uneventful and over very familiar ground, had given me many fine views of distant places that I would be visiting in the coming weeks.

## The Coniston Fells

The Coniston fells were the hills of my youth—the first mountains I learned to know well and to love. Going back there now seems very like going home. Everything is familiar, little has changed and the return down the old track to Coniston in the evening sunshine, with the shadows lengthening across the turf, the crags turning purple, and the larks singing, is still the perfect ending to a mountain day. Nearly fifty years ago when we used to come down this way after a day on the crags I always felt curiously sad—sad with a fullness of beauty that I could not really comprehend; sad that it would be at least another week before I could again savour the beauty and the adventure. Nowadays, some of the sadness has gone—perhaps I have learnt to come to terms with the beauty of mountains—but the perfection of it all, the grey rocks, the quiet tarns, the soaring heights, still remains, and there are memories around every corner. How many times have I sheltered under the arch of Cove Bridge, eating damp sandwiches in the rain, how often have we completed our last climb at dusk and continued on to the summit to watch the sunset over the Scafells, and when did we last trot down the winding track in the darkness to catch the last train home? Every few yards of track, almost every climb on Dow Crag, and every beck and pool has its memories, for this was where some of us spent the best years of our lives.

Out of hundreds of visits to the Coniston fells the majority have been climbing days but I must have done the round of the tops dozens, or even scores, of times. Even after a day's climbing we would usually finish off with a visit to one or several summits. This, perhaps, did not happen so often after climbing crags elsewhere in Lakeland but at Coniston it was part of the ritual for we liked to think we were complete mountaineers, and not merely gymnasts—on our home ground, at least. There are about a dozen summits in the Coniston fells—the number varying according to what you regard as separate summits and which ones you can fairly miss out. If you count tops like Buck Pike, Great How Crags or Little How Crags you can swell your total. Falkingham, being more accurate, does not count these, but includes the two summits of Walna Scar to make twelve and this was the round I did one cold and windy mid-week day towards the end of June.

You can go round the Coniston fells clock-wise or anti-clock-wise and I have never decided which way I prefer. If you leave your car at the fell gate above Coniston the clock-wise round may seem more direct but you are then faced with a rise of a few hundred feet at the end of the day from Church Beck and round The Bell or by way of Boulder Valley, which can be rather awkward in the dark—as I have often discovered in winter time. Possibly, I have done the round more often in this direction, for I like the scramble up the quarries above Blind Tarn and the walk in the morning sunshine along the top of the crags, with the Scafells straight ahead. But, this time, I felt like finishing off with the Walna Scar summits and the old, familiar walk across the slopes of Little Arrow Moor, joining the well-remembered track down from the crags. Perhaps I felt it was a sort of pilgrimage. And, for similarly vague reasons, I started from the Sun Hotel in Coniston—and not from the fell gate. We started from Coniston in the old days—from our hut on the lake shore at Coniston Old Hall, in fact—for the fell road was then too rough and difficult for our rather primitive vehicles and, in any case, motoring up fellsides to the crags seemed, in our youthful wisdom, to savour of cheating. With advancing years I am sometimes tempted to ignore my principles and must admit that, although slightly ashamed, I nowadays often leave my car at the fell gate, or even beyond it. But, on this June day, at least, I did the proper round from the village.

The woods by Church Beck have been thinned out since we first went this way in the late 1920s. Higher up the fell the former mines cottages have become holiday homes. One of them was acquired as a climbing hut by an old friend many years ago, and perhaps others are used in this way. There are also two climbing huts high up on the slopes of Coniston Old Man facing Dow Crag—one of them the former gunpowder hut for Cove Quarries; the other, a former quarry building that several of us restored. I remember helping to drag the roof timbers up the fellside. The route towards my first summits took me up the zigzags from the mines—there used to be an overhead cable here carrying huge iron buckets—and over Lad Stones on to Wetherlam. I think Lad Stones was misnamed by the Ordnance Survey when they first did the maps—probably through mishearing the local pronunciation. This has always been La'al Gladstone to the locals—Little Gladstone—but the derivation seems obscure.

Wetherlam is a sad mountain for me for the remains of my brother Leslie—my closest mountain companion of a lifetime—are scattered among the summit rocks where there is a view of the highest land in England, looking north-west across Wrynose. I passed the little tarn where we often ate our sandwiches and then across the Hen Crag summit to my private memorial. The distant views were remarkably clear. Not only were distant hills like Ingleborough easily identifiable but you could see all the land in between. Much closer was the lovely Brathay country—rounded hills, scattered woodlands and sparkling waters. A particularly rewarding summit experience occurred on Wetherlam in January 1978. Two of us had done a snow climb between the cliffs on the eastern face in fog so dense that we had to steer by compass. Fifty feet below the summit we were still in cloud, with visibility no more than two or three yards, but a few steps from the cairn we suddenly emerged into dazzling sunlight. At first only the summit rocks, steaming in the heat, were in sunshine, with a ceiling of blue sky above our heads, but, a few minutes later, the surrounding bank of fog sank slightly and the rocky, snow-flecked summits of the Scafells peeped over the top. The highest land in

England is at least five straight miles from Wetherlam but that day the summits seemed within throwing distance. Between the Scafells and our sunlit eyrie fleecy cotton-wool clouds billowed and writhed in the sunshine and all the rest of Lakeland lay hidden below in the dark fog.

It was a remarkable sight but the revelation was not yet over. Turning round to descend Wetherlam Edge into the fog there was a perfect Brocken Spectre straddling an outcrop perhaps 100 yards away—a ghostly apparition, seemingly at least fifty feet high, surrounded by two concentric rainbows, or 'glories'. In more than fifty years of wandering the hills it was only the fifth Brocken Spectre I had seen, and my fourth in Lakeland. I had never seen one so close before; all the others had seemed a mile or more away, astride some distant ridge. Last century the early climbers in the Alps were sometimes alarmed by the sudden appearance of the Spectre but, today, the apparition is dismissed as a simple reflection phenomenon, caused by the shadow of the observer being cast on to mist or fog by sunlight. But the generally unexpected appearance of the Spectre is always an exciting moment in the hills for the figure, obeying every movement of the observer, sometimes appears to be hundreds of feet high. The phenomenon appears when there is strong sunlight, at a particular angle, directly behind the viewer when facing thinning mists.

On my round of the Coniston fells in June 1977 I had two summits on Wetherlam to collect and then the separate rocky top of Black Sails before the descent to Swirl Hause and the easy staircase of Prison Band to Swirl How. On a previous round many years before I walked through a thunderstorm with torrential rain—stone walls were swept away in the dales—and on Swirl How hailstones, the size of mothballs, were falling out of the sky and rolling down the slopes towards Grey Friar. All this is easy walking country and you can rattle off the summits at speed, viewing the dales in turn as you box the compass. In some of my rounds of the Coniston fells I have included Little Carrs but Falkingham rightly ignores it as a separate summit and I missed it out this time. The remains of the aircraft in Broad Slack still lay as pitiful witness to man's fallibility with machines—the plane just failed to clear the summit—as I walked on to Great Carrs and looked down the rough, grey crags that provide such interesting routes to the summit out of Greenburn. Grey Friar came next—a superb viewpoint for the whole line of the Scafell range and westwards to the sea. I could also see most of my remaining summits, with the prominent dip of Goat's Hause in between. The wind was still quite strong and the purple shadows of the clouds were racing across sunlit fells, changing the pictures every minute. Distant lakes and tarns looked surprisingly blue—almost royal-blue ink blots in places—and the rocks light grey in the sunshine, shortening apparent distances. It looked as if I could be round in another hour, but I knew it would take much longer.

Back, then, to the main ridge and the bracing high-level tramp to Coniston Old Man. How many times, I wondered, have I walked along this ridge—summer and winter, sunshine and snow, in the wind and rain? It must be one of the most traversed walks in the Lake District, but still, after all these years, wonderfully worthwhile. Seathwaite Tarn, down to the west, looked quite full—there'd be no water shortage at Barrow—and the sun was lighting up the crags of Great Blake Rigg where we have sometimes climbed. It was amusing to recall that my first visit to Seathwaite Tarn, in, I think, 1928, had been by taxi, accompanying a waterworks inspection party. To the east were the fine, rocky coves above Levers Water and Low Water with their many sporting routes—especially in winter—to the ridge. The ascent to Brim Fell, although far from steep, always seems quite a trudge—perhaps because the slope is fairly featureless. Coniston Old Man is often a crowded viewpoint but there were few people about this day and I had the familiar scene of mountains and sea, with the deserted mines and the still active quarries immediately beneath, almost to myself. The cairn on the summit is a considerable edifice, varying in height according to the activities of the vandals, but on one of my early visits was completely buried in snow—the greatest depth of snow I can remember on any summit in this country. The year might have been about 1930.

On this recent visit I looked across to the fine precipice of Dow Crag and remembered the first time I had seen the crag—grey, steep and forbidding beneath a huge black cloud. Tiny figures were scurrying like ants down the screes below the crag that day in the 1920s and I learned they had been climbing. It seemed exciting—a completely new world for an imaginative boy—and, within a year, I was making my first visits to a crag that was to play a big part in my life. But there was nobody climbing on the crag this June day as I rounded

Harter Fell, Eskdale (left) and Green Crag

Brown Pike and Buck Pike from Cove Bridge

Crinkle Crags from Oxendale

Browney Gill and Crinkle Crags
(*below*) Side Pike and Mickleden from Lingmoor Fell

(*overleaf*) The Langdale Pikes

Summit rocks of Pike o' Blisco

Coniston Old Man and Brim Fell

Mark Atkinson memorial on Caudale Moor; Red Screes behind

Grisedale and ridge of Dollywaggon Pike and Nethermost Pike

Birkett Fell memorial cairn

Fairfield from Rydal Fell

the fine Goat's Water corrie and followed the easy track to the splendid rocky summit. I peered down all the buttresses and gullies in turn, tracing many of the routes in imagination, and once more looked down the long length of Dunnerdale and Eskdale to the sea. No sign of the Isle of Man, even on such a clear day. Sea-haze was probably obscuring the island. Then, easily past the rock window beyond Great Gully that makes such a superb photograph, on to Falkingham's rejected Buck Pike, and round the ridge above Blind Tarn to Brown Pike. There is a fine scrambling route up through the quarries to this airy top but I didn't go down that way as I had to pick up two summits beyond the pass of Walna Scar. Blind Tarn—blind because it has no visible outlet—is one of the most dramatically-sited mountain tarns in Lakeland and I have often sat in the quarries and looked down at the fish rising and the circles widening across the whole width of the pool.

My last two summits were the top of Walna Scar itself, just beyond the pass, and the little peak of White Maiden, some distance to the south-west. White Pike, further on, just fails to reach the required height. And now there only remained the track down the pass and across Little Arrow Moor to Coniston and the car. In the 1920s or 1930s an MG sports car was driven over the pass by a friend of mine—I believe as an advertising stunt for the manufacturers—but in 1977 there was a more serious threat to the peace and quietude of the area. The sport of boggling had been invented—driving up and down the passes, and over mountain tops in some cases, in especially adapted four-wheel-drive vehicles. Vehicles had been reported in many remote parts of the fells and the British Mountaineering Council, as well as most climbers and fell walkers, were showing considerable concern. It would be a sad commentary on modern values if our lonely fells were allowed to become a playground for motor sportsmen. There was another controversy in 1977 about a threat to 'improve' the Walna Scar track below Cove Bridge to enable vehicles to transport material for the strengthening of the bridge. In the end, following widespread opposition from amenity interests, the work was done without any alteration to the track.

In the days of my youth there used to be a rifle range near Boo Tarn but today there's no sign of it and the tarn, too, has also disappeared. On the other side of the track there is a Bronze Age burial mound and stone circle—surprisingly little-known to most walkers. And it was on these slopes many years ago that a local doctor's son photographed what he thought was a flying saucer—supposedly, one of the outstanding 'sightings' in this country. I have a copy of the photograph which is certainly remarkable, but I still do not know the explanation. Perhaps Coniston Old Man *is* a mystery mountain. Certainly, members of the Aetherius Society think so; they say it has special properties of spiritual energy, and used to hold services on the summit ridge near a flat slab of rock. But I am not competent to discuss these matters.

On a rather more mundane note I remember once trotting down these slopes and finding a lot of money—shillings and half-crowns, as they then were—every few yards. Later, in the Sun Hotel, I was honest enough—or unwise enough, depending on your outlook—to boast of my find, only to be introduced to the owner of the money who had just reported its loss, through a hole in his trouser pocket. But I found nothing on this latest round—other than the discovery that there are always new sights and experiences to be won in familiar hills, even if you have been exploring them for a lifetime.

## Glaramara Circuit

Although set among some of the most popular and impressive mountains in the Lake District Glaramara has no clearly recognizable or remembered shape. Some of us don't even think of Glaramara as a mountain or peak, but more as a long, straggling line of fell, and we tend to talk of going over or along the top, rather than up it. Seen from afar Glaramara seldom obtrudes on the skyline and, more often than not, is only recognized after the surrounding hills have been identified—"so that lump over there must be Glaramara". And yet this shy but beautiful mountain is a magnificent viewpoint, with a splendidly varied, switchback ridge and, hidden among the crags and outcrops, some of the finest mountain tarns in the district. Glaramara—the word is Celtic, not Norse—is also one of our loveliest mountain names. And, fortunately, there seems no danger of its being renamed Switchback or something equally silly—a fate that seems to be overtaking Blencathra.

Glaramara, with the linking fell of Allen Crags, is really the long northern spur of the Scafell range, and the ridge, from Rosthwaite or Seatoller, makes perhaps the most exhilarating approach to the roof of England. This ridge fills most of the high land between Langstrath Beck and Styhead Pass and there are ten summits in the area above 2,000 feet. I planned to collect these in an easy round from Seatoller one sunny day in early June. It was the week of the spring holiday—two days after Jubilee Day—and, judging by the number of people seen on the fells, half the country seemed to be making the most of it.

Forty years ago there were no tracks over Glaramara, and, because of the hummocky nature of the ground, the many crags and outcrops, several stretches of bog, and the deeply-cut ravines on either side, it was always a good place for compass practice in bad weather. Nowadays, however, there is a clear track all the way—it was made, I believe, by walkers staying at the holiday guest-house that borrowed 'Glaramara' as its name—and no excuse for getting lost. Even so, if the ridge is being crossed by an unconventional route in thick mist, some care might be needed. My first summit was Cam Crag, the little rocky peak at the top of Cam Crag Ridge that soars entertainingly out of Langstrath, and it seemed best to collect this from the entrance to Comb Gill—the wonderful hanging valley that faces northwards up the length of Borrowdale. I remembered some rewarding climbing days when we have made a circuit of this corrie, ascending a succession of rock routes in turn, but on this perfect June day I went up the fellside to Bessyboot and then, past Tarn at Leaves, to take Cam Crag in the rear. There were processions of walkers on the ordinary route up Glaramara but nothing moving on my side of the fell except sheep. I scrambled up the miniature waterfalls of a little, rocky gill, walked round the remote tarn and then found a pleasant rock route up a succession of bluffs to my first top. Cam Crag is a fine, airy viewpoint with Borrowdale and Skiddaw straight ahead and the deep trough of Langstrath to the right.

Just across this trough were the rocky summits of Sergeant's Crag and Eagle Crag—to be traversed later on a walk to satisfy a reader who had been puzzled by an engraved inscription on the summit cairn of the latter peak. The inscription was reported to have read "This is Wolfman Country", but the stone had disappeared by the time of my visit. Apparently—I found out later—the incised plaque had been taken up from Stonethwaite and affixed to the cairn as a joke of rather limited appeal, but had been removed after a complaint that it had 'frightened' a woman walker.

From my eyrie on Cam Crag I also looked down to Dove's Nest caves—one of the most remarkable formations in Lakeland. Hundreds or thousands of years ago a great buttress of rock slipped down the fellside but, surprisingly, came to rest againt its parent crag, leaving great fissures and holes underneath at the back. These are the caves and, for those with some climbing skill—and candles, torches or headlamps—their exploration can provide an energetic, and even exciting, half-day. It is a good place on a wet day—the dark interior is always dry—and adventurous children, under an experienced leader, can have the time of their lives there. I have heard it said that this was the wolves' last lair in Lakeland.

Raven Crag, with its well-known gully and other rock routes, faces Dove's Nest across the corrie and, as I crossed Comb Door, I wondered if anybody was climbing there. For extra interest I scrambled up the rocks direct to the secondary summit of Glaramara, looking across at Raven Crag as I went up, but could see nobody. A few hours later I descended to Seathwaite at the end of my round to be told by Stan Edmondson, the farmer, that two climbers had been killed on Raven Crag during the day. Whether the tragedy happened before or after I had been within hailing distance I never found out.

Francis Falkingham credits Glaramara with two summits of more than 2,000 feet and Allen Crags with four, but three of his Allen Crags summits are really on the Glaramara ridge before the depression that marks the division between the two mountains. However, this is not very important and I agree there are six summits along the ridge to Esk Hause. There are also at least six tarns on or near the ridge—the one-inch Ordnance Survey map only names one, High House Tarn—and their presence makes this upland walk especially enjoyable. Almost all of them are real jewels of the mountains. There are two at the northern end and a fine collection beyond Pinnacle Bield, the largest of these being High House Tarn, with its trout. A few hundred yards away to the south lies Lincomb Tarn, cradled in steep, little crags—one of the most dramatically-sited pools in Lakeland. Some of these lovely tarns have to be sought out for they are hidden behind rock outcrops but all are worth visiting. Around a few of the pools are stretches of boggy ground, flecked here and there, in season, with stonecrops and saxifrages and perhaps bog asphodel and cotton grass. All this colour—the tarns, the grey rocks and the flowers—and the splendid mountain views combine to make this a very special promenade. The highest land in England is opening out ahead of you and, if you turn round, there is the curve of Borrowdale with its woodlands, the lake and its islands, and, as backcloth, the bulk of Skiddaw.

Once over Allen Crags and down to the Esk Hause path I had a curious diversion to make—to the rounded top of Tongue Head, at the head of upper Langstrath and almost on the well-trodden tourist track. I thought I had better collect this since I had not decided how I was going to tackle the Scafell summits later. As it turned out I could have collected it much more easily when I did Rossett Pike, Esk Pike and the Scafell outliers from Langdale a few weeks later. Anyway, I trotted down the Esk Hause track to the Tongue Head summit and then trudged back up again before dropping down to Seathwaite Fell for my last two tops.

The views were outstanding—Bowfell looking very craggy, with the sun on Flat Crags, the soaring bulk of Pillar, the sideways-on view of Langdale Pikes, and Base Brown, beyond the Styhead track, with its carpet of bright green bilberry. I had never noticed Base Brown looking like this before—a bald mountain of rock and scree with a green cap. Rather like custard on a Christmas pudding, if the colours had been different. There was still snow in Central Gully and Cust's Gully on Great End and a last tiny patch at the very top of South East Gully.

From the shore of Sprinkling Tarn I looked across at Great Gable and could pick out Napes Needle quite easily. And the two summits of Seathwaite Fell each provided strikingly different views of the biggest mountains in the country, with the great gash of Piers Gill especially prominent. Not many people go over Seathwaite Fell but it provides a splendid way down from the heights. One day I set out to count the tarns on this little fell and located a dozen. There may easily be more. Indeed, this little-visited fell has more tarns than almost any other, and one of them at least—beyond Sprinkling Tarn—must be one of the most photogenic in the district. There are no tracks on Seathwaite Fell and I just wandered about the little crags in a delightfully haphazard way and then trotted down the broken rocks to the familiar Styhead track, where I joined the homeward-bound processions.

Stan Edmondson told me about the tragedy on Raven Crag and then said something that, in a different way, surprised me even more. He'd never seen so many visitors and cars at Seathwaite in his life and, since he was born at the farm—the Borrowdale base for trips to Great Gable and the Scafells—and this was a mid-week day, this seemed remarkable. Walking down the lane to Seatoller I could see what he meant. Both sides of the lane were packed with vehicles all the way down to the main road and there were school camps in the intake fields. Clearly, Jubilee Day had become Jubilee Week for many and I was glad my little round had taken me away from the more popular fells.

# 6. The Eastern Fells

The Lake District is split into two, very roughly, by the A591, the Kendal to Keswick road, and the following two chapters deal with the summits that lie to the east of this main artery through the district. These mountains may be further divided, more to the east, by the gap of Kirkstone Pass and its northward continuation of the Dockray to Troutbeck road, and all the two-thousanders within this segment—thirty-eight of them—have been designated the eastern fells and are now described. The remaining summits, to the east of the pass and reaching out towards the road over Shap Fells, have therefore been styled the far eastern fells which makes them seem curiously distant and remote. In fact, these fells in the far east are the nearest to my home and some of them I can see every day—except when the clouds are down.

The arbitrarily-named eastern fells embrace, oddly, the north-south backbone running through the middle of Lakeland—the mountain barrier of Fairfield, Helvellyn and the Dodds, which is the biggest single mass of high ground in the district. This backbone stretches for twelve miles from Rydal to Threlkeld, only falling below 2,000 feet at Grisedale Pass, once the ridge has been gained. Much of the ridge is above 2,500 feet and Helvellyn is one of the tiny handful of three-thousanders in the Lake District. Helvellyn Lower Man is also more than 3,000 feet in height and is listed as a separate two-thousander by Nick Wright in his *English Mountain Summits* but excluded—and I think rightly, as the rise is so slight—by Falkingham. But, of course, this fine top is always traversed when walking the ridge.

Non-mountaineering motorists driving along the main highway through the district may not fully appreciate the height or the splendour of the long mountain barrier for the highest summits are set well back from the road and the lower slopes, alongside Thirlmere, thickly forested with conifers. From some points along the road, within five miles of Keswick, much better views of the range may, however, be obtained and the sight can be especially dramatic in winter. But the finest views of these fells and, by far, the best approaches, are from the east, the Patterdale area. Looking west up any of the valleys, especially Dovedale, Deepdale and Grisedale, the Helvellyn range appears as a rocky mountain wall and, under snow and ice, these views are as exhilarating as anything in Lakeland. The range is buttressed by crags and ridges that enclose wonderful corries, each containing its own mountain tarn. Further north the lonely switchback line of the Dodds has its few crags tucked, low down, on the western side of the barrier—a curious circumstance in Lakeland—but the Fairfield crags face north and east, making the head of Deepdale a particularly impressive place.

All these eastern fells are old friends. The Fairfield Horseshoe is a convenient afternoon or evening walk and the eastern corries of Red Screes, which I can see from my house, are within a short drive. Especially, however, the eastern wall of the Helvellyn range is a constant delight. The corries—or coves as they are called here—are rewarding retreats in summer time—remote from the processions going over Striding and Swirral Edges, and generously equipped with rock for climbing, ridges for scrambling, tarns and pools beneath waterfalls for bathing, and grassy belvederes in which to doze away a sunny afternoon.

In winter time, however, the 'best' side of the Helvellyn range comes into its own. This is where we do most of our snow climbing and skiing, when the possibilities for adventure can be added to the enjoyment of winter beauty. On dozens of occasions each winter Kirkstone Pass is traversed in the search for snow and ice—journeys of high hope but often of some doubt for only the south-facing slopes of the hills may be seen from my home. We wonder: "What will we find today?" If the day is clear there may be a view of the snow-capped Coniston and Langdale hills from the Ings to Troutbeck road—one of my favourite Lake District views. Sometimes these fells, under snow, can appear like a line of fairy castles made out of icing sugar, sparkling and magical in the sunlight. The eastern-facing gullies on Crinkle Crags and Bowfell can be seen, and the distant white gashes assessed for possible snow climbing, but the sight of indifferent sporting prospects on these slopes does not necessarily mean that Helvellyn will prove unrewarding. The Helvellyn range attracts greater accumulations of snow, and longer-lasting winter conditions, than any other part of Lakeland with the possible exception of some of the deepest gullies on Great End. You can often find snow on Helvellyn when the rest of the district is moving from spring to summer. So we pass over Kirkstone Pass, often still doubtful about whether we will find snow for climbing or skiing around Helvellyn. The first clue may be obtained by the backwards view into Dovedale from Brotherswater, the north-facing crags seen for the first time, and then, a few miles further on, come peeps up Deepdale and Grisedale when more may be revealed. But the conditions on the east face of Helvellyn, above Red Tarn—one of the best of the winter areas—cannot be judged until 2,000 feet of height has been won and sometimes the skiing potential cannot be judged from the valley, but has to be sought out.

The possibilities for horseshoe rounds in the eastern fells are considerable. Besides the popular Fairfield Horseshoe there is the even more popular circuit of Red Tarn by way of Striding and Swirral Edges—undoubtedly, the finest mini-horseshoe in Lakeland, especially in winter. Then there are the circuits of Dovedale, Deepdale, Grisedale and Glencoyndale, with, further south, the round of Scandale from Ambleside. The Deepdale round is one of the best of these—Hart Crag by way of Hartsop above How, Fairfield, St Sunday Crag and down the long ridge of Birks, with its splendid views of the curving length of Ullswater. There is also the circuit of another Deepdale, the valley that bites into the Dodds, which can easily be done from Dowthwaitehead—different sort of country but rewarding for its seclusion.

### Helvellyn Days

Helvellyn is the most popular mountain summit in the Lake District—probably in England. During the Tuesday of a rather wet and windy week in July 1966 a total of 614 people were counted on the summit in daylight hours, and it is likely that on some sunny weekends up to a thousand walkers have reached the top on a single day. No other Lakeland mountain—not even Scafell Pike or Great Gable—has so many devotees. The attractions of Helvellyn are fairly obvious. It is the highest mountain in Lakeland outside the Scafells and much more accessible—either from the main road through the district alongside Thirlmere or from Patterdale or Glenridding to the east of the summit ridge. Further, there are at least fourteen tracked routes to the summit—seven from each side—and one of these, the airy, rock ridge of Striding Edge, is by far the most popular mountain ascent in the country. All sorts of people go up Helvellyn—for some it is their only mountain, their first and last summit—and, many years ago, hundreds rode up on ponies. Bicycles and motorcycles have also been ridden—or carried—to the summit, and an aeroplane made its historic landing near the shelter in 1926.

But despite all this humiliation—and the assorted monuments to a faithful dog, a foxhunter and the aeroplane pilot—Helvellyn is a very fine mountain. Its north–south summit ridge is the longest, lofty roof-tree in the district and its east-facing corries and ridges are superb examples of mountain architecture, dramatically sculptured. Seen from the west the Helvellyn range is not strikingly impressive—mostly high, grassy slopes above the Thirlmere conifers—but, from the east, the true character of the mountain and its satellite summits is at once apparent. There are six coves or corries facing east—successively, Keppel Cove, Brown Cove, the unnamed cove between Striding and Swirral Edges in which lies Red Tarn, Nethermost Cove, Ruthwaite Cove and Cock Cove—and I have never been able to decide which is the best. All are impressive—steep, hanging valleys, enclosed by rocky ridges and backed by crags.

Helvellyn is at its best in winter time. There is no worthwhile rock-climbing in summer on the mountain itself—although there are several worthwhile routes on the eastern crags of Nethermost Pike and Dollywaggon Pike—but, under snow and ice, the whole four miles of the eastern face of the range presents remarkable scope for the winter mountaineer. At its best, the centre of the face between Striding Edge and Swirral Edge can give up to 800 feet of snow climbing—generally with a steep cornice—and, in addition, there are at least a dozen gullies, often well-iced, and almost innumerable variations up through the crags. The gullies of Great End used to be considered the best in the district for winter climbing but, in a good winter, there is much more variety on Helvellyn—although nothing of the very highest standard. As the mountain is so readily accessible from my home I spend a great deal of time each winter in these eastern corries—so much more convenient for the shorter days than the major crags to the west of the Lake District. Browncove Crags to the west of the main Helvellyn ridge—oddly named, because Brown Cove is to the east—can also provide worthwhile snow and ice climbing.

But all this invigorating work with ice-axe and crampons seemed a long time away when I walked the Helvellyn tops on my traverse of the two-thousands for the round was made on a mid-week day in July—in the middle of a heatwave. Curiously, however, although the preceding and following days were hot and stifling, this day was unexpectedly cloudy and cool. There was not a hint of sunshine all day and the cloud was so thick on Dollywaggon Pike that, at one time, even on so familiar a summit, I had to use my compass. It was also the only day for weeks when I had worn a shirt on the tops.

There were thirteen summits to be collected on this walk—the figure inflated by a succession of 2,000-foot tops on Birkhouse Moor—and the round completed, quite easily, within eight hours, starting and finishing at Glenridding. Out of the many thousands of visitors to Helvellyn each year I don't suppose many go up there three times in one day, but this is what I had to do. Of course, I didn't go up and down the mountain three times—that would have been quite a performance—but I had to go to the top three times from neighbouring summits. Perhaps there are easier ways of doing the round without having to go to the top of Helvellyn three times, but I couldn't think of one. So I went up Birkhouse Moor and along Striding Edge to the summit, down Swirral Edge and up to Catstycam and then back the same way to the summit again, and then on to Low Man, Whiteside and Raise and back the same route to the summit a third time. By this time I was getting a little tired of Helvellyn but I'd still plenty more to do—along the ridge to Nethermost Pike, High Crag and Dollywaggon Pike, down to Grisedale Tarn, up to Seat Sandal, back to the tarn, and then down the long miles of Grisedale to Glenridding.

A year earlier the round would have been two or three miles shorter but the Grisedale car-park had now been closed and you had to leave your vehicle in Glenridding, adding nearly an hour to the walking, there and back. This Grisedale car-park had become something of an eyesore and I believe had led to some vandalism, but it was certainly convenient for those doing the longer mountain walks and its closing is regretted by many.

From Glenridding, at the start of the round, I managed to

select quite an interesting rock-scrambling route through the crags on the north-east ridge of Birkhouse Moor. There is a zigzag track up through the juniper and among the outcrops but it was possible to find a more direct route on rock nearly all the way which enlivened what would otherwise have been a tamely pedestrian round—up and down mountains which I must have ascended scores of times. Just before starting the scramble I found a newish pair of sunglasses underneath a boulder. The loser may have them on application, if he can provide proof of ownership.

Falkingham found four summits on Birkhouse Moor so I had to seek them out but the low cloud concealed all the views. The most notable feature of the panorama from this long, bulky spur of Helvellyn is the sight of the east face of the mountain enclosed between the twin ridges of Striding Edge and Swirral Edge—especially in winter time. Indeed, you have to ascend to this viewpoint or to the upper reaches of Red Tarn Beck from the former Greenside mines before you can properly assess, in season, the chances of reasonable snow climbing on the face. The face is hidden from everywhere else, except the two rock ridges. But this day nothing was to be seen—not even the dark pool of Red Tarn. The turrets of Striding Edge were quickly traversed, and the first visit to the summit of Helvellyn achieved. I hadn't been over these edges since the previous winter and was appalled at the increasing erosion. The whole mountainside is being kicked away by clumsy walkers. At one time the only track went over all the towers, but now less-exposed routes have been trampled out along each side by the over-cautious or inexperienced and both edges, as well as the scramble up to the summit, are now in a sorry mess. How satisfying it is to be up here in winter time when all the sliding scree and rubbish is covered in snow and ice.

Perhaps a word of warning about the potential dangers on Helvellyn for ill-equipped or inexperienced walkers in winter-time would be appropriate. In summer-time these ridges are perfectly feasible for most people; in winter—especially when there is ice concealed beneath the snow—they demand proper equipment and experience. Ice-axes should be carried and walkers should know how to use them and, under certain conditions, crampons should be worn on the boots. Ordinary vibram-type, rubber-soled boots, without crampons, can be lethal on hard, polished snow or ice—indeed it is impossible not to slip, wearing these uncramponned boots, on rock-hard polished snow set at even the slightest angle. Every year there are accidents in winter on these ridges—some of them fatal. Four months after my round a father and his young daughter fell to their deaths in Brown Cove from a point just beyond the summit of Swirral Edge. At the inquest it was stated the tragedy would not have happened if they had been wearing crampons. And yet, every winter, I meet people on the Helvellyn ridges without either ice-axes or crampons, and, more than once, have had to go to the assistance of walkers unable to move because of their lack of proper equipment or experience. People should realize that the weather in the valley in winter-time is no indication of the conditions on the tops and that, in any case, the weather can change dramatically within minutes.

Returning to more pleasant topics it was interesting, during my round, to observe the sheep on the summit of Helvellyn. These creatures have long struck me as being far from ordinary sheep. They don't, for example, scatter or walk away when you approach but come right up to you. Obviously, they see more human beings than most other mountain sheep and have grown accustomed to our ways. They know, for instance, that many people stop for lunch on top, and so they lie in wait, hoping for titbits. These sheep will eat anything you care to throw them—cheese, sardines, cake or jam butties—and are the only sheep encountered on the fells that will eat out of your hand. On my three visits to the summit this day what looked like the same sheep was waiting at the summit shelter for me every time, but it got nothing for I'd had my sandwiches on Catstycam. It reminded me of a goat I once met when camping in the Alps that pounced on a tiny cube of soap that was supposed to last two of us for a fortnight, and ate it at one gulp—although I've never tried the Helvellyn sheep with soap.

It was odd, too, to bump into geologists on Swirral Edge—chipping away with their little hammers with what seemed great interest and concentration. And there was another of them hammering away in Brown Cove, half a mile away. I had heard the tapping long before I saw them and couldn't understand it, knowing they couldn't be climbers hammering in pitons for there's no rock worth climbing in these parts, except in winter. I hope they had a successful day. Even if there'd been dozens of them they couldn't do as much damage to the mountain as that already done by walkers' boots.

The walk to Raise seemed a long way that day—and even longer, coming back—mostly, I suppose, because of the poor visibility. A short distance down the north-east slopes of Raise is the hut of the Lake District Ski Club and, in Savage's Drift, the site of the ski run which is improved with snow fences set up each winter. This is a place of particularly happy memories for me extending back more than thirty years, and to before the days when several of us erected the pre-fabricated hut and installed the ski-tow machinery. The slope provides some of the most consistent skiing snow in the Lake District and there were five months of skiing here during the winter of 1976/77.

Having reached the summit of Helvellyn a third time I continued south along the remaining summits, being forced to find the cairn on Dollywaggon Pike by compass—the summit being some distance from the usual track. No water was found until I reached Grisedale Tarn so that, had the day been hot—as forecast—I could well have been dehydrated as I had been on some other rounds. The pull up to Seat Sandal was rather trying after a longish day but, eventually, my last summit was bagged and I was down at the tarn again in a few minutes. It took exactly an hour and a half from the summit of Seat Sandal to the Glenridding car-park which looks something like six miles on the map so I can't have been dawdling, but I found the stones on the pass rather hard on the feet.

It had been rather a lonely, sad sort of day—no views, no sunshine, no cloud shadows dappling the heights, and few people about—and, as if to echo the general gloom, the Grisedale sheep near Elmhow sounded as mournful that evening as any I have heard. First, the cries of the lambs and then the deeper-throated moans of their mothers as if, between them, they were carrying all the troubles of the world. How different, I thought, from the sheep on the summit, 3,000 feet up, who never make a sound but just wait patiently for the next walker to come along, and the chance for a change of diet. My only stop all day had been for lunch in a corner of rock on Catstycam. There's no excuse to stop when you're alone and there's no view and all you're doing is humble peak-bagging over familiar ground.

**The Traverse of the Dodds**

The Dodds are among the least-frequented fells in the Lake District—and, therefore, not very rewarding for devoted collectors of litter. You can walk over all the summits in summer and sometimes never see another person—indeed, the only occasions when I have met people on these fells have been when traversing the tops in winter, either on foot or on skis. The reasons for this comparative neglect of these considerable fells—the highest, Great Dodd, is more than 2,800 feet high—are fairly obvious. The Dodds are smoothly-rounded, grassy and almost featureless, and the valleys that reach up to the heights—Deepdale and Mosedale—boggy and rather dreary. If you look at the map the area appears curiously bare—even of printing—and there are fewer crags, woods, tarns or other interesting features than almost anywhere else in Lakeland—except, possibly, the 'back o' Skiddaw' country. There are, in fact, some fine crags—Castle Rock of Triermain, Wanthwaite Crags and Bram Crag—but these are down by the road through St John's in the Vale and are not seen from the tops. Indeed, when you are doing the round of the Dodds you come upon the little, rocky summit of Calfhow Pike with some relief—the only place where you can get your hands on rock. And, except for the bogs in the dales, you will only find a couple of shallow pools. Again, there are some splendid ravines, including Stanah Gill and Mill Gill with their waterfalls, but these also are crowded down on the western sides, just above the road—a most unusual feature for Lakeland.

But, although the Dodds are so smooth, featureless and neglected these very circumstances provide their charm. You can hardly expect any excitement, and you have to search hard even for interest, on a round of these fells, but the rounded Dodds can provide you with quietude and peace in an often-crowded Lakeland, and the summits make one of the best promenades from which to view the northern fells and dales. From these rounded tops, largely free from cairns, litter and evidence of the passage of feet, you can look out, as if from some high terrace, at more spectacular mountains and, on the splendid, springy turf, cover the distances with ease. This is what the Scafells and Great Gable were like fifty years ago, mostly free from tracks and erosion, and the Dodds are worth seeking out for this reason alone.

The Ordnance Survey prefer 'Dod' in the summit names although 'Dodd' is more widely accepted nowadays, and the group, Great Dodd, Watson's Dodd and Stybarrow Dodd and their outliers, are popularly known as the Dodds. They are really an extension of the Helvellyn range—separated from it by the high col of Sticks Pass—but the Helvellyn pilgrims rarely continue the northern traverse of the heights, which really requires the use of motorcars at each end. In winter time the Dodds become more attractive for snow heightens the scenery and these fells can often have considerable accumulations. The head of Deepdale, facing north-east, can often be a snow trap for months on end, and the northern slopes of these fells can sometimes provide some of the best opportunities for advanced skiing, because of their steepness, in the Lake District. And the traverse of the tops, on skis, makes a fine cross-country expedition.

The collection of these summits was made at the beginning of July. I saw three people in the distance on Watson's Dodd but nobody else all day. But the song of the larks accompanied me nearly all the way and the day gradually improved from morning mist and hazy blue-grey shapes to the brightest of summer evenings. The mists lay low over Ullswater as I drove to Dockray and even from High Row, more than 1,300 feet above sea-level, it was impossible to see the tops. But there was a strong south-west wind blowing and I knew the summits would clear later. Sometimes, in the snow, High Row resembles a winter sports centre with ski-tows on the slopes and much noise and excitement. It is one of the best viewpoints from a road in the district but, that day, just a lonely corner in the clouds. I had ten summits to collect, including the outliers of Sheffield Pike and Clough Head, and the best round was not immediately obvious. The circumnavigation of Deepdale, including Hart Side, is straightforward enough but, to include the outliers, a certain amount of backtracking seemed inevitable. In the end I decided to collect Randerside, on the ridge of Great Dodd, first, followed by Clough Head, before picking up the highest of the Dodds. Sheffield Pike would have to be a digression later. There may be neater ways of doing this round but they were not apparent at the time.

Groove Beck was selected as the best way to Randerside—an easy walk along a sheep-trod, slightly marred by several sections of bog which ensured that my feet were wet from the start. I was wearing one of my oldest pairs of boots that day—others are reserved for more demanding expeditions—and, before the end of the walk, was annoyed at my choice for, besides letting in water, they proved unduly restricting and badly blistered my feet. The rest of my walks, I decided, would be in better boots. From Randerside the grassy slopes of Great Dodd were traversed to the track towards Clough Head and the second summit collected. Here I met the wind, now almost gale force, and was glad of the little wall-shelter and, better still, of the metal container, a few yards away to the north, besides which I crouched to eat my sandwiches. This metal container, remarkably, is used for the collection of hundreds of yards of rusty wire taken from old fences on the fells—the only such receptacle met in my traverse of the two-thousands. It might be an ugly intrusion on the heights but not nearly so ugly, nor so dangerous to sheep, as the miles of old wire that litter some of the fells. Whoever put it there showed some public spirit.

The views were improving, with the ridges and ravines of Blencathra beginning to rise through the mist beyond the trough of the Keswick plain, and the western skyline of the Lakeland fells starting to take shape. It was now necessary to retrace my steps and walk over the little, rocky staging-post of Calfhow Pike on to Great Dodd. Here I wondered—and not for the first time—whether, in fact, the Ordnance Survey people had actually ever been on these tops—or whether they measured them on a bad day. For the cairn on Great Dodd does not seem to be on the highest point—nor, in fact, does the cairn on Stybarrow Dodd. Watson's Dodd is not regarded as a separate two-thousander by Falkingham—not enough of a depression from Great Dodd—but I went there all the same, wondering who on earth was Mr Watson. The summit is rather undistinguished but the mountain has the magnificent Castle Rock of Triermain on its western flank—one of the steepest crags in the district. And there are many other curiosities of nomenclature on the Dodds. What, for instance, is the story behind Fisher's Wife Rake on Clough Head and who was Jim of Jim's Fold, and why was Nameless Fell so called—before they changed it to Birkett Fell in honour of the late Lord Birkett who did so much to save Ullswater from becoming another reservoir?

Stybarrow Dodd was next traversed—its two indicated summits and the other one—and by now the day was improving, but not my feet. The views were now clear—I could nearly pick out the ski hut on Raise—and the fells were dappled with sunlight and racing cloud shadows. I looked down the northern slopes where I have enjoyed some of the steepest skiing in the Lake District and south to the winter playground of Helvellyn—both looking tamely innocuous in the sunshine. Greenside was the next summit—an easy walk—and I continued, above the old quarries, down to the depression before Sheffield Pike. The gale was now blowing in quite fierce gusts, making walking rather difficult. In fact, much of the day's walking was rather tiresome—a lot of it trackless and mostly traversing over tussocks. Not the best country for tired feet. It was pleasant, though, on Sheffield Pike to be on a bit of rock for a change, and the sight of the long length of Ullswater was stimulating. Glenridding, at the foot of the mountain, is one of the most familiar parts of the Lake District to me—largely because of frequent winter climbing and skiing days—but, curiously, Sheffield Pike was one of the last of the Lake District two-thousanders to be ascended—for the first time, less than ten years ago. I think, too, it was the only Lake District mountain I specially sought out because I had never done it before. All the others had been done, incidentally, on more or less long walks or climbs. Then, one day, I discovered I had never been up Sheffield Pike and quickly remedied the omission. My principal memory of that day is of eating a large farmhouse tea, provided by a farmer friend, and, especially, of the bilberry tart.

But this July day was not quite so pleasant, I still had the steep trudge up towards Greenside again, two Hart Side summits and the walk back to High Row before I could take off my confounded boots. To help, I took off a pair of socks and obtained some relief but this simple walk, because of the wrong footwear, proved the most trying of all my peak-bagging days, instead of one of the easiest. The remarkable ditch on the main summit of Hart Side was examined, and once again I wondered who had done this tremendous excavation and why, finally deciding it had probably been miners many years ago. Then, on to the secondary summit and down, on a lovely evening, now sheltered from the wind, to the lonely hamlet of Dowthwaitehead and the trudge back up the road to the car. Dowthwaitehead, surrounded by fells, has some claim to be the most sunless place in the Lake District—it is said the sun avoids the hamlet for months at a time—but it was certainly sunny that July evening and, amid its sparkling waters, a little jewel of a retreat. There are also said to be more buzzards than people at Dowthwaitehead, but all I saw that evening were cows and sheep. The first job on reaching the car was to change my boots and the second to drive down the hill to the pleasant inn at Dockray for some much-needed refreshment. My ten summits had been collected at the cost of a few bits of skin and I remembered happier rounds of these fells, but the Dodds will always have their attraction on the right sort of day, when you feel you want to get away from worries or crowds, or just need to think.

## The Fairfield Horseshoe

Perhaps the best-known horseshoe round in the Lake District, and one of the easiest, is the circuit of Rydale—the Fairfield Horseshoe. Most summer weekends there are people doing the round from Ambleside or Rydal—often a surprising variety of pedestrians, ranging from elderly gentlemen with sticks to youngsters in sandals, as well as babies slung on rucksacks and far-ranging dogs. The walk is about ten miles long but the only steepish places are at the beginning and the end; otherwise it is all very easy and straightforward going, mostly on grass. The usual time for the round is between four and six hours, depending on fitness or the number of stops for viewing, photography or food, but some people, not wanting to be rushed, take a whole day over it. Going round non-stop at an ordinary, though steady, pace and trotting down all the steep bits, I have done it in three hours, but this is quite unexceptional. Runners in the annual Fairfield Horseshoe race take about an hour and a half to get round, and the record, still standing in 1977, is one hour, eight and a half minutes.

There are generally held to be eight summits on the Round—Heron Pike, Rydal Fell (or Erne Crag), Greatrigg Man, Fairfield, Hart Crag, Dove Crag, High Pike, and Low Pike—but Falkingham finds ten two-thousanders. Naturally, Low Pike, being too low to count, is excluded, and he also eschews High Pike, not being satisfied that the dip between this summit and Dove Crag is sufficient to qualify it as a separate summit. On the other hand, Nick Wright in his *English Mountain Summits* accepts High Pike as a two-thousander, although, after a close perusal of both the one-inch and 1:25,000 maps with a magnifying glass, I think this very doubtful, and have excluded it from my tally. But all this is hardly relevant for you go over the top, anyway. Falkingham, however, more than makes up for his exclusion of High Pike, by counting the slightly knobbly, but still rounded and grassy, hill of Rydal Fell as no fewer than four summits and, if you are sufficiently interested, you can pick them out on the map. It is in circumstances such as this that the seeker after the two-thousands realizes the ridiculous nature of his task. On our peak-bagging round we dutifully ticked off these silly tops, located after some debate, but felt rather ashamed of ourselves, particularly since Erne Crag is included as a separate summit, in addition to the multi-crowned Rydal Fell.

I had the pleasure of the company of my friend, Ted Stacey, for the Fairfield Horseshoe round and, since it was mid-week and he had his job to do, we did it in the evening. It was the middle of May—my last walk before snow-climbing in Scotland—and the evening was dull but dry. The walk took us four hours which left us with sufficient time at the end to enjoy some ale, brewed in the wood, at the Golden Rule, Ambleside—a fitting conclusion to any round of the fells.

There is no 'right' way round the Fairfield Horseshoe. I have been round dozens of times, both clockwise and anti-clockwise, and have always found the circuits equally enjoyable. For this evening walk, however, we decided to go anti-clockwise, thinking that the sunset views might be slightly better from the Rydal Fell ridge and the breakneck run down Nab Scar a suitable appetizer before refreshment. My previous visit, a couple of months earlier, had been made in the opposite direction and had proved especially noteworthy, since we failed to get round. A friend from the south, on a fleeting visit to Lakeland, wanted some fresh air so I said we would go round the Fairfield Horseshoe. It was a wet, cloudy day, with some menace in the sky, but it was not until we reached the top of Nab Scar that we met the wind which, thereafter, increased to gale force. Somewhere on Rydal Fell we met a man, struggling in the opposite direction and seeking his wife who had given up earlier, and it was some time before this domestic contretemps could be sorted out and the couple dispatched to the valley by a less exposed route. The wind was coming out of the east and the rain was torrential—great curtains of it being swept across the ridge. I had told my friend that this was a very easy walk but, by now, neither of us was so sure about this. The difficulty—apart from the drenching rain and impenetrable mist—lay in placing one's feet on the ground. Once lifted up, to take a step, the foot was blown sideways and could only be placed on the ground with some effort. On one of the easiest ridges in the Lake District we progressed like drunken men, literally fighting for every step. You would have thought we were retreating from the South Pole, Everest or Moscow. We didn't go where we wanted but where the wind decided.

Eventually, we reached the top of Greatrigg Man but the slight descent to the dip before the rise to Fairfield proved our undoing. Several times we had been blown away for several yards but, looking round, after one particularly ferocious gust, I saw my companion lying on the ground. He had been blown completely off his feet and had come to rest, some distance away, fortunately without injury. Not worth it, we decided—without discussion—and; in a moment, we were running down to Stone Arthur and Grasmere. Immediately, sheltered by the ridge, we were out of the wind and merely had to contend with the downpour and the mist which, by then, didn't matter. This is the only time I have been blown off a mountain, been forced to abandon a walk because of the wind. More than once I have been blown off a rock-climb—not literally, but effectively—but it was humiliating to be blown off the Fairfield Horseshoe—and, literally, in my companion's case. I remember we dried out in the Swan at Grasmere and then, to redeem ourselves, went up Helm Crag in the rain, and back along the main road to the car at Rydal in the dark.

But this May evening in 1977 we had none of these problems and the walk went very easily. It was pleasant ambling round the familiar circuit in the cool of the evening, avoiding the sticky heat of the day, and watching the fells turning blue and shadowed before they melted into the night. Gradually, the length of Windermere extended as we rose higher over Low Pike and High Pike and most of the Lake District was visible, although dimly seen, from the summit of Dove Crag, reached after the last easy mile of gently-shelving grass. Nothing is seen, from the summit, of the noble crag that gives this fell its name—one of the steepest cliffs in England—and this is the main weakness of this otherwise rewarding round—the splendid northern precipices that buttress the curve of the horseshoe for nearly two miles are out of sight below the easy plateau. The top of Dove Crag is about a quarter of a mile away to the north and it is possible to lie on the very edge and drop a stone straight on to the screes—300 feet below. One of the routes on the crag—most appropriately named Hangover—is one of the hardest climbs I have ever done, but much harder routes have been made through the overhangs in recent years by the new breed of rock experts. A particularly interesting feature of the crag is a large cave, to one side near the top, where up to a dozen people can sleep comfortably and completely dry. Inside the cave is a metal box containing visitors' books, methylated spirits and, sometimes a little food, which should not be disturbed since it has probably been left by a temporary resident. The books contain an interesting record of many visits and climbs; outdoor-activities groups often use the place as a bedroom. It would not be wise for me to give the exact location for inexperienced walkers could find themselves in trouble trying to reach the cave. Sleep-walkers, too, are not advised to sleep there; a walk of two or three yards would be their last.

Further round the northern curve of the horseshoe are, successively, the cliffs of Hart Crag, Scrubby Crag, Hutaple Crag and Black Crag and the gullies of Black Tippet and Flinty Graves. It was down one of these places and over a cliff that two girls fell to their deaths, probably during a snowstorm, several years ago, and, for a long time, their bodies lay undiscovered in the snow. Bloodhounds were the first to locate the tragic remains. In bad weather, therefore, walkers should keep away from the top of these cliffs but, in good conditions, the walk is made much more rewarding if it is made along the edge of the crags, from which dramatic views of the wild, upper corries of Deepdale may be obtained. For winter mountaineers these cliffs and gullies can provide good snow and ice climbing. Many years ago I was involved in several modest first ascents on these crags in summer—their'discovery' as a climbing ground came rather late—but, nowadays, my visits there are mostly in the wintertime. Beginners can have excellent snow-climbing practice when the scree shoots are well filled; the steeper gullies need more experience.

It was rather chilly on the top of Fairfield on our evening round and we ate our sandwiches lower down the mountain, out of the wind. Somebody had placed a Union Jack on the summit cairn—probably in anticipation of the forthcoming Queen's Jubilee—but there was nobody about and, as expected, we saw no people at all throughout the walk. The distant views were clouding over but we could still pick out the Scafells and Great Gable, High Street and the Coniston fells and the toe of Windermere reaching towards Morecambe Bay. I remember Angle Tarn above Patterdale could be seen—a smudge of blue among the shadows.

The most notable feature of that early summer evening in the fells, however, was the constant noise of aircraft. Fairfield must be below the flight path of commercial aircraft for I hear them every time I go there, but that evening the droning was incessant. No sooner had one passed over than another followed it and, often, there were several aircraft overhead at the same time. Aircraft noise is a discordant note in the high fells, especially on an otherwise quiet evening, and when the droning is continuous the intrusion is particularly irritating. A few years ago I found the noise, above my house, so annoying that I wrote to my M.P. about it and he forwarded my letter to the ministries involved. The constant droning was bad enough during the daytime but it also continued throughout the night, often making sleep difficult. And, once awake, you couldn't get off again—waiting for the next droning to start and then continue, slowly, into the distance. I learned from Whitehall that my house happens to be situated exactly on the line of one of the most-used aircraft corridors, carrying the traffic between Ringway and Prestwick, and that an average of 240 aircraft passed over my house each day. There was nothing they could do about it, although my M.P. had already suggested—there were many other complaints—that the corridor should take the line of the M6. More recently, the aircraft noise above my house has not been so bad—perhaps they are now flying higher—but the noise in the fells seems to be getting worse—especially on Fairfield. Perhaps there is no easy answer to this modern pollution of the Lakeland air, but the marked increase deserves recording.

We came easily down the long ridge towards Ambleside, conscientiously ticking off the absurd tops of Rydal Fell, and finished, at a run, down Nab Scar, avoiding the zigzags and coming straight through the steep bracket. Rydal Water looked a sombre pool at the darkening, and the last visitors had paid their money to look through Wordsworth's home. The exercise had been useful but we had missed the sunshine and the changing pattern of cloud shadows on the fells. Far more memorable was a round during the following winter in crusted snow and thick mist when we had to use compasses on Hart Crag and Dove Crag and the rock step below Low Pike was thick with ice. In these conditions the Fairfield Horseshoe can be an interesting challenge; in perfect weather, you can take your children round—or, even, your grandparents.

**Summits from Kirkstone**

Five summits in the delightful but familiar country west of the Kirkstone Pass to Patterdale road, missed out in my unplanned and casual collection of the two-thousands, had to be picked up in a rather indiscriminate day towards the end of the series. If my peak-bagging had been properly planned I could have finished my longish Helvellyn day with the ascent at St Sunday Crag from Grisedale Hause, returning to Glenridding along the ridge of Birks. This would have made a more demanding round, with fifteen summits, but would have been perfectly feasible and is commended as a more sensible method of including the summits south of Grisedale. As it was, these tops remained unvisited until nearly the end of July, sticking out of the record like a sore thumb, and Red Screes and Little Hart Crag had also to be collected. These last two might have been added to the Fairfield Horseshoe round, finishing with the easy descent of Snarker Pike to Ambleside or Rydal, but, it may be remembered, we had done the Horseshoe in the evening and this would have meant a return in the dark. Truth to tell, however, we never thought of this at the time—so careless, or, indeed, non-existent, had been my planning. The missing tops, therefore, had to be fitted in somehow and, since there seemed no very obvious way of linking them into a horseshoe round, it was decided to stoop to the use of a car in between, and do them in two unconnected bits. Wiser walkers doing the series will arrange things better.

My son Robin was my companion on this day of picking up previously unconsidered trifles—a dreary day of mist and rain that failed to do much uplifting of the spirit. We started from a lay-by on the Patterdale side of Kirkstone Pass—to save a mile or two of road walking—crossed Kirkstone Beck by some gymnastic leaping, and contoured round the slopes of Middle Dodd into Caiston Glen. Up above us was the rocky bield where, in 1948, a Lakeland terrier named, I seem to remember, Butcher, was trapped for something like a fortnight but eventually rescued alive in a blaze of national newspaper publicity. I remembered standing at the excavations—many tons of rock were prized out of the fellside—and watching the little chap being brought out by the kindly rescuers. Perhaps more pints of celebratory beer were consumed that day around Brothers Water and Patterdale than ever before or since.

We trudged up Caiston Glen in the rain and then mounted easily from Scandale Pass to the twin rocky summits of Little Hart Crag. Why we always call it Caiston Glen—a Scottish, rather than a Lakeland, appellation—I can't say, for the Ordnance Survey does not do so on its tourist maps. Little Hart Crag is a worthy little mountain, much rockier than many, the guardian of lonely Scandale, and a magnificent viewpoint for the Hartsop valley. There is good scrambling, and even some climbing, on the rocks and a long wall of crags, Black Brow, to the west of the summits, overlooks the fine ravine of Hoggett Gill. Nick Wright, in his *English Mountain Summits*, includes Black Brow, on the track to Dove Crag from Little Hart Crag, as a separate two-thousander but this seems rather doubtful. Falkingham does not include it and a close perusal of the 1:25,000 map does not persuade me to add it, either. Nor does a study of the ground; there is not enough of a depression between Black Brow and Little Hart Crag.

Descending to Scandale Pass we continued the nearly 1,000-foot ascent to Red Screes and ticked off our third summit—Little Hart Crag counting as two. This, of course, is the least interesting way of ascending Red Screes. Far better to go up from the summit of Kirkstone Pass through either the south-east or the north-east corrie—particularly in winter time. The gullies in these rocky corries, especially the former, make quite interesting snow-climbing routes and the ravine of Kilnshaw's Chimney, between the two, can also be quite entertaining when blocked with snow. Since the summit of Red Screes can be reached from my house in one hour this eastern face makes a useful winter playground for a short morning or afternoon visit. On this wet July day, however, there was no temptation to linger on top and we trotted down the ridge to Middle Dodd which does not count as a separate summit since the rise from Red Screes is imperceptible. Here, remarkably, the rain stopped and we ate our sandwiches in an airy, rocky corner in five minutes of rare sunshine—the only ration of the day, and the only break in the rain which soon resumed.

Knowing of a bridge across the upper reaches of Kirkstone Beck we made straight for this, down steep screes, believing this would provide a quick route to the car, but it probably took longer than the easy trot down the ridge would have done. It was then a short drive into Deepdale where we tackled the ascent of Birks from Wallend. This route is not commended to anyone, especially on such a wet, misty day. It is an incredibly dull plod, steep and trackless and, until we struck the ridge at St Sunday Crag, we had to use a compass. We were wearing cagoules which meant that we were just as wet through inside, from condensation, as we were outside, from the rain. All we could do was trudge on, fortified by the probably mistaken belief that, at least, summit-bagging must have some benefits. St Sunday Crag was duly collected and then its subsidiary summit of Cavel Pike before a break-neck, squelching descent to Deepdale. It was so wet underfoot that splashes rose from our feet as we plunged down, careless of the bogs since we knew we now couldn't get any wetter.

St Sunday Crag is a fine, lofty mountain of more than passing interest, nowadays, to mountaineers. At one time the mountain was regarded as little more than an interesting route to Fairfield and, especially, a magnificent way down to Patterdale, but in 1954 the potentialities of the long line of crags overlooking Grisedale were first discovered by climbers. Earlier, the crags had been ignored for, from the valley, they looked too broken and insignificant, but exploration proved this to be far from the truth. Since then, many worthwhile routes have been put up on these crags, including the 600-foot-long Pinnacle Ridge which can provide an interesting, moderate route to the summit, in both summer and winter conditions. Other routes, especially those on the Nose, are much harder. The fellside below the crags is one of the steepest in Lakeland and this fact, combined with the situation of the crags, just below the summit ridge, had concealed the real quality of these cliffs during fifty years of climbing exploration elsewhere.

# 7. The Far Eastern Fells

The smoothly-rounded far eastern fells of the Lake District—all the heights east of Kirkstone Pass and Ullswater—are, pre-eminently, walking country. There is rock-climbing on Buckbarrow Crag in Longsleddale, Rainsbarrow Crag in Kentmere, Raven Crag above Pasture Beck and in a few other places but, mostly, these fells lend themselves to easy walks along undulating, grassy ridges, often above steep, craggy slopes and, sometimes, in very lonely country. This is also the country of the golden eagle—the birds having selected one of the quieter areas for their return to Lakeland after an absence of 200 years—the Martindale red deer, with their own sanctuary, and the native fell pony, some of them still living almost wild. But, although this is fine walking country it is hardly thronged with tourists or even large numbers of walkers. You will probably meet people on the Kentmere Horseshoe or on Caudale Moor most summer weekends but never crowds of them, as on Helvellyn, Gable and the Scafells, and even the long ridges of High Street are rarely 'wick wi' foak'. When the lovely hamlet of Mardale was drowned about forty years ago, and Haweswater doubled in size to become England's largest reservoir, this area below the eastern ridges and lonely valleys of High Street became a place for the mountain connoisseur—a retreat where he could find the peace and quietude so often lacking in the more crowded part of Lakeland. A small car-park at the south end of the reservoir, tucked underneath the northern crags of Harter Fell, is still large enough to accommodate these discerning visitors.

In a sense, this is reservoir country—Haweswater, Hayeswater, further to the west, Kentmere Reservoir and Wet Sleddale Reservoir, close to the Shap Fells road—but we have grown accustomed to them. Haweswater has an ugly, white shore-line when drawn down and sometimes the ruins of the drowned buildings and the walls around the former intake fields appear above the retreated waters*, but Hayeswater always seems full and hardly changed from a mountain tarn. Kentmere Reservoir, too, can be accepted as a mountain tarn in a fine setting although there was one recent occasion—as later described—when the pool had to be emptied for a month or two for urgent repair work. But, in addition to these waters, adapted for public and industrial needs, the far eastern fells can boast some of the most splendid mountain tarns in Lakeland—especially Small Water, Blea Water and Patterdale's Angle Tarn. Some writers have described Small Water, underneath Nan Bield Pass, as the most perfect of all our tarns and Blea Water, below the High Street crags, is the deepest in the district.

There are thirty-five two-thousanders in the far eastern fells, with High Street (2,719 feet) the highest, and Grey Crag the most easterly summit in the Lake District. Several can be seen from my house and their shapes are as familiar to me, in the changing seasons and lighting, as nearby streets are to the townsman. As I write this chapter Yoke, Ill Bell, Thornthwaite Crag, Mardale Ill Bell and Harter Fell are deeply plastered in snow—a great ring of sunlit, white peaks circling the head of Kentmere and looking twice their real height. Tomorrow, if the weather holds, I hope to be traversing the round on skis.

The finest walk in these far eastern fells is along the Roman 'road' over the High Street fells, the best horseshoe round, the circuit of the Kentmere hills, while the loneliest country is among the rounded heights that look down to the Shap Fells. It was among these fells to the east of Kirkstone Pass where, nearly fifty years ago, I met some men of the Ordnance Survey building a triangular column on one of the summits—which one, I cannot now recall. They had brought up their materials on the backs of ponies and were camping out on the site. To a youngster it seemed a wonderfully, exciting job—working and living up in the fells—and it was the first triangulation column I had ever seen. That day long ago had other excitements, too. We saw our first red deer—only a few yards away, climbing out of Riggindale on to the High Street Ridge—and, later, down by Hayeswater, our first fell ponies, almost certainly living wild in those days. Even now, the walker is more likely to see red deer, fell ponies and the golden eagle in these lonely

* Possible plans to increase considerably the storage capacity of Haweswater by the building of a much higher dam were still being discussed in 1978.

fells than in any other part of Lakeland.

Besides the horseshoe rounds described in this chapter there are several other opportunities in the far eastern fells for circuits of the valleys. The circuit of Longsleddale from Sadgill embracing Shipman Knotts, Kentmere Pike and Harter Fell to the west and Branstree, Tarn Crag and Great Howe to the west is one of these, while another includes the Troutbeck fells, Thornthwaite Crag and Caudale Moor, starting and finishing at Troutbeck. In addition, the valleys of Boardale, Martindale, and Fusedale, can all be circumnavigated along the heights. Especially rewarding, too, can be the round of several of the valleys running eastwards from the High Street ridge—Riggindale, Randale, Whelterdale and the dale down which flows the splendid waterfalls of Measand Beck. The round of Riggindale from the head of Haweswater, along Rough Crag and Long Stile to the summit of High Street and down Kidsty Pike makes one of the best short days in the district. Immediately south of this round lies Mardale Waters, an idyllic corner of Lakeland, still unspoiled despite its proximity to the artificially flooded dale. Herein lie the fine pools of Blea Water and Small Water, backed by a ring of crags, and a tumult of becks and waterfalls. Even the water-board direction signs nearby cannot take away the magic and music of the mountain heights and streaming fellsides.

## Walking High Street

The long, north–south spine of the far eastern fells from the Penrith–Pooley Bridge area to Troutbeck and Windermere is the highway in the clouds the Romans used nearly two thousand years ago. They called it High Street and this is the name still used for the highest point, 2,719 feet above sea-level—a splendid, uplifted plateau with crags to both east and west and rocky ridges, enclosing deeply-gouged dales, reaching down to Haweswater. This is the way the Roman soldiers went, sometimes in chariots or in slave-borne litters, between their garrisons at Brougham and Ambleside—something like fifteen miles along the eastern edges of the mountains, most of them, at more than two thousand feet above the sea. Before the soldiers, the ancient Britons also knew these fells, building their homes, their stone circles and their burial mounds around the valley heads and you can still see the remains today, mostly around Moor Divock at the northern end of the 'street'. And after the Romans, marauding brigands and raiding Scots crept along the ridge, to be followed by more peaceful travellers—pack-horse trains and the more energetic dalesfolk. Men from Mardale and Longsleddale used to drag barrels of beer and mountains of food up the fellside and race their horses along the grassy ridges. Indeed, the Ordnance Survey still name the summit or its southern slopes, Racecourse Hill, on their large-scale maps.

Some of the highway was flagged with rock, much of it sandstone, dragged up to the ridge by the Romans or their slaves, but nothing of this can be seen today, although two great stones, south of the summit, are believed to have marked the way. In places the route is grooved, as if by thousands of marching feet, but elsewhere the 'street' is not even tracked and the northern miles are difficult to trace, especially in bad weather. You have to use your imagination, traversing High Street, to get the flavour of this ancient route. Try to imagine the marching legions rounding the steep crags above the surrounding valleys and the high tarns, often in bad weather, or the Scots invaders working southwards along the ridge to make their raids into the dales. The faint track that goes up the steep side of Froswick from Troutbeck Park is where the raiders came down from the heights, and today we call this 'the Scots' Rake'.

The High Street walk above the scooped valleys that line the flanks from Penrith to Windermere can be one of the delights of a Lakeland visit—a longish but not particularly tiring day, along miles of history with much to be seen in good weather, and plenty to think about. A few years ago I did the walk with my brother from Celleron, just south of Penrith, to Troutbeck, north of Windermere and can still remember every mile—not because of the views, for we saw nothing, but because of the appalling weather. Leaving a car at the southern end we were dropped from another near Tirril and left to our own devices. This transport had been specially arranged so we didn't feel like abandoning the walk when we saw that the clouds were down to about 500 feet and, once committed, had to continue. Very soon the drizzle became a downpour which continued all day and, as we got higher, the wind increased in strength until it almost reached gale force—right in our faces, the whole way. We had to steer by compass throughout but, towards the end, missed the Scots Rake in the thick cloud, got badly off route, and then, to plot a new course, had to climb several hundred feet back to the ridge. It was one of the most exhausting walks we had ever done and when we got down to Troutbeck Park we found the fields about a foot deep in water. I remembered I had told my brother: "We'll do it from north to south so that we're facing the sun the whole way", but, in fact, we saw little more than our feet all day, let alone the sun.

There are twelve summits of more than 2,000 feet in the High Street fells but their collection does not necessitate doing the whole length of the Roman way. It does, however, involve one or two diversions and, perhaps, the use of two cars. The problem was solved by recruiting the willing services of my friend, Ted Stacey and, by a little ingenuity, we were able to manage with one vehicle. He drove me to Howtown, leaving me to traverse the northern section of the ridge alone, and then drove round to Haweswater, leaving the car at the Mardale car-park, and later joining me on the ridge, after walking over Kidsty Pike. The arrangement was to meet on High Raise at a certain time—it might have been one o'clock—and we did, in fact, meet exactly on the summit at the right moment. Casual planning sometimes works out like this; if we had gone into the thing in more detail our meeting would probably have been much less effectual.

It was a day of warm sunshine and excellent views but with a very strong west wind on the tops. The comparison with my previous traverse could hardly have been more marked. Most northerly of the High Street two-thousanders is Loadpot Hill and this was collected by taking the prominently grooved track out of Fusedale, walking above Brock Crag, crossing the Roman 'road' where it is reasonably distinct, and then ascending easily to the summit. On the way up the fellside there were views down into Howtown Bay where some water skiers were disporting themselves and the noise of the motorboats accompanied me for some time. Loadpot Hill is a sprawling fell and I recalled the difficulties we had had in locating the summit when we had been up there in the cloud and rain. Actually, there are two summit cairns—one of them adorned, oddly, with a flagstaff—but the main one is a boundary stone with a bench-mark and the letter 'L', almost certainly for Lowther, the big landowners in these parts. There is now an Ordnance Survey pillar which I don't remember seeing on previous visits.

The most remarkable feature of Loadpot Hill is, of course, the remains of the chimney of Lowther House which, at one time, was a shooting lodge with stables. This, I believe, was mostly built of wood but was dismantled some time ago, although the stone-built chimney stack remained. Some years ago this chimney stack was complete, a tall finger pointing, incongruously, to the sky, but each time I have been there it has been increasingly reduced in height and, this time, was only a few feet high. The chimney is some distance south of the summit but still has its value, as a navigational aid in bad weather, as my brother and I discovered on our epic traverse. But, this day, there was no need for aid for the views, eastwards to the Northern Pennines and, west, to the Lakeland hills, were superb. Helvellyn, the Scafells and Skiddaw were tipped with cloud but the cloud shadows were chasing across the sunlit lower fells. There was the dramatic, 'end-on' view of Great Gable and the prominent track on to Striding Edge. Especially noticeable was the ravine of Redgate Gill on the east-facing crags of Place Fell which, from this angle, looks a much more formidable place than it actually is. All the extensive moorland country, northwards to Penrith, could be seen—a rather lonely, desolate landscape traversed mostly by sheep, fell ponies and, now and then, the Martindale red deer.

The next summits southwards were the twin tops of Wether Hill, another sprawling grassy fell that is quite featureless, except for the boundary stone and short wooden stake that marks the northern and higher summit. Both summits, however, are listed by Falkingham for there is a depression between them. I doubt whether many people ascend Wether Hill—the hill where wethers, or castrated rams, are kept—for its own sake, but you can cover the ground quickly when doing the High Street walk. And the following summits of Red Crag and Raven Howe were easily traversed, the mountain views improving all the time. Here, the course of the Roman road is clearly visible and you have the feeling you are getting somewhere. New fencing has been placed along this section in recent years. High Raise, and my meeting with Ted, was the next summit and I walked up the last gentle rise wondering whether he was already there. Then, fifty yards away, I saw him approaching the summit from the opposite direction and we met exactly at the cairn, where we devoured our sandwiches, and complimented each other on our timing. He had already passed over Kidsty Pike but we went back there together to collect my next summit and to admire the splendid view down into Riggindale. We were now in golden-eagle country but did not see the birds, although I have seen them two or three times in the eastern fells on other occasions. Kidsty Pike is a fine rocky summit, worthy of a practice climb. I once saw three or four fell ponies silhouetted on the summit rocks. When they saw me they scampered down the side of the rocks at great speed and disappeared into the dale. The shape of the summit peak makes the Pike easily recognizable from the east, and the eyrie is a wonderful viewpoint for the huge bulk of High Street.

We went back to the next summit of Rampsgill Head, above the great trough of Rampsgill and the Martindale red deer country. Sometimes you can hear the deer roaring in these corries at rutting time and it is a stirring noise. Once, hearing them, I first thought it was a motorcycle being ferociously revved in the distance, until I realized how far away I was from any road. Then I saw a great stag a few hundred feet below me, picking his way across the scree and roaring as he went.

The next summits were The Knott and Rest Dodd, the latter some distance away beyond a considerable descent but I didn't want my companion to do this unnecessary slog so left him to stroll on to The Knott while I picked up the Dodd. The idea was to do this at the trot—for the exercise—but it was warm work, now sheltered from the westerly wind, walking up Rest Dodd at speed and then struggling back to The Knott, stripped to the waist. Rest Dodd is principally notable as a viewpoint for the Martindale deer sanctuary but, since it is an off-shoot from the main High Street ridge, it seemed rather a trying diversion that day. Perhaps people planning a round of the two-thousands with more care than I did could fit it in more appropriately with something else.

My companion was rejoined on The Knott and then we only had to walk over High Street itself and descend Long Stile to Rough Crag, the last of the twelve summits, and down to the car. This was the best part of the day. There was a handsome new cairn on High Street and several walkers on the summit—the first people we had seen. Long Stile is a splendid rocky ridge—undoubtedly the finest approach to High Street—and, having plenty of time, we dawdled on the way down, stopping every now and again to enjoy the exhilarating views. The ridge provides the best close-up views of Blea Water Crag, the eastern buttress of the mountain, Blea Water far below, the deepest of our mountain tarns, and the cliffs of Mardale Ill Bell, that transform an otherwise dull mountain into quite a dramatic one. The reservoir of Haweswater showed a thin white line around its shore but, for the middle of July, was satisfactorily full. Earlier, from The Knott we had looked down on Hayeswater, Penrith's reservoir, which always seems full, no matter how dry the season.

Down to the left was the steep-sided trough of Riggindale and we counted fifteen fell ponies grazing there. But no golden eagles or red deer that day. Easily we trotted down the pleasant ridge of Rough Crag and round the promontory of The Rigg to the lake and the car. I remembered the Mardale of forty years earlier, before the flood—the church, the inn and the farmsteads. Now, in time of drought, you can see some of the old walls and recall the once peaceful hamlet of Mardale Green—before it was drowned to provide distant Manchester with water.

It had been a satisfying day, amid scenery that improved at every mile, with views across many counties, sunshine all day, the sky full of lark song, and the strong gusting west wind making the cheeks burn. The last hour, in evening sunshine, with the great crags in blue shadow, and Mardale Waters, under the Nan Bield, a clamour of waterfalls, foaming pools and tumbling becks, had been a special delight. Perhaps the Roman soldiers, in those distant days long before mountains were 'discovered' as places for recreation, might even have sometimes enjoyed their passage over these fells, when the sunshine and the views allowed them to forget for a while the hardships of their sojourn in a foreign land.

## The Kentmere Horseshoe

Much of the Kentmere Horseshoe is visible from my home—the shoulder of Harter Fell, the nick of the Nan Bield, the dome of Mardale Ill Bell and the tops of Ill Bell and Yoke—although today, as I write, the clouds are down and I can barely see across the neighbouring fields. But I can still picture, in imagination, nearly every yard of the round—a comfortable, twelve-miles' walk over shapely heights, buttressed on their eastern flanks by crags and rocky corries—that I have traversed so many times, summer and winter. The horseshoe is the circumnavigation of the upper reaches of the Kent—the river, one of the fastest flowing in England when in spate, that passes through the centre of Kendal—and takes in eight two-thousanders. Upper Kentmere is a glorious dale head, especially to the west where scattered crags, reaching down to the intake fields, can provide excellent rock-climbing practice. There are several fine old farms with rookeries in their tree belts and the dale, so close to the main Kendal-to-Keswick road and to urban centres on the fringe of the national park, still retains an atmosphere of peace and seclusion. The round of the tops takes you away from this pastoral quietude to splendid heights that look down on Haweswater and some of the finest of our mountain tarns, and across to the High Street fells and the home of the golden eagle.

Since the entrance to the dale is so close to my home I tend to drive past it, on the best days, and make for central or western Lakeland, too often reserving the Kentmere tops for short days or bad weather. But there have still been a variety of wonderful, rewarding days on these familiar fells—often in mist, rain or snow but, occasionally in sunshine with unbroken views. Two recent trips—since the round to be described—were, respectively, in deep snow and thick cloud. In the former, two of us, stupidly forsaking our skis, attempted the round on foot and had to abandon it half-way to avoid a descent in the dark. Most of the way we were up to our knees in new powder snow and, now and again, nearly up to our waists. Two or three days later, when the snow had consolidated, two friends did the round on skis—one of the finest expeditions of its kind in the district. On the cloudy day we had to steer by compass almost the whole way round and saw nothing but, even so, it had seemed a good day.

The round of the Kentmere two-thousands was one of the earliest in the series, in the middle of May, and, again, I had Ted Stacey as my companion. It was a sunny day, with wonderful views—one of them of Gragareth, the highest summit in the 'reorganized' Lancashire, still topped with snow. (Before Whitehall altered the counties Coniston Old Man was the highest summit in the county palatine—a far worthier mountain.) We started from Kentmere church, crossed the valley and the Kent to the eastern side and went past Hollowbank and Withered Howe, up along the old grooved path, to Kentmere Pike. This bare, rounded summit shares with Snarker Pike, above Kirkstone Pass, the distinction of looking less like a pike than almost any other Lakeland fell. The top is more like a plateau than a peak and is further humbled by having a wall right across it. But, although the summit and the Kentmere slopes are unexciting, the Longsleddale flank of the fell is buttressed by crags and deep gullies—a wild rocky scene above the winding waters of the Sprint and so close to the pastoral quietude of Sadgill. A better but longer approach to Kentmere Pike is by way of the cart-track that links Kentmere with Longsleddale and thence over the intervening summit of Shipman Knotts. The round of the Longsleddale heights can also be started from this track, reached from Sadgill, or finished along this way in an anti-clockwise round. By going over Shipman Knotts there are good views of the Longsleddale cliffs and, looking back, the pools of Skeggles Water near Green Quarter Fell and Kentmere 'Lake'. Many years ago, perhaps centuries back, there was almost certainly a lake in Kentmere in the low meadows south of the present hamlet. Today, there is a straggling pool, little more than a widening of the river, where diatomite is worked. Some time after the last war there was also a proposal to win diatomite from Skeggles Water but, following a public inquiry, the suggested venture had to be abandoned—on environmental grounds. From the tops the diatomite pool in Kentmere assumes a curious, and obviously unnatural, shape.

We passed over Kentmere Pike and the undistinguished summit of Brown Howe, enjoying the splendid views across the dale of the 'best' sides of Yoke, Ill Bell and Froswick. These eastern flanks of the shapely Troutbeck hills are steep and craggy, with several fine corries enclosed between the ridges. The biggest cliff is Rainsbarrow Crag, the shoulder of Yoke—for generations a retreat for foxes but 'discovered', in recent years, as a climbing crag. The right-hand edge of the crag, looking up from near the head of Kentmere, provides an excellent scrambling route to a tiny tarn and then the summit of Yoke and, seen from the northern corrie, this edge, with its rocky towers, has something of the appearance of a ridge in the Cuillin of Skye. Several years ago I wrote about this ridge, commending it as far better than Striding Edge with the additional attractions of being untracked and free from orange peel. Deliberately, I avoided identifying the place but was so deluged with letters pressing me to reveal its location that, finally, to save the mounting postage costs, I disclosed the situation. To do the full length of the ridge requires, initially, a rock climb of ten or fifteen feet, although the ridge can be reached, higher up, by simple scrambling. I was glad to notice, on a recent visit, that the ridge was still, fortunately, untracked and unscratched so, clearly, it had so far escaped the hordes. Excellent winter climbing may also be enjoyed in some of the nearby gullies.

Ted and I traced the route from the opposite side of the valley and then continued over The Knowe on to the summit of Harter Fell, where the summit cairns are decorated or defaced, according to your point of view, by old iron fencing posts. Harter Fell is another rounded summit but a noble fell, nevertheless, for the northern face is an imposing front of shattered cliffs, providing a fine backcloth to the head of Mardale. This craggy face is a favourite resort of mine for solitary scrambling—but not to be commended to the inexperienced—and interesting routes through the crags may be devised, summer or winter. Harter Fell Gully itself is best avoided in summer, since it is very loose and dangerously eroded, but can make a fine snow climb. One of the best 'surprise' views in Lakeland may be obtained from a cairn on the ridge when approaching the summit from Adam Seat, to the south-east—a sudden view, down the crags, of the length of Haweswater. nearly 2,000 feet below.

Our view from the summit was of the High Street fells and a corner of Blea Water, the deepest mountain tarn in the district, and, south and west, a wide panorama of the Lakeland fells, Windermere and Morecambe Bay. We trotted down to Nan Bield pass, the gap of the old pack-horse trail I can see from my home, and looked down on the lovely jewel of Small Water, one of the most splendidly-sited of the fell tarns. There were two summits of Mardale Ill Bell to collect before we swung southwards for Froswick, leaving out Thornthwaite Crag since I had decided this would fit more neatly into a later round of the fells above Pasture Beck. Somewhere along this section of the route we looked down into Kentmere and had quite a shock. The reservoir of Haweswater, seen earlier from Harter Fell, had been full, with no suggestion of the obtrusively white line which spoils the scene when the level is drawn down, and Small Water was brimming over, but Kentmere reservoir was strangely empty and ugly. This half-mile-long, square-shaped pool that normally washes the lower slopes of Froswick and Ill Bell in tasteful symmetry was just an unsightly area of grey rock and mud, with a puddle in one corner. From the heights it looked rather like a bomb-site or city clearance area—a huge scar in the heart of the hills.

On our return from the round, concerned and puzzled about this new intrusion, I sought out the reason for the empty reservoir and the answer was reassuring. The reservoir had apparently been emptied so that the valve that controls the release of water down the River Kent could be inspected and repaired. When the job was done the reservoir would be allowed to fill up again and, indeed, by high summer of that year, Kentmere Reservoir was back to normal. Apparently two million gallons of water a day had been seeping out of the reservoir but, once the wastage had been stopped by the repair of the valve, the pool replenished itself—a feat it can achieve even in drought. The capacity of the reservoir is something like 250 million gallons. A year or two ago the reservoir was advertised for sale—it seemed, at the time, a possibly welcome storage bonus for the then hard-pressed water authorities—but the response was disappointing to the commissioners. I understand, however, that by the time this book is published the local paper manufacturing firm of James Cropper and Co. Ltd will have taken over the responsibility for the maintenance of Kentmere Reservoir. Water from the River Kent that flows out of the reservoir is used in paper making and also by other companies to drive a water turbine and a water wheel. When you walk along the edge of Mardale Ill Bell between Harter Fell and Froswick, as we did that day, you pass just above the source of the River Kent which, in spate and ten miles further south, can become a very fast moving torrent. The river has its birth just below Bleathwaite Crag in the fine corrie of Hall Cove. We could see the source among the bright green mosses below the crag which are always wet and boggy because of the hidden springs.

We were not very far away from golden eagle country that day but had no sight of the great birds. Several young eagles have been produced in recent years—for first time in the district for nearly 200 years. The policy of the Royal Society for the Protection of Birds, in providing watchers and wardens and keeping the exact location of the site a secret to the general public, has proved very successful. Few people, however, may be aware that golden eagles have also nested in western Lakeland. The nest was there in 1976 on a remote crag in a little-visited part of the fells but the birds had no success with their hatching on that occasion. The following year this second pair of eagles—one of them conceivably one of the young birds born in the eastern Lakeland fells a few years earlier—bred successfully on their western crag, not far from the sea. There were possibly two eggs but, unbelievably to decent people, the nest was robbed. Some unscrupulous people, with greed their only motive, had probably wrecked the chance of a second location in Lakeland for Britain's finest bird.

Our traverse of the cone-like summits of Froswick and Ill Bell, followed by the stroll over Yoke and down the Garburn Pass back to Kentmere went easily and quickly. The summit of Ill Bell is decorated with a cluster of tall cairns that, with the mountain's soaring shape, make the fell easily recognizable from several angles. From the south the fell seems shaped like a bell, rounded and symmetric, and this is almost certainly the derivation of the name. But Ill has nothing to do with 'hill' although the mountain is named Hill Bell on some maps, and in old guide-books. The most likely derivative is Eel or E'il, meaning evil—nothing to do with eels, but suggesting a dark or foreboding place, although it has never seemed like that to me. The same word crops up in several parts of Lakeland—Eel Tarn, Eel Crags, Ill Crag and so on.

Sometime we call this switchback skyline the Troutbeck fells—one of the neatest progressions of little hills in the fell country, and perhaps the best ridge walk in eastern Lakeland. From my house I see them end-on, with the black shape of Rainsbarrow Crag most prominent, but the motorist driving over Kirkstone Pass can see the whole switchback—a magnificent sight under snow. Many years ago a motorcyclist traversed their length, although not over the tops; to do the traverse on skis—as two of us did in February 1978—is a delight. We came down the ridge to Kentmere, this sunny May day, looking down on a sparkling picture of silvery waters, neat woodlands and bright meadows. Over to the right were the Coniston fells and, further away, Black Combe and the estuary of the Duddon. Somewhere among the woods and the meadows were crowds and traffic, towns and villages, but to us it seemed a mainly pastoral scene. The noise and the bustle were silenced, the cars hidden, nothing moved except the grazing sheep, and Kentmere was just a sleepy corner on a sunny evening.

## The Fringe of Lakeland

The most easterly two-thousander in the Lakeland fells is Grey Crag, a remote height above Longsleddale and about four miles west of the summit of the main road over Shap Fells. It should not be confused with Gray Crag, above Hayeswater—a much rockier and far more impressive mountain. Grey Crag is the nearest two-thousander to my home—perhaps eight miles away, as the ravens fly, and marginally closer than Kentmere Pike and Yoke—but I can't have been on top more than two or three times. You are immediately aware, on Grey Crag, of being really on the verge of Lakeland. Desolate valleys reach eastwards across Shap Fells towards the Eden valley and the long line of the Pennines and, southwards, Morecambe Bay silvers the horizon all the way round to the dark bulk of Black Combe. Few Lake District walkers bother with Grey Crag; most of them have never even heard of it. All the same, it is a splendid viewpoint, not so much of the Lake District but of wider horizons, and the seeker after solitude may find some solace in its untracked, grassy slopes. This is where the moorlands end and the mountains begin—within two hours of lonely walking from the former main road to Scotland.

Ted Stacey and I planned to fit six summits around Longsleddale, including Grey Crag, into a short day in mid-June. A far better round would have been the complete circumnavigation of the dale, embracing Harter Fell and the heights to the east of Kentmere, but we had done the Kentmere Horseshoe a month earlier and were now merely filling in gaps in my collection. It was a wet, misty morning although the clouds were fairly high on the tops and the rain stopped later, even giving us a few patches of sunlight on the last trot down to the valley. Leaving the car by the fine pack-horse bridge at Sadgill in Longsleddale we went straight up the steep slopes to the rocky shoulder of Great Howe and then over tussocky grass and peat hags to the cairn on Grey Crag. There is a much larger cairn on Harrop Pike, nearly a mile to the north-east, but Grey Crag is clearly the summit by a few feet and Falkingham rightly avoids any claim for the inclusion of the Pike as a separate summit. The views through the thin mist and drizzle were limited but Windermere could be seen beyond the sprawling foothils of south Lakeland and, north-west, we could see new snow, that had fallen during the night, on High Street, High Raise and Harter Fell, making these fells seem much higher than they are. Immediately below us was the little side-valley of Stockdale—sometimes known locally, for some reason, as La'al London. This is along the route of the Haweswater aqueduct and in the upper reaches of the valley is a band of rock which the dalesfolk call Stockdale grit. At one time pieces of this 'gritstone' were used for sharpening scythes.

Tarn Crag was the next summit, reached by an easy descent, avoiding the marshes of Greycrag Tarn, and then a curving rise. Greycrag Tarn is hardly a pool any longer, being completely overgrown with rushes, and can be a nasty place when partially concealed with snow. The only interesting feature of the summit plateau of Tarn Crag is the high, stone survey post built during the construction of the Longsleddale tunnel that carries the Haweswater aqueduct south towards Manchester. It is sited about 100 yards from the summit cairn and used to be surrounded by a wooden platform but most of the timbers have now rotted away—or been stolen. Tarn Crag is principally notable for the fine precipice of Buckbarrow Crag, low down on its western slopes, just above the track to Gatescarth Pass. This is a good climbing crag, with several quite exposed routes and I remember many happy days spent there. I happened to be involved in the first ascent of one of the best routes, Sadgill Wall, not long after the war, and sometimes we used to go there to mark peregrine eggs with dye—roping down to the nest—so as to make them useless to collectors. Perhaps the peregrine, fighting to retain its home in Lakeland, no longer nests there. The whole of the fellside around Buckbarrow Crag is particularly craggy and on a more recent descent of Tarn Crag through the cliffs two of us had quite an exciting time. We had no rope, being merely on a walk, and kept finding ourselves above impasses, necessitating retreats and frequent searches for other ways.

The views were clearing as we left Tarn Crag on our June round and the rain had stopped. South and east we could see the Pennines stretching to Ingleborough and beyond, but there was little to be seen of Lakeland, except the Coniston fells. The two summits of Branstree—the present generally accepted name—came next, easily reached by quite a long, featureless walk, finishing up the tedious slope of Selside Brow. The name is derived from Brant Street—brant meaning steep—but the Ordnance Survey fail to name the summit although giving the name to the steep slopes above Haweswater. Again, the summit is quite featureless—sometimes without even a cairn—but, a few hundred yards to the north-east, is the fine cairn of Artle Crag, with some spatterings of rock nearby to brighten the otherwise rather drab surroundings. This cairn also provides the finer viewpoint, with Haweswater far below and the Mardale fells stretched across the western skyline. On our way up Selside Brow we had admired the new fencing along the fellside, splendidly firm and straight, but were saddened by the miles of old, rusty wire and fence posts left scattered about the grass—an obvious hazard to both sheep and human beings, as well as being unsightly. This disregard for the environment seems to be an increasing practice on the Lakeland fells these days—only on Clough Head have I seen evidence of the rusty wire being collected. It occurred to us that, if the collection of the old wire was impracticable, it could, at least, be stowed along the foot of the fences or, better still, tied there. We now had to make a diversion to collect the summit of Selside Pike, about a mile and a half away to the north-east—encountering further long lengths of untidily-abandoned fencing materials. On the way we passed another of the survey posts built by Manchester Corporation during the construction of the Haweswater aqueduct. Selside Pike is an old favourite for we often used to walk over it years ago after a day's climbing in Swindale, a perfect little valley enclosed by crags and threaded by pools and waterfalls. In more recent years the water engineers have taken over the dale but it is still largely unspoiled and, fortunately, not yet opened to the motorist. South of the summit of Selside Pike is Mosedale Cottage, sometimes occupied by shepherds or lost walkers—a remote residence in one of the loneliest valleys in Lakeland.

All we had to do now to complete our tally of six summits for the day was to return to Branstree, drop down to Gatescarth Pass and scramble up to Adam Seat, a shoulder of Harter Fell, and our last top. There is an old boundary stone on the summit of Adam Seat but nothing else except a fine view down into Longsleddale and across to the minor heights we had just traversed. Surprisingly, the sun came out and we ran all the way down to the old Wrengill quarry and the track over the pass in much more cheerful weather. At one time you could spend a comfortable night in the abandoned cottages in the quarry but now the roofs have fallen in and the sheep seem to have taken over. The walk down the pass and underneath Buckbarrow to Sadgill makes a wonderful end to a summer day in the eastern fells. On your right is the River Sprint, one of the most adventurous becks in Lakeland, with magnificent pools for bathing and impressive waterfalls, to the left the soaring cliff of Buckbarrow Crag, and, straight ahead, the long road down one of the least-spoiled dales in the district, loud with bird song and the cries of sheep. It seemed a most peaceful evening scene, coloured by memories of many youthful days on the crags, but the sight of an old quarry bogie jammed in one of the best of the waterfalls, was an ugly reminder of man's foibles. It had been an easy day of improving weather on little-known fells with not very obvious appeal, but all of the Lake District is rewarding if you can be humble enough to treasure placid scenery and the sight of rather desolate wastes that were just the same a thousand years ago.

## Around Pasture Beck

The circuit of the fells around Pasture Beck, east of the Patterdale side of Kirkstone Pass, makes a delightful, short horseshoe round—easy walking with changing views of quite craggy scenery. Pasture Beck, with its pools and tiny waterfalls, rises just below the prominent gap in these rather lonely eastern fells known as Threshthwaite Mouth and the perfect, little side-valley is saddled with the mouthful of a name, Threshthwaite Mouth Glen. There is another glen, a few miles or two away on the other side of Kirkstone Pass—two strange Scottish intrusions into fell country nomenclature. The round embraces seven summits, but three of these are located, oddly, on Gray Crag which, from most directions, looks an almost level ridge. I did the round on a very hot day in July—two days after my dehydrating circuit of the Mosedale Horseshoe. It was just as hot on this much shorter walk but a breeze on the tops made conditions more pleasurable. Without considering the route I made an anti-clockwise round; the opposite circuit is rather easier and might be preferred by some.

The short day began with the usual summer motoring frustrations on Kirkstone Pass—caravans, mostly, driven with infuriating slowness and taking up most of the road. It was a relief to turn into the wonderful, old-world hamlet of Hartstop, with its quaint spinning galleries on some of the houses—a place that manages to retain the real Lakeland atmosphere despite its proximity to a tourist highway. The old name of Hartsop is Low Hartsop—presumably to distinguish the place from High Hartsop, further up the dale. Only old-stagers like myself speak of Low Hartsop nowadays but the distinction is still applied to the nearby fells. Hartsop Dodd, the fell above Low Hartsop, is, properly, Low Hartsop Dodd, while High Hartsop Dodd is still the official name of the fell above Hartsop Hall, rather further up the Kirkstone valley. The fact that Low Hartsop Dodd is more than 300 feet higher than High Hartsop Dodd is not a mistake by the map makers; the terms do not apply to elevation but to situation.

The summit of Low Hartsop Dodd, or just Hartsop Dodd, as it is now known, was reached in well under one hour—a steep ascent up the delightful north ridge and then easily to the cairn by the wall that crosses the grassy top. Hartsop Dodd is marked by several grooves that might have been pony tracks to old quarries or mines. The route to Caudale Moor by the fell wall is long and dull so, instead, I followed the edge of the crags above Threshthwaite (locally 'Threshet') Glen. The main crag below me was Raven Crag on which, many years before, Jim Birkett and I put up a few undistinguished first ascents but failed, largely through my incompetence, to make a first traverse of the crag. This remarkable traverse, below overhangs, has since been done by other climbers.

Caudale Moor is a great, sprawling fell with six spreading ridges of which Hartsop Dodd is one. Seen from Kirkstone Pass the fell is comparatively featureless but, on other sides, it is seen as a considerable craggy mountain, with several lines of cliff facing north, east and south. The fell also has the dubious distinction of being possibly the easiest in the district to ascend—only a little over a thousand feet of height to be gained in two and a half miles if the walk is made from the inn at the summit of Kirkstone Pass. As youngsters we knew the mountain as John Bell's Banner but this is really the name of the lower summit of the moor. Stony Cove Pike—a little cairn on a rather desolate plateau, with grey rock outcropping the grass—is the higher summit. Almost certainly, John Bell was the Rev. John Bell, curate and schoolmaster of Ambleside, who was born in the sixteenth century. Banner is the old word for boundary and since, at one time, the parishes of Windermere, Grasmere and Patterdale met on the top of Caudale Moor, it is probable that the summit or thereabouts became known locally as the limit of the sphere of Mr Bell's ministrations. This was before the days when Ambleside became a separate parish. It is sometimes said that the name has a hunting derivation but I think this unlikely.

During the round I walked across to the Mark Atkinson monument, erected by his son Ion in memory of his father, a well-known farmer and former licensee of the Kirkstone Pass Inn, who owned that part of the fell. The holding has since been acquired by the National Trust, so that Caudale Moor now belongs to the nation. Ion Atkinson is a friend of mine and I was glad to see that the cross on the cairn, missing on previous visits, had been replaced.

The two summits were collected and I scrambled down to Threshthwaite Mouth to find a suitable rocky coign for my lunch. A heat haze hung over the hills and I dozed away in my pleasant eyrie, remembering many other visits to this wild gap in the fells. They used to say that many years ago a squirrel could have passed from the edge of Windermere to the rocks at Threshthwaite Mouth without touching the ground, but that was before most of the trees disappeared from the fells. I recalled an occasion one winter when I had sat among the same rocks and watched a fox slowly walking up the snow-covered screes beneath Thornthwaite Crag, the other side of the gap, his long tail brushing a trail through the powder. It was warm work, plodding up the steep 600 feet of ascent, stripped to the waist, to the beacon cairn on Thornthwaite Crag—the 14-foot high column of stone that identifies the summit so clearly from many parts of Lakeland. I can just see the cairn from my house on a clear day and this often means that the following day will be wet—exceptional clarity in Lakeland is often a sign of deteriorating weather shortly.

The walk from Thornthwaite Crag over Gray Crag to Hartsop must be one of the easiest mountain rambles in the district, but splendidly rewarding. Gray Crag has cliffs on both its eastern and western flanks—an unusual feature in Lakeland—and its north–south ridge is a smooth, uplifted spine with fine views down each side into 'Threshet' Glen and Hayeswater. I could clearly see the traverse on Raven Crag, the wide rocky corrie of Threshthwaite Cove, and the shattered cliffs of Hartsop Dodd. On the other side was the long, black pool of Hayeswater in its narrow trench, backed by the line of High Street fells. As I looked into the reservoir there was a sudden, jarring sound and a helicopter swept down the dale above the tarn, passing just over the shoulder of High Street before disappearing towards the south-east. I wondered what it was doing, so low over the fells. Was it on a mountain rescue? The machine, perhaps half a mile away, was flying at my height, 2,000 feet, and I could easily see the pilot, sharing with me almost the same view.

It was an easy trot down the nose of the fell to Hayeswater Gill, flowing out of the tarn, and, profusely perspiring, I sought out a suitable pool for a bathe. The gill, above and below the filter house, has several picturesque cascades and inviting pools but most of them seemed too visible from the well-used Hartsop track for my purpose. For years I have meant to buy myself a bathing costume for these mountain dips and, some day, this might be done, although I've managed without one for fifty years. Fell bathing may be an acquired taste but it can often transform a mountain day. Enterprising people can sometimes achieve a number of immersions during a mountain walk on a hot day—my brother would think nothing of doing three or four in an afternoon—but, ideally, the last one should be arranged close to the car, so that you finish your walk like a giant refreshed, ready to push over mountains.

One perfect pool after another had to be rejected on this stifling day for, although the tops had been deserted, the track above Hartsop was alive with family parties. But, finally, about half a mile from the car, I found a quiet pool—only ten yards from the track but completely concealed. It was hidden by a ring of rowans, edged with turf, a waterfall at one end, and six feet deep. Within two minutes I was in—a bath for the gods, invigorating, cool and immensely soothing to jaded muscles. I could hear people coming down the track, but my bathe was undisturbed, and I luxuriated under the waterfall for perhaps a quarter of an hour. Many years ago two Grasmere friends of mine achieved the curious record of bathing in every one of the nearly 500 mountain tarns in Lakeland—sometimes in winter. My modest total would be less than fifty, but I think the pools have been the best—quiet places for bringing you back to life rather than for swimming practice. This one completely restored me and even the drive home over Kirkstone through the holiday traffic failed to destroy my animal sense of well-being.

## Place Fell

Place Fell, circled by the southern crook of Ullswater, happens to be last of the Lakeland two-thousanders to be herein described but is, by no means, the least significant summit. Indeed, Place Fell, despite its modest height, is a worthy, bulky mountain of some character—the ideal grandstand from which to spy out the Helvellyn range and the far eastern fells. Its broad-shouldered massiveness, the steepness of its flanks plunging straight into the lake or down towards lonely Boardale, and its detachment from surrounding loftier peaks gives it a dignity not often found in such a relatively low hill. The valleys to the east—the red deer country—are among the least-visited in the district, the maps show only one main track across its slopes and you are unlikely to find crowds up there. I believe I have seen more red deer on Place Fell than people—once a herd of ten trotting over the summit from Boardale. They say in Patterdale that when the Martindale red deer appear over the skyline of Place Fell they can expect worsening weather, and this particular sighting was followed by days of storm and high winds. As it happened my visit during the collection of the two-thousands coincided with my worst wetting of the series, although we saw no deer this time.

The summit and its satellite top of Round How were collected on an evening trip in mid-July—the evening before my wet round of Red Screes and St Sunday Crag with my son. Again, I had the companionship of Ted Stacey. Instead of taking the familiar track to Boardale Hause we zigzagged straight up the fellside near Grey Crag and then turned right over The Knight to the summit. This side of Place Fell is remarkably steep and rough and the slopes are most attractively scattered with juniper—splashes of dark green against the heather and bracken. Here and there were banks of thyme, giving off a fragrant scent when trodden, and the huge, tumbled boulders and the rough rocks of Grey Crag suggested, as they always do, a fine practice ground for the scrambler or climber. It was raining and the clouds hung low over the high tops but the visibility was good enough to see across the lake and admire the splendid sculpturing of the valleys that bite into the Helvellyn range. This is a superb view on a clear day—the curving reaches of Ullswater with the houses, farms and hotels of Patterdale and Glenridding looking like toys nearly 2,000 feet below, saucer-like hollows below encircling mountain ridges and, immediately beneath, glimpses of the wonderful lake-shore path to Sandwick, through the birches. There are few more interesting low-level walks in Lakeland than this shore path, with new views every time you top a rise or turn a corner—the ideal easy afternoon for a family party or for elderly walkers.

Soon after we had admired the western views, and before reaching the summit plateau, the clouds came down and the downpour increased. The red deer country to our left was completely blotted out, the rocks were soon streaming and we concentrated on getting the job finished as quickly as possible. There are three or four tarns just below the summit of Place Fell but we never saw them or, indeed, anything else, apart from the splashes from the sodden ground as we ran, full tilt, down the slopes. Round How was collected on the way and then it was non-stop all the way until we came to the track by the sturdy, well-built houses, nestling with their lawns, yew trees and pines into a fold in the fellside. A peaceful place this corner near Goldrill Beck, between the mountain and the lake, but all we had thoughts of that drenching evening were to get out of our soaking clothes and have a drink. We didn't time ourselves that evening but we went up without a stop, and ran all the way down, so we can't have wasted much time.

My memories of Place Fell are of rather pleasanter visits—summer days of bathing in the lake and scrambling on Grey Crag, wandering across the sprawling top, exploring down Scalehowe Beck, lazing on grassy belvederes and looking across to the parallel valleys beyond the lake, or ambling along the Sandwick shore track with my children. Place Fell, on the right sort of day, can be one of the most satisfying little mountains in Lakeland—a place to take the family to look for the red deer, birds or foxes when the higher, more popular, fells are too crowded for enjoyment.

St Sunday Crag, Cofa Pike and Fairfield from Seat Sandal

Sheffield Pike from Keldas

Dove Crag, Fairfield and Helvellyn from Caudale Moor

Summit of Harter Fell, Mardale

Place Fell

Summit beacon on
Thornthwaite Crag

High Street, Long Stile and Blea Water

Froswick, Ill Bell and Yoke

Gray Crag and Pasture Beck

Brothers Water from Angletarn Pikes

Haystacks above Buttermere

Summit rocks of Helm Crag

# 8. Other Ways Up

There are, fortunately, no 'correct' or 'official' routes up Lake District mountains. The traditional freedom to wander at will over the high fells is still, in almost all cases, permitted by landowners and tenants. Afforestation limits access to a few fells and parts of Martindale deer forest are out of bounds to walkers but, nearly everywhere else, you can go any way you like—restricted only by your ability, or lack of it, to surmount difficult places. This is not to imply that all the *approaches* to the high fells are open; in several places, across private land—including intake fields—the walker must keep to accepted tracks. But, once above the last intake wall, the mountains themselves become, generally, open country—a facility to be treasured and respected. The area is a national park and much of it, through the National Trust, belongs to the nation but we are walking over somebody else's land—even on the tops—and we should all behave as if we were in our own gardens.

The high fells, therefore, once through the approaches, may mostly be ascended from all directions—except where crags bar the way—but, over the years, accepted routes to the summits have become established and maps and guide-books channel walkers along these tracks, leading, especially in recent years, to increasing erosion. These routes are, mostly, the easiest or the most obvious ways to the top; in a few cases they also happen to be the most interesting. But the more determined walker, anxious to get into untracked country, can easily devise alternative routes and taste the joys of minor exploration. Gills, for instance, can be followed to their source or quite adventurous ways made up through outcrops or crags. Indeed, you may only have to go a quarter of a mile away from the popular, eroded tracks to find yourself in surprisingly different or rewarding scenery.

The walker collecting the two-thousands and trying to link them into horseshoe rounds, however, is generally picking up his summits by the easiest ways, along their spines, since—perhaps not being a peak-bagger by nature—he is probably seeking to get the job over, as quickly and neatly as possible. This was the case when I revisited all the two-thousands for the purpose of this book so that the routes described are, by no means, necessarily the best ways up these mountains, but merely the ones that seemed the most convenient at the time. Undoubtedly, this is one of the weaknesses of such an exercise; you have been up all the mountains but not seen the best of them. To get the full flavour of all these fells you need to ascend and descend them all, separately, in all directions, whereas my intention was merely to revisit them all, in fairly quick succession, to give an indication of the horseshoe-round possibilities of the district. But now, to remedy the situation to some extent, I thought it might be helpful to some readers to suggest other ways up some of the higher or more interesting fells. Some of these routes are much more rewarding than the convenient ways taken when I trotted round the two-thousands. All have been walked by me at some time—most of them many times—and some are favourite walks.

The lords of the northern fells are Skiddaw and Blencathra and both are freely scored by summit routes. There are many finer ways to the top of Skiddaw than by the time-honoured route from Keswick over Jenkin Hill. Slightly more direct routes lead from Millbeck and Applethwaite and there are quiet, untracked ways from Bassenthwaite village where you may find yourself alone with the sheep. An even more interesting route, revealing a possibly unexpected corner of Skiddaw, can be enjoyed by tackling the mountain from the north—leaving the track to Skiddaw House from Bassenthwaite, and gaining the summit ridge by way of Dash Falls and Dead Crags. This is fine, wild country, quite out of character with the rest of the mountain, and well worth seeking out by those who prefer secluded places. But the most rewarding way of all up Skiddaw is to ascend Ullock Pike from the Bassenthwaite area and continue over Long Side to the summit. The edge of Ullock Pike makes a splendid staircase to the heights—an undulating track among the heather giving increasingly extensive views of the valleys on either side and, backwards, across the plain of Cumbria, to the Galloway hills.

Blencathra has its popular ascent over Sharp Edge from Scales but some of the ways up the steep, south-facing ridges or the ravines that lie in between are at least as good or even better. One of the best is by way of the ridge of Hall's Fell, landing you exactly on the summit—an exhilarating route, over rocky tors, keeping on the crest all the way, with especially glorious views into the ravines. All these clefts—the ravines of Blease Gill, Gate Gill, Doddick Gill and Scaley Beck—may be used as routes of ascent and will commend themselves to scramblers. Doddick Gill provides perhaps the most challenging ascent, Scaley Beck the easiest, but all of them are places where you are away from the beaten tracks, on rough ground and among dramatic scenery. The south wall of Blencathra is, of course, by far the best side of the mountain. Other ways to the summit saddle may be taken from Threlkeld and Mungrisdale but they are tame in comparison.

For Lonscale Fell, the north-east ridge provides an interesting scrambling route and there are more rewarding ways to the summit of Carrock Fell than the one taken on the round described in an earlier chapter, which is probably the easiest. From Mosedale, this unusually varied little mountain can be ascended through the rocks, gorse and heather to the summit, with the remains of its ancient fort, and there is a shorter route from Stone Ends, a mile further on, leading, interestingly, past old mine workings and through the crags. Bowscale Fell is another of the northern fells that should not be dismissed by the horseshoe ascent described which avoids the northern face of the mountain—its best side, by far. Ascents are better made from Mosedale or Bowscale so that lonely Bowscale Tarn can be visited and a scrambling route worked out through Tarn Crags. Alternative routes up the remaining northern fells may be selected from the map. Few are of outstanding interest but worthwhile, unusual walks can be worked out in the old mining areas, especially around High Pike and Great Sca Fell, where there are several quite fine ravines.

In the north-west fells the routes along the ridges—largely those already described—are generally the most stimulating. This is a section of Lakeland where most of the fells are naturally linked together and where walkers normally traverse several in turn. Causey Pike, Eel Crag, Hopegill Head or Grasmoor, for example, are more often ascended as part of a traverse of one or more of the spines than as separate walks. In the same way, Hindscarth is generally linked with Dale Head and Robinson while the Buttermere fells, on the opposite side of the valley are usually included in a ridge walk—at least, along the more easterly summits. There is no need for me to deal more thoroughly with Hindscarth since the mountain's finest feature—its splendid north ridge—was traversed on the round described and a direct, scrambling route from Honister Pass has also been suggested. The usual route up Robinson is to take the well-used track from Buttermere over the marshy ground of Buttermere Moss, but there are other routes from Gatescarth, Hassness and Newlands Hause, the last of these being interesting in its lower reaches by Moss Force and Robinson Crags but rather featureless higher up. Much the best route up the mountain is from Newlands church by way of High Snab Bank and the edge of Robinson Crags. This is quite an airy way, through changing scenery and can also provide a fast run down. When Bob Graham established his Lakeland 24-hours fell record in 1932 by running up and down forty-two mountains this was the way he came down from Robinson, his last peak, reaching Keswick, his starting point, in about forty minutes from the top. His record stood for twenty-eight years but, in more recent times, something like 100 fell runners have equalled his performance, or, in a few cases, considerably improved upon it.

Dale Head is very easily reached from Honister Pass—an ascent of merely 1,300 feet—but there are better routes of ascent from Seatoller or Rosthwaite, by way of Rigghead quarries or High Scawdel. From the north the summit may be reached from Little Town in Newlands by the obvious route up the valley to Dalehead Tarn or, for the more enterprising, by the old copper mine under the north-facing crags of the mountain—an interesting route through fine rock scenery, traversed, in places, by ancient tracks used by the miners hundreds of years ago. High Spy, too, has its ascents from Little Town and through Rigghead quarries on the Borrowdale side, or can be reached from Grange by routes skirting, or going through, the cliffs of Blea Crag.

Grisedale Pike, Hopegill Head and Whiteside, normally traversed by their splendid linking ridge, may also be reached from the north—from Whinlatter Pass or High Lorton, through thickly afforested areas, for the first two summits, and from High Lorton (or Hopebeck) for the last-named top. The ascent of Hopegill Head from High Lorton, by way of Swinside and Ladyside Pike, is a fine mountain walk, improving as it progresses, while the northern ascents of Grisedale Pike may be found attractive by those who enjoy the charms of woodlands and unfrequented ways. Whiteside is best reached from Lanthwaite Green, at the northern end of Crummock Water—an enjoyable ascent, through heather and juniper, along the edge of the crags that overlook Gasgale Gill. The bulky mountain of Grasmoor, with its bold, craggy front overlooking Crummock Water and its fine cirque of Dove Crags high above Gasgale Gill is a tame, grassy mountain when reached from Coledale Hause, but much more interesting when tackled direct from the west or the north. From Lanthwaite Green you select your way up through the cliffs, according to your ability as climber or scrambler. There is nothing very difficult but, for the ordinary walker, nothing really easy; handholds of juniper may be found useful by the cautious. All ways are steep but I've never found anything worth a rock-climb, although two gullies look promising. Perhaps, under snow and ice, this western prow of the mountain provides a challenge, but I've never been up there in winter. There is some severe climbing on Dove Crags but the routes are limited and some of them rather poor. For walkers there is a good route to the summit from Gasgale Gill to the right of Dove Crags by way of a grassy ridge.

The wonderful, little peak of Whiteless Pike and the neighbouring height of Wandope can both be easily ascended from Buttermere. One of the more interesting ways up Wandope skirts the remarkable crater-like formation of Addacomb Hole. Eel Crag is usually ascended by the excellent Causey Pike–Sail Ridge, but an interesting route from Coledale may be made by following the terraces or ridges among the crags, instead of the more pedestrian ascent by way of Coledale Hause. It should, perhaps, be mentioned that the Causey Pike–Eel Crag range can be reached from Newlands Hause by the ascent of the pleasant ridge of Knott Rigg and Ard Crags and the descent to a high pass above Rigg Beck that provides a useful connection with the main track along Scar Crags.

The fine ridge of High Crag, High Stile and Red Pike may be reached from Ennerdale up steep, unplanted ground between the forests but these ways are tedious and lacking in interest. In contrast, the ascents from Buttermere, either through the north-facing corries or by their containing ridges, are mostly varied and exhilarating and, in some cases, enlivened by dramatic rock scenery. The corries of Birkness Combe, Bleaberry Combe and Ling Comb, each one ringed with crags, are exciting places with many opportunities for scrambling and mild exploration. Of the Red Pike ascents the one that follows the cascades of Sourmilk Gill, or an easier path through the woods, and then passes Bleaberry Tarn is the most popular, but the routes through Ling Comb or along Lingcomb Edge, being more secluded, are worth seeking out. For High Crag and High Stile more direct ascents may be made through the corries and up along ledges between the crags or, for High Stile, straight up the north-east ridge. Birkness Combe is a climbing area, with many routes up all the surrounding crags, and mountain campers will find delightful sites in the corrie on turf patches between the becks. I have many memories of wonderful, long summer days on these crags, finishing with a visit to the summit of High Stile, and then the trot down the ridge in the evening to the valley. But determined walkers can also reach the summit from the corrie by tackling the screes and working their way up between crags—trackless, and not detailed in the guide-books, but all the better for that.

The over-cairned, eroded routes to the Scafells, the highest land in England, can be avoided, to some extent, by the walker seeking different ways. Grains Gill, for instance, is a less-crowded approach than Styhead Pass from Borrowdale, and the walker with some rock-climbing experience may then reach the summit ridge by one of the Great End gullies—Cust's Gully is the easiest—or by the interesting scramble up Skew Gill. Snow will often be found in these gullies in June—sometimes on the hottest days. From the popular Corridor Route to Scafell Pike interesting ways to the ridge may also be found past Round How or the charming tarn of Lambfoot Dub. The summit of Styhead Pass, and thence the range of Scafells, may be reached from Wasdale, more attractively than up the stony pass itself, by the simple expedient of keeping to the floor of the valley and taking the old path alongside the pools and cascades of Lingmell Beck. Reference has been made earlier to the problems presented to ordinary walkers—and especially young people—by the Broad Stand route to Scafell from Mickledore, and the eroded screes of Lord's Rake, but the trudge up Brown Tongue, for Mickledore or the Pike, is still the best route from Wasdale. The easy run down from Scafell over Green How, avoiding the crags, can often prove useful.

Of the many approaches to Scafell the one from Wha House in Eskdale, following the Terrace Route over Slight Side, is perhaps the easiest and a magnificent walk. I once went this way on a cloudy, muggy day, hoping eventually, to get above the fog that filled the valley. Reaching the summit of Scafell I suddenly stepped into bright sunlight—and an unforgettable scene. Everything below me was hidden in a sea of cotton wool cloud stretching, in all direction, to the horizon, and the sun blazed down on the white, swirling sea out of a bright blue sky. All that could be seen, apart from the white and the blue, were the summit rocks of Scafell Pike, more than a mile away, with people standing there and, in between, the top five feet of Scafell Pinnacle.

A very fine direct route to the Scafells may also be taken from Hardknott Pass by way of Mosedale, crossing Lingcove Beck and the Esk and then ascending steeply by Little Narrow Cove to the Broad Crag col. This route takes the walker through magnificent rock scenery and past some of the most splendid mountain camping sites in the district. But the Scafell range provides more opportunities for exploratory walking than any other part of the Lake District; routes away from beaten tracks may be found in many places. The sport of rock-climbing has been developed to an extraordinary extent during the last fifty years—and especially within the last twenty—but walkers, for the most part, still follow the tracks that were in use a hundred years ago—most of them, the easiest ways up the fells. It should, however, be emphasized that untracked ways should not be sought out by inexperienced walkers, or in bad weather.

Great Gable is too popular a mountain to need much elaboration of its routes. A direct route to the summit may be made from the traverse beneath the Napes Ridges, by way of the screes of Great Hell Gate, to the east of the crags, or Little Hell Gate, to the west. Scramblers may take to the upper rocks in places. Both routes lead to Westmorland Crags, just below the summit which may be by-passed or climbed by an easy gully. The mountain lends itself to an easy traverse from the top of Honister Pass—over Brandreth, Grey Knotts and Green Gable to the summit and down by Beck Head and Moses Trod, or in the reverse direction. Scramblers with some climbing experience may vary this route with the ascent of Central Gully on Gable Crag, which has the remains of the old smuggler's 'hut' in its upper reaches—now little more than a pile of stones. The descent to Beck Head from the summit of Great Gable can be confusing in bad weather, some walkers getting too far to the left or west and finding themselves committed to the rough screes above Gable Beck. It is best, in thick mist, to keep fairly close to the edge of Gable Crag, which will be on your right.

The lofty wall of the Pillar range, including Steeple and Scoat Fell, is most often traversed by the Mosedale Horseshoe round, perhaps in abbreviated form, but the approaches from Ennerdale—once the forest has been negotiated by a ride or drove-way—are particularly dramatic and exhilarating. Ways are generally steep and often rocky but often prove easier than they appear from the valley. The direct route up Steeple, for instance, is a suitable walkers' track, with fine views into the coves on either side, and there is a good way, past Tewit How and round the crags of Mirklin Cove, to Scoat Fell. Pillar mountain may also be reached from Ennerdale, either through Windgap Cove to Wind Gap or over White Pike, and the climbers' route, through the ride immediately below the Rock, may also be followed as far as Robinson's Cairn. This prominent memorial cairn—so often wrecked by vandals in recent years—is probably more often approached by walkers along the famed High Level Route from Looking Stead, reached from either Ennerdale or Wasdale from the summit of Black Sail Pass. After passing Looking Stead, and just before the first steep rise to Pillar on the ordinary ridge route a track will be seen traversing right underneath the crags of Green Cove. This track should be followed, up and down easy rocky sections and below the crags of Hind Cove to the cairn—a delightful traverse through superb country high above the forests and the Liza. From the cairn, walkers should mount, through boulders and across a section of scree, to the Shamrock Traverse—an easy track rising to the right above the Shamrock crag—which leads to a final steep slope of scree and an ascent of about 400 feet to the summit of the mountain. During the ascent from Robinson's Cairn Pillar Rock will be seen to the right—an imposing, cathedral-like precipice, with its successive skyline features of Low Man, High Man and Pisgah.

The usual route to Pillar from Wasdale is by way of Black Sail but an alternative route is to go up from Mosedale Beck to the steep screes of Wind Gap—the prominent col to the left of the summit. Further to the left along the summit Ridge is the combe of Blackem Head where Mosedale Beck has its source and this steep way, through impressive rock scenery, may be used for the ascent from Wasdale of Scoat Fell or Red Pike. Scoat Fell can be reached most easily from Nether Beck and past Scoat Tarn while climbers and scramblers can work out mountaineering routes among the crags and outcrops to the summit of Red Pike by leaving Mosedale Beck near the easily identified Y Boulder, or some distance beyond it. The splendid rocky peak of Yewbarrow, commanding superb views of Wastwater and the Scafells, is far better traversed in its entirety than merely topped as in the round earlier described. The route from Overbeck bridge on the shore of Wastwater can be taken right up the ridge to the summit but this involves the climbing of Bell Rib, a rock tower *en route*, which should not be tackled by walkers without climbing experience. These non-climbers should traverse left, before reaching Bell Rib, and scramble up an easy gully between the tower and Dropping Crag. Both routes lead to the remarkable cleft of Great Door and then, pleasantly, to the summit, and eventually, the descent, by way of Stirrup Crag—a steepish scramble—to Dore Head.

The glory of Glaramara is the walk along its switchback, tarn-clustered ridge, described earlier, and the usual ascent from Borrowdale, over Thornythwaite Fell, is deservedly popular. This route may be varied by walking, instead, up the attractive valley of Comb Gill to reach Comb Door and an alternative track to the summit by scrambling up the side of the upper reaches of the ravine. Climbers may prefer to tackle the pitches in the ravine—a route that can provide some interest when the waterfalls are not in spate. Ways to the summit can also be found from Langstrath, one of the more adventurous being by climbing the moderate rocks of Cam Crag—a route demanding some climbing knowledge but without any real difficulty. Langstrath Beck is one of the finest mountain streams in Lakeland, with its magnificent confluence with Greenup Gill and its wonderful pools—Blackmoss Pot, Swan Dub and Tray Dub, each one a perfect place for a bathe on a warm, summer day. A pleasant, easy walk for such a day would be to walk up the valley, bathing in the pools *en route*, and then to follow the beck to Angle Tarn, striking right towards Pinnacle Bield and the main track to the summit of Glaramara and the well-marked path down to the start. Better still is to do this walk in the opposite direction, with the bathes towards the end of the day—a round I have often enjoyed on a hot day. Really determined tarn and pool bathers could probably fit in up to a dozen different immersions on this round.

Several of the walking opportunities around Bowfell and the Langdale Pikes have been suggested earlier and most of this country is too familiar to need embroidery. The ascent of Bowfell from Eskdale, by either Ore Gap or Three Tarns, should be specially commended—first past the glorious pools of the Esk and then to the almost equally splendid waters and falls of the Lingcove Beck. Another favourite route of mine follows the south ridge of Esk Pike from Lingcove Bridge and over the rocks of Yeastyrigg Crags and Pike de Bield to the summit. Both these routes can be joined by walking up Mosedale from Hardknott Pass, and Crinkle Crags can also be reached from Lingcove Bridge and Eskdale, by a variety of ways, including an easy ascent through Adam-a-Cove or a scrambling approach up Long Top.

The varied potential of the Coniston fells for walking and scrambling is also well known to most visitors and the usual routes up Coniston Old Man and Wetherlam too eroded or tracked to require further commendation or description. Some other ways, however, might be briefly mentioned. Swirl How or Great Carrs, for instance, can be approached from Little Langdale by way of Greenburn Tarn and the lovely pools of Greenburn Beck. Sometimes, when I have gone this way, I have climbed up one or other of the ridges of Great Carrs where simple rock scrambling can be enjoyed. In winter, the gullies between these ridges can provide interesting work for ice-axe and crampons. The rocky country north of Levers Water and to the east of the main ridge from Brim Fell to Swirl How is also well worth exploring. Great How Crags can provide several interesting mountaineering routes and the ridge of Raven Tor, to the west of Levers Water, makes an exhilarating ascent or descent for those with climbing experience. The easiest approach to the Coniston fells is from the summit of Wrynose Pass and along the well-graded ridge of Wet Side Edge to Great Carrs and Swirl How. A pleasant sheep walk known as Fairfield conducts the walker from the ridge to Grey Friar—a fine, rather neglected mountain that is well worthy of exploration from Tarn Beck in the Duddon valley, especially round the cliffs of Great Blake Rigg where some climbs have been made. Wetherlam presents interesting attractions on the Tilberthwaite side—old copper workings, some little-visited crags and one or two notable ridges. In particular, the east ridge presents a fine, natural route—up easy rock in its final stages and reaching the usual summit track close to a small, secluded tarn. Again, the winter possibilities of this side of the mountain are worth seeking out, the usual descent being by way of Wetherlam Edge to Birkfell Hause.

The unrivalled winter attractions of Helvellyn range have already been mentioned and there is no need to elaborate on the usual summer routes to the most frequented mountain summit in England. All that need be added is that all the east-facing coves are among the most entrancing places in Lakeland in summer time, and the most potentially dangerous—to those without proper equipment and experience—in winter. While I was writing this book four people were killed in this area, through slipping on hard snow or ice, and about a dozen others injured. Several others, wearing Wellington boots or low shoes, were, quite rightly, turned back by national park wardens. The huge amount of publicity underlining the danger, to the inexperienced, of our fells in winter time does not seem to have made much impact in the towns and cities remote from the Lake District but, nowadays, within a few hours drive.

Fairfield and its associated summits can also be a rewarding winter climbing area and, in summer time, the northern flanks of the mountain, reached from Deepdale, present a wonderfully dramatic area with great sweeps of crag and high, lonely corries. You can often laze away a summer's afternoon in these rocky corners and see nothing move except the sheep and the buzzards. People walking the familiar Fairfield Horseshoe sometimes fail to appreciate the real character of this fine mountain. To them it seems a high, grassy traverse; only a walk over Cofa Pike to Deepdale Hause or St Sunday Crag reveals the mile of crags that overlooks the upper reaches of Deepdale Beck.

Further to the east, the High Street range is chiefly remarkable for its lonely valleys reaching eastwards towards Haweswater, all of which can provide quiet and lonely routes to the ridge where you are just as likely to see red deer, fell ponies or even the lordly golden eagle as fellow-walkers. The best route to the summit of High Street is from Haweswater along Rough Crag and Long Stile, with the fell ponies of Riggindale grazing far below to the right and the black pool of Blea Water down to the left. An easy descent can be made across Mardale Ill Bell and down, past the lovely tarn of Small Water, by Nan Bield Pass. Kentmere, further to the south, is a curiously neglected valley for many visitors, hastening to the fells from the towns and cities, tend to drive through Staveley to the centre of the district and miss the turn-off to the dale and its fine ring of mountains. One day in February 1978 two of us traversed most of the Kentmere Horseshoe on skis—much of it in glorious sunshine, but Ill Bell and Yoke in thick cloud. Before the clouds came down it might have been an Alpine day, with sunlit snows stretching to the horizon, not a breath of wind and not a sound, except the swish of the skis. Later, we had to steer by compass—a tricky business on skis—and we came down to Hartrigg Farm at the darkening in falling snow and a bitter wind out of the east.

These are fells I see every day and, further east, the tip of Grey Crag, peeping over the rising height of Potter Fell. The further east you go in the fell country the more lonely the hills and the dales. How many visitors know the perfect little valley of Swindale, with its crags, pools and scattered woodland, the eastern Borrowdale and Wasdale—so unlike their counterparts to the west—the trough of Bannisdale, or the seclusion of Mosedale and Wet Sleddale? All this is part of the old Westmorland that disappeared, at the whim of Whitehall, a few years ago, but is still treasured by those who live here. An unspoiled part of Lakeland, where the dales look much the same as they did 100 years ago, and where there is no need for car-parks or litter bins. Kirkstone Pass is the real line of demarcation in Lakeland—much more so than the main road over Dunmail Raise. Westwards lie the weekend processions over Helvellyn, and the crowded popularity of Langdale and Borrowdale; eastwards—save for the Roman way over High Street—is a different country of lonely valleys and largely untracked heights. But, increasingly, these eastern dales will become more sought-after and important. We want our wildernesses and our quiet places but, in time, we may have to pay the price. The red deer and the fell ponies still have their homeland here and the golden eagles are back but their future may be insecure. Truly, we destroy the things we love but, hopefully, the far eastern fells of Lakeland will remain untouched by commerce and development and the worst excesses of mass tourism for many years to come.

# 9. The Little Mountains

Mere height has little to do with the charm or even the challenge of mountains. Everest is a far less attractive, distinctive or shapely mountain than the Matterhorn, and the ordinary way up Mont Blanc—the highest mountain in Europe—is a far easier climb than many of the routes up mountains only half as high. And you can be more severely tested on a 60-foot Lake District rock climb on, say, Kern Knotts, than on many ascents six times this length elsewhere. In the same way, the mountains of Lakeland should not be judged or, still worse, rejected, merely because of their height, or lack of it, above sea-level. A 2,000-foot elevation to signify mountain status in England is far too arbitrary and inaccurate a definition for serious acceptance since it embraces dreary Pennine peat hags, completely without mountain form, and indeterminate summits in distant Dartmoor, but excludes such heights as the splendid bulk of Black Combe or the perfect little peak of Haystacks. Better by far to forget all about definitions—whether a height is a mountain, a hill or a fell—and judge them all, large or small, on their attractiveness, challenge, variety and character. And, assessed this way, some of the two-thousanders of Lakeland will be seen to have limited appeal while many of the 'little mountains'—the fells below 2,000 feet—become wonderfully rewarding heights, much more deserving of exploration than some of the grassy domes that might pass for mountains in the lists.

Get out your maps and you will find 100 or more of these little mountains in the Lake District. Not all of them, by any means, are especially worth seeking out for their own particular appeal—although it is always a joy to be high up anywhere in Lakeland—but many are distinctive, dramatic, even challenging, and others strikingly varied in feature, presenting fine, unusual views, threaded by delightful tracks or refreshingly devoid of paths. Before writing this chapter I jotted down the names of about 100 of these little mountains and, looking through the list and remembering walks over all these places, I believe it is the intimacy of these fells that provides most of their appeal. The walks to the summits are, mostly, relatively short and can often be started from places remote from the main tourist area. Often you are going into little-visited country and seeing views of fells and dales not experienced from the well-worn tracks on the larger, and more familiar mountains. Sometimes you are looking *up* at the better-known fells from unfamiliar angles and, because these little mountains are often more compact than the giants, with a great deal of variety crowded into smaller space, there can be surprises round every corner—a perfect jewel of a tarn, perhaps, the steep, grey rocks of an unexplored crag, or a ravine dropping through woodlands of rowan and birch.

For the statistically inclined it could be mentioned that several of these little mountains only fail to reach the 2,000 feet contour by quite small margins. High Seat, for example, the highest point of the indeterminate ridge between Thirlmere and Borrowdale, is only four feet short of a dictionary-defined mountain, but a most uninteresting, even dreary, summit, only reached after squelching through bogs. Hardly a notable mountain, despite an extensive summit view, although the top of the Ordnance Survey column that adorns the summit is probably more than 2,000 feet above sea-level. According to the one-inch maps Seathwaite Fell is a little mountain, with a summit cairn at 1,970 feet, but a study of larger-scale maps and the ground itself shows that this point is not the summit for there are two other areas above the 2,000-foot contour. These 2,000-foot tops were included in my collection so, for once, the summit cairn builders were wrong.

Among the highest of the little mountains are Illgill Head (1,983 feet), Black Combe (1,970 feet), Shipman Knotts (1,926 feet), Brae Fell (1,920 feet), Middle Fell (1,908 feet) and Haystacks (1,900 feet) and several of these are notable fells in any company. Illgill Head is the summit of the Wastwater Screes, one of the most dramatic walls in the district, and the walk along the top of the cliffs from the lower summit of Whin Rigg provides splendid views down the crags and ravines to the lake nearly 2,000 feet below your feet. There is also a splendid summit view of the beautifully proportioned head of the dale—Wasdale Head, with its noble ring of mountains, the very heart of the shrine. This fine cliffs walk can easily be tackled from either end of the deepest lake in

England and combined with a scramble, in the reverse direction, along the foot of the screes, for closer examination of the gullies that provide demanding climbing routes.

Black Combe was my first mountain—it had always looked a mountain from my boyhood home in Furness and certainly seemed like one as we trudged up from the Whicham Valley road, with several apparent summits to be surmounted before we finally topped the real one. This modest ascent—my first real mountain after many walks up lower hills—happened more than fifty years ago but I can still remember most of that day very clearly and, especially, the view of the Furness peninsula spread out below us like a map. We didn't know Black Combe was a famous summit, or that Wordsworth had been up there and written that the view from the top was the best and the longest in Britain. All we knew was that this was the mountain we could see every day from our home—we believed in those days the combe was an extinct volcano—and that we ought to go to the top. So Black Combe will always be a real mountain for me, and I suppose it is also a mountain for people who glimpse it from sitting-rooms in Morecambe or many places along the Lancashire coast, or from the North Pier at Blackpool or from the tower of Liverpool Cathedral—a great, sprawling, whale-backed summit on the edge of the sea. There are several other hills in this remote, south-west corner of Lakeland, ancient stone circles, old burial-grounds, lonely moors, the fine road winding over Bootle Fell—one of the least-visited parts of the national park. How many people, I wonder, have walked from Devoke Water to Black Combe? It could be the loneliest walk in Lakeland.

Shipman Knotts, rising from the Kentmere-Sadgill pass, is really a shoulder of Kentmere Pike but a surprisingly rough and craggy little mountain as I have found to my cost when skiing up there. Brae Fell in the Caldbeck hills is an undistinguished, grassy mound of little character but from the summit there is a superb view of the Cumbrian coast, the Solway Firth, the border country, the Scottish Lowlands and the long sweep of the Northern Pennines—the sort of view that makes the dull trudge from the north or from the neighbouring height of Great Sca Fell to the south so worth while. Compared with these rather disappointing little mountains, however, Middle Fell, half-way along the northern shore of Wastwater, is a very fine hill, rugged, wild and rocky, providing many opportunities for adventurous exploration.

And the summit view straight across the lake to the rampart of The Screes and leftwards to the highest land in England—is quite superb.

The last of the highest of the little mountains is Haystacks—my favourite of them all. No other of the smaller fells of Lakeland has so much variety within less than a square mile—dark crags, with several redoubtable climbing routes, smaller, clean, grey crags and outcrops with many easier climbs and scrambles, ravines and waterfalls, heather tracks, and some of the finest mountain tarns in Lakeland, including one on the summit. I have written earlier about this perfect, little mountain, so easily reached from the top of Honister Pass and even closer to Scarth Gap, so there is no need for further eulogy, except to say that if little Haystacks was a thousand feet higher it would be one of the most important mountains in England.

So far I have dealt, in the briefest detail, with only about half a dozen of the hundred or so fells in the Lake District that are largely ignored in most guide-books—although Wainwright seeks them out—simply because they are of modest height. Within the confines of one short chapter I cannot describe, or even mention, all the others but perhaps I can refer to some of my favourites, leaving the many routes to their summits to be chosen by those interested through a study of the maps. Anybody, by studying the excellent productions of the Ordnance Survey, can find his way up Blea Rigg or Stone Arthur or Great Cockup or a score of others and discover new corners. As an example, he can wander over Great Cockup and, while wondering about its strange name, come upon the lovely, little gap of Trusmadoor with its much more euphonious nomenclature. Or he can walk round the splendid circuit of Far Easdale, picking up, in turn, the neat, little summits of Helm Crag, Gibson Knott, Calf Crag and, on the other side of the dale, the soaring height of Tarn Crag. Helm Crag is one of the most distinctive of the little mountains of Lakeland, with its rocky top—'The Lion and the Lamb' or 'The Old Lady at the Organ'—that provides the only summit in all our mountains that can only be reached by climbing. You can get up the Scafells or even rocky Harter Fell without using your hands but not the highest point of little Helm Crag, although it is only a simple scramble of a few feet. Tarn Crag, dropping steeply towards Easdale Tarn, always seems higher than its modest 1,800 feet suggest. It provides an excellent ridge route down to Grasmere from High Raise, along a delightful track winding among the heather and around tors of grey rock with a vista of tarns and widening valleys below. And, on the other side of the fell, is the dark cliff of Deer Bield Crag, with its cluster of demanding rock-climbs—some of them the most difficult in the district.

Black Combe was my very first 'mountain' but Stickle Pike, above the Duddon, my first hill—as a schoolboy of eleven or twelve years, in short trousers and wearing a school cap. Curiously, I did not go up there again for fifty years, although I had been across its shoulder on the way to Caw and the splendid high ridge leading to the Coniston fells many times. Perhaps this second visit was a sort of pilgrimage. I recalled the summit photograph and how the master in charge had emphasized the dangers of boulder trundling and, for some strange reason, the perils of drinking from the becks. Ever since, I have obeyed his stricture against rolling boulders down the fellsides but have always drank copiously from becks whenever I felt like it, without any apparent harm. The pointed peak of Stickle Pike, on the strength of only two, widely separated ascents is, nevertheless, to be commended, and Caw, with its commanding views of Dunnerdale; has long been a favourite fell. Eagle Crag and Sergeant's Crag, above Langstrath, are dramatic, little peaks, with memories of climbing days and wonderful bathes in the pools below, while Loughrigg Fell and Lingmoor Fell, nearer home, have memories for me of easier, more relaxing days—often in winter. We have often gone over Loughrigg or Lingmoor on Boxing Day, sometimes catching a glimpse of the traditional hunt, and generally finishing up, at dusk, in some old, low-raftered inn. Few fells are more criss-crossed by easy paths than Loughrigg—a tourist's hill if ever was—but, out of season, it is a wonderfully relaxing place, with its views of lakes and woodlands and the higher fells, its great caves and its springy turf. A pleasant place, away from the traffic, for grandparents and grandchildren. Lingmoor, buttressed by quarries and cliffs, is a superb viewpoint for the Langdale hills. One photographer friend of mine says it has more potential for colourful pictures than many of the higher fells.

Wansfell and Latrigg, the nearest lungs to Ambleside and Keswick, require no particular description or commendation; in season, they can have their delights for the elderly or the very young. Catbells, too, is a very popular summit. To me, it has always seemed the children's little mountain—and not only because it was my daughter's first hill, at the age of two. Every time I cross the top there are children up there and Hugh Walpole peopled the fell with youngsters in his books. It is a shapely hill, with steep, short ascents and wide views from the top of lakes and plains and mountains, with the toy town of Keswick set delightfully in the middle. And Catbells leads to the exhilarating ridge of Maiden Moor, High Spy and the Derwent fells.

Among the lesser-known little mountains of Lakeland is Green Crag above Eskdale, a rocky ridge leading over to Dunnerdale. This sturdy fell has a serrated skyline, almost reminiscent of Skye from some angles, and there are several tracks up through the heather and among the crags leading to the rough summit. On the way, the fine waterfall of Birker Force can be visited and the view from the top of the highest mountains in Lakeland makes the ascent a particularly suitable choice for a short day's excursion. Many Lakeland visitors know Barf, the rocky ridge above Bassenthwaite Lake and the Bishop of Barf—a rock pinnacle that is whitewashed every year—but not all of them scramble to the top. You can go up from Thornthwaite, either alongside the forest, or straight up, past the Bishop, the screes and the steep heather, by a scrambling route that lands you, more directly, on the summit. This is a striking viewpoint—especially of the great massif of Skiddaw across the lake, looking its full height from this angle. Further to the west, the twin-peaked little mountain of Mellbreak, overlooking Crummock Water is a fine, rough fell of considerable character, with plenty of rock and airy tracks and especially fine views of the lake and the lovely vale of Buttermere. This is a fell deserving of detailed exploration; one visit will not reveal the wealth of crags, ravines and hidden combes. Best of all, Mellbreak stands on its own, with no links to other fells, and must be regarded as among the most arresting and independent of the smaller mountains of the district.

Looking through my list of little mountains, by no means complete, I see that I have still not mentioned half of them, but old memories come tumbling out. Hot, lazy days on Angletarn Pikes, for instance, with bathes in the tarn every half-hour, or getting lost on Souther Fell—the ghost mountain—in thick cloud, or scrambling about on Buckbarrow to find new climbs, or skiing on Sallows above

Kentmere on untouched powder snow. There was an afternoon on The Nab above Martindale with the red deer roaring in the valley and another day on Knott Rigg and Ard Crags when I accompanied some fell-running record-breakers for a time—until I realized they were about twice as fit as myself. Or a short afternoon in the sunshine on Hallin Fell with the children, many years ago, a wet day on Armboth Fell looking forward to afternoon tea at Watendlath, or searching for skiing snow on Great Mell Fell. There are so many of these little mountains and so many pictures of happy days—Nab Scar, Rosthwaite Fell, Rannerdale Knotts, Outerside, Bleaberry Fell, Steel Fell and Glenridding Dodd. The list is as evocative as a diary.

These, therefore, are a selection of the little mountains of Lakeland, all of them wonderful places, but some more wonderful than others. Seek out every one—when you have traversed all the higher tops—and you will add a variety of scenery and experience to your knowledge of Lakeland that might surprise you. All Lakeland mountains, the largest and the smallest, are magical places on the right day, and in the right mood. Your reward may come on some remote, grassy summit—perhaps a break in the sky to reveal a distant glimpse of Scotland—or on the east face of Helvellyn in winter, or on a sunny, summer's day half-way up a rock-climb in Birkness Combe. Suddenly you realize how fortunate you are—to be active and healthy, far from motorcars and television and strikes and violence, high up on a Lakeland mountain in sunshine, rain, cloud, wind or snow. Every day throughout the seasons the hills are different, every day you can find something new. Surely, it is all a matchless heritage to be guarded with constant devotion and common sense. Whatever happens, the hills will always be there and, in time, if we approach the heights with humility, respect and experience, we can win the freedom of the most wonderful mountain country in England.

# Appendix

A list of Lake District summits of 2,000 feet or more in height compiled by Francis G. Falkingham and reprinted, with permission, from the 1966 *Journal of the Gritstone Club*. Some of the nomenclature may be queried—I have referred to this, where appropriate, in the book—but the list is printed unaltered, in its original form. The first set of figures in each group is the six-figure map reference taken from the Ordnance Survey's one-inch map. The second set of figures is the height of the summit in feet. A cross(+) signifies that the height is higher than the approximate figure given.

*Note.* The heights in the list are those in existence when the list was compiled. Since then the Ordnance Survey have revised their mountain heights and the more accurate figures, given on the latest maps, may be slightly different from those in this list. Scafell Pike, for instance, has no longer the easily remembered height of 3,210 feet, but is now a mere 3,206 feet.

HIGH STILE GROUP

| | | |
|---|---|---|
| 35/124164 | 2019 | Great Borne |
| 125165 | 2000+ | Great Borne (north top) |
| 142157 | 2085 | Starling Dodd |
| 160154 | 2479 | Red Pike |
| 165158 | 2050+ | Dodd |
| 170148 | 2644 | High Stile |
| 164150 | 2400 | Chapel Crags |
| 180140 | 2443 | High Crag |
| 206142 | 2126 | Fleetwith Pike |
| 211141 | 2050+ | Fleetwith Pike |
| 213141 | 2050+ | Fleetwith Pike |
| 219126 | 2287 | Grey Knotts |
| 215119 | 2344 | Brandreth |
| 225114 | 2120 | Base Brown |

PILLAR-GABLE GROUP

| | | |
|---|---|---|
| 35/140084 | 2266 | Seatallan |
| 145107 | 2618 | Haycock |
| 132110 | 2288 | Caw Fell |
| 124119 | 2100+ | Iron Crag |
| 140110 | 2350+ | Little Gowder Crag |
| 154111 | 2750+ | Scoat Fell |
| 158114 | 2750+ | Scoat Fell |
| 160114 | 2760 | Scoat Fell |
| 164116 | 2689 | Black Crag |
| 158116 | 2687 | Steeple |
| 166106 | 2707 | Red Pike |
| 176093 | 2009 | Stirrup Crag |
| 173085 | 2058 | Yewbarrow |
| 171121 | 2927 | Pillar |
| 172124 | 2500+ | Pillar Rock |
| 186118 | 2058 | Looking Stead |
| 195105 | 2630 | Kirk Fell |
| 199108 | 2550+ | Kirk Fell |
| 215107 | 2603 | Green Gable |
| 211103 | 2949 | Great Gable |

SCAFELL GROUP

| | | |
|---|---|---|
| 35/227084 | 2984 | Great End |
| 224079 | 2950+ | Ill Crag (North) |
| 223075 | 3040 | Ill Crag |
| 219076 | 3054 | Broad Crag |
| 215072 | 3210 | Scafell Pike |
| 221068 | 2500+ | Scafell Pike (Pen) |
| 220069 | 2500+ | Scafell Pike |
| 209082 | 2649 | Lingmell |
| 207063 | 3162 | Scafell |
| 209059 | 2850+ | Cam Spout Crag |

| | | |
|---|---|---|
| 210050 | 2499 | Slight Side |
| 237075 | 2903 | Esk Pike |
| 250075 | 2106 | Rossett Pike |

ALLEN CRAGS GROUP

| | | |
|---|---|---|
| 35/237085 | 2572 | Allen Crags |
| 241092 | 2200+ | Allen Crags |
| 243097 | 2350+ | Allen Crags |
| 246102 | 2550+ | Allen Crags |
| 247106 | 2560 | Glaramara |
| 250108 | 2300+ | Glaramara |
| 256114 | 2000+ | Cam Crag |
| 227095 | 2025+ | Seathwaite Fell |
| 230093 | 2000+ | Seathwaite Fell |
| 241080 | 2250+ | Tongue Head |

LANGDALE PIKES GROUP

| | | |
|---|---|---|
| 35/282073 | 2403 | Harrison Stickle |
| 274074 | 2323 | Pike o' Stickle |
| 279081 | 2351 | Thunacar Knott |
| 279079 | 2362 | Thunacar Knott |
| 281095 | 2500 | High Raise |
| 286089 | 2414 | Sergeant Man |
| 292122 | 2370 | Ullscarf |

BOWFELL-CRINKLES GROUP

| | | |
|---|---|---|
| 35/245064 | 2960 | Bowfell |
| 245067 | 2850+ | Bowfell |
| 245069 | 2825+ | Bowfell |
| 249054 | 2650+ | Shelter Crags |
| 249052 | 2680 | Crinkle Crags |
| 249051 | 2730 | Crinkle Crags |
| 249054 | 2740 | Crinkle Crags |
| 248049 | 2816 | Crinkle Crags |
| 250046 | 2733 | Crinkle Crags |
| 260043 | 2200+ | Great Knott |
| 251034 | 2426 | Red How |
| 264035 | 2259 | Cold Pike (near) |
| 271042 | 2304 | Pike o' Blisco |

CONISTON GROUP

| | | |
|---|---|---|
| 35/289008 | 2400+ | Wetherlam |
| 288011 | 2502 | Wetherlam |
| 283008 | 2400+ | Wetherlam |
| 270010 | 2575 | Great Carrs |
| 260004 | 2536 | Grey Friar |
| 273005 | 2630 | Swirl How |
| 34/271986 | 2611 | Brim Fell |
| 272978 | 2635 | Coniston Old Man |
| 263978 | 2555 | Dow Crag |
| 261966 | 2237 | Brown Pike |
| 258964 | 2000+ | Walna Scar |
| 254957 | 2000+ | Walna Scar |
| 218997 | 2140 | Harter Fell |

HELVELLYN GROUP

| | | |
|---|---|---|
| 35/334225 | 2381 | Clough Head |
| 330211 | 2166 | Calfhow Pike |
| 342204 | 2807 | Great Dodd |
| 349211 | 2250+ | Randerside |
| 343189 | 2750+ | Stybarrow Dodd |
| 341186 | 2756 | Stybarrow Dodd |
| 353187 | 2600+ | Greenside |
| 359197 | 2481 | Hart Side |
| 362195 | 2350+ | Hart Side |
| 369182 | 2232 | Sheffield Pike |
| 343174 | 2889 | Raise |
| 338166 | 2832 | White Side |
| 348158 | 2917 | Catstycam |
| 341151 | 3118 | Helvellyn |
| 351149 | 2832 | Striding Edge |
| 360157 | 2300+ | Birkhouse Moor |
| 361158 | 2300+ | Birkhouse Moor |
| 363159 | 2350+ | Birkhouse Moor |
| 365163 | 2318 | Birkhouse Moor |
| 344141 | 2920 | Nethermost Pike |
| 343136 | 2850+ | High Crag |
| 346130 | 2810 | Dollywaggon Pike |
| 344115 | 2415 | Seat Sandal |

HIGH STREET GROUP

| | | |
|---|---|---|
| 35/405169 | 2154 | Place Fell |
| 409166 | 2000+ | Round How |
| 457181 | 2201 | Loadpot Hill |
| 456167 | 2200+ | Wether Hill |
| 455163 | 2210 | Wether Hill |
| 450153 | 2328 | Red Crag |
| 450144 | 2358 | Raven Howe |
| 448134 | 2634 | High Raise |
| 444128 | 2581 | Rampsgill Head |
| 447126 | 2560 | Kidsty Pike |
| 437127 | 2423 | The Knott |
| 432136 | 2278 | Rest Dodd |
| 441110 | 2718 | High Street |
| 454113 | 2062 | Rough Crag |
| 431100 | 2569 | Thornthwaite Crag |
| 429110 | 2331 | Gray Crag |
| 428114 | 2286 | Gray Crag |
| 426118 | 2250 | Gray Crag |
| 418100 | 2502 | Stony Cove Pike |
| 413100 | 2474 | John Bell's Banner |
| 411118 | 2018 | Hartsop Dodd |

FAIRFIELD GROUP

| | | |
|---|---|---|
| 35/355083 | 2003 | Heron Pike |
| 357087 | 2000+ | Erne Crag |
| 356092 | 2022 | Rydal Fell |
| 356104 | 2513 | Greatrigg Man |
| 358117 | 2863 | Fairfield |

cont.

| | | |
|---|---|---|
| 369134 | 2756 | St Sunday Crag |
| 382145 | 2040 | Birks |
| 369112 | 2698 | Hart Crag |
| 356091 | 2000+ | Rydal Fell |
| 356093 | 2000+ | Rydal Fell |
| 356095 | 2000+ | Rydal Fell |
| 374104 | 2603 | Dove Crag |
| 384101 | 2000+ | Little Hart Crag |
| 387100 | 2091 | Little Hart Crag |
| 396087 | 2541 | Red Screes |

YOKE-MARDALE GROUP

| | | |
|---|---|---|
| 35/438067 | 2309 | Yoke |
| 436077 | 2476 | Ill Bell |
| 435085 | 2359 | Froswick |
| 448101 | 2496 | Mardale Ill Bell |
| 448098 | 2400+ | Mardale Ill Bell |
| 460098 | 2539 | Harter Fell |
| 461083 | 2300+ | Brown Howe |
| 465077 | 2397 | Kentmere Pike |
| 471090 | 2180 | Adam Seat |
| 488078 | 2176 | Tarn Crag |
| 497072 | 2093 | Grey Crag |
| 478100 | 2333 | Branstree |
| 487103 | 2200 | Branstree |
| 491112 | 2142 | Selside Pike |

GRASMOOR GROUP

| | | |
|---|---|---|
| 35/199226 | 2593 | Grisedale Pike |
| 193221 | 2300+ | Grisedale Pike |
| 186224 | 2525 | Hopegill Head |
| 185228 | 2300+ | Ladyside Pike |
| 171219 | 2317 | Whiteside |
| 174222 | 2250+ | Whiteside (east top) |
| 175203 | 2791 | Grasmoor |
| 193203 | 2749 | Eel Crag Hill |
| 188197 | 2533 | Wandope |
| 199203 | 2500+ | Sail |
| 208206 | 2205 | Scar Crags |
| 219209 | 2000+ | Causey Pike |
| 180190 | 2159 | Whiteless Pike |

DALE HEAD GROUP

| | | |
|---|---|---|
| 35/202168 | 2417 | Robinson |
| 214160 | 2200+ | Hindscarth (south top) |
| 216165 | 2385 | Hindscarth |
| 223153 | 2473 | Dale Head |
| 234162 | 2143 | High Spy |
| 236170 | 2050+ | Nitting Haws |

BLENCATHRA GROUP

| | | |
|---|---|---|
| 35/333305 | 2306 | Bowscale Fell |
| 340310 | 2200+ | Bowscale Fell |
| 329296 | 2100+ | Bannerdale Crags |
| 336290 | 2200+ | Bannerdale Crags |
| 323277 | 2847 | Blencathra |
| 312270 | 2600+ | Knowe Crags |

SKIDDAW GROUP

| | | |
|---|---|---|
| 35/286271 | 2344 | Lonscale Fell |
| 267278 | 2837 | Little Man |
| 255281 | 2400+ | Carl Side |
| 249284 | 2405 | Long Side |
| 261291 | 3053 | Skiddaw |
| 277286 | 2200+ | Sale How |
| 291312 | 2265 | Great Calva |
| 291342 | 2050+ | Great Sca Fell |
| 292338 | 2100+ | Great Sca Fell |
| 296330 | 2329 | Knott |
| 311327 | 2058 | Coomb Height |
| 310339 | 2000+ | Great Lingy Hill |
| 303338 | 2000+ | Great Lingy Hill |
| 319350 | 2157 | High Pike |
| 342336 | 2174 | Carrock Fell |

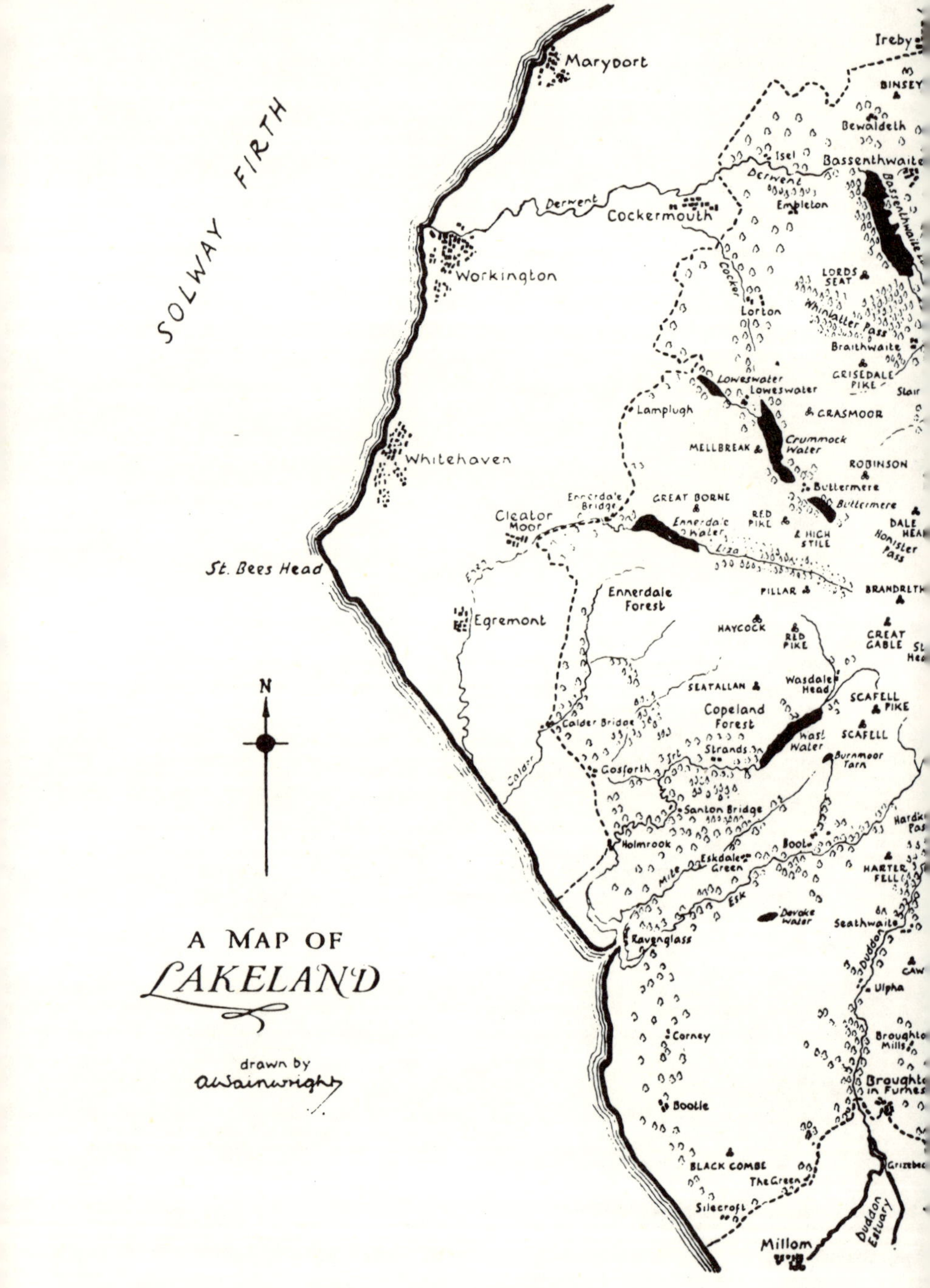


A MAP OF
LAKELAND

drawn by
A. Wainwright

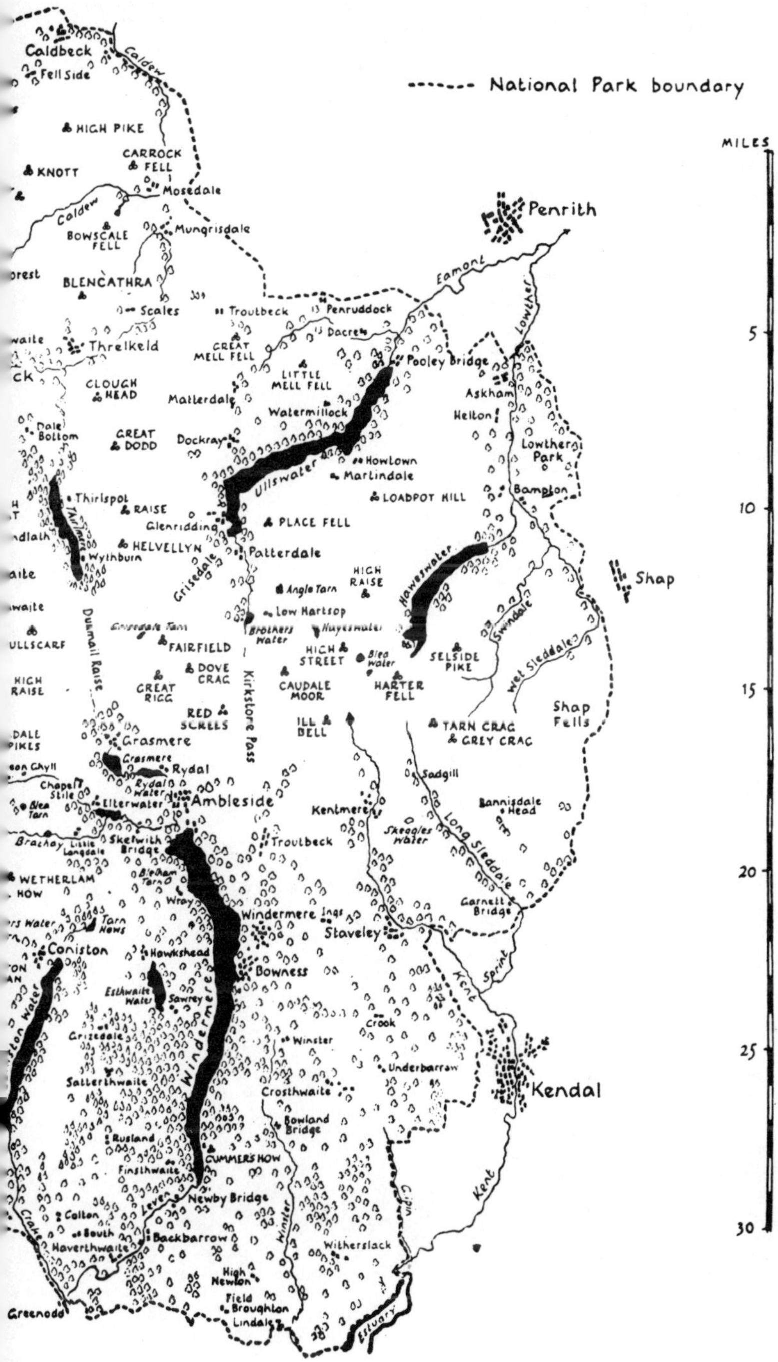

National Park boundary
MILES
5
10
15
20
25
30
Caldbeck
Fell Side
Caldew
HIGH PIKE
CARROCK FELL
KNOTT
Mosedale
BOWSCALE FELL
Mungrisdale
BLENCATHRA
Scales
Troutbeck
Penruddock
Dacre
Penrith
Eamont
Lowther
Threlkeld
GREAT MELL FELL
LITTLE MELL FELL
Pooley Bridge
Askham
CLOUGH HEAD
Matterdale
Watermillock
Helton
Dale Bottom
GREAT DODD
Dockray
Lowther Park
Howtown
Martindale
Ullswater
Bampton
Thirlspot
RAISE
LOADPOT HILL
Glenridding
PLACE FELL
Wythburn
HELVELLYN
Patterdale
Haweswater
Shap
Grisedale
HIGH RAISE
Angle Tarn
Low Hartsop
Swindale
Dunmail Raise
Grisedale Tarn
FAIRFIELD
Brothers Water
Hayeswater
HIGH STREET
Blea Water
SELSIDE PIKE
Wet Sleddale
DOVE CRAG
GREAT RIGG
Kirkstone Pass
CAUDALE MOOR
HARTER FELL
RED SCREES
ILL BELL
Shap Fells
TARN CRAG
GREY CRAG
Grasmere
Rydal
Rydal Water
Sadgill
Chapel Stile
Blea Tarn
Elterwater
Ambleside
Kentmere
Bannisdale Head
Skelwith Bridge
Troutbeck
Skeggles Water
Little Langdale
Long Sleddale
Blelham Tarn
WETHERLAM
Wray
Windermere
Ings
Garnett Bridge
Tarn Hows
Staveley
Coniston
Hawkshead
Bowness
Kent
Sprint
Esthwaite Water
Sawrey
Crook
Grizedale
Winster
Underbarrow
Satterthwaite
Windermere
Crosthwaite
Kendal
Bowland Bridge
Rusland
CUMMERS HOW
Finsthwaite
Leven
Newby Bridge
Colton
Winster
South
Backbarrow
Haverthwaite
Witherslack
Gilpin
Kent
High Newton
Field Broughton
Greenodd
Lindale
Estuary

# Index

# Index

BCJ